DIFFERENTIATION:

SIMPLIFIED, REALISTIC, AND EFFECTIVE

How to Challenge Advanced Potentials in Mixed-Ability Classrooms

BERTIE KINGORE, Ph.D.
AUTHOR

Jeffery Kingore
GRAPHIC DESIGN

Professional Associates Publishing
www.kingore.com

Current Publications by
Bertie Kingore, Ph.D. ————————

Alphabetters: Thinking Adventures with the Alphabet (Task Cards)
Assessment: Timesaving Procedures for Busy Teachers, 4th ed.
Assessment Interactive CD-ROM
Bertie's Book Notes 2008
Centers in Minutes!
Centers CD-ROM Vol. 1: Grades K-8
Centers CD-ROM Vol. 2: Literacy Stations, Grades K-4
Developing Portfolios for Authentic Assessment, PreK-3
Differentiation Interactive CD-ROM
Engaging Creative Thinking: Activities to Integrate Creative Problem Solving
Integrating Thinking: Strategies that Work!, 2nd ed.
Just What I Need! Learning Experiences to Use on Multiple Days in Multiple Ways
Kingore Observation Inventory (KOI), 2nd ed.
Literature Celebrations: Catalysts for High-Level Book Responses, 2nd ed.
Reaching All Learners: Making Differentiation Work!
Reading Strategies for Advanced Primary Readers: Texas Reading Initiative Task Force for the
    Education of Primary Gifted Children
Reading Strategies for Advanced Primary Readers: Professional Development Guide
Recognizing Gifted Potential: Planned Experiences with the KOI
Recognizing Gifted Potential: Training Trainers Presentation CD and Guidebook
Teaching Without Nonsense: Translating Research into Effective Practice, 2nd ed.
We Care: A Curriculum for Preschool Through Kindergarten, 2nd ed.

FOR INFORMATION OR ORDERS CONTACT:
PROFESSIONAL ASSOCIATES PUBLISHING ————————
PO Box 28056
Austin, Texas 78755-8056
Toll free phone/fax: 866-335-1460
info@kingore.com

VISIT US ONLINE!
www.kingore.com

DIFFERENTIATION: SIMPLIFIED, REALISTIC, AND EFFECTIVE
How to Challenge Advance Potentials in Mixed-Ability Classrooms

Copyright © 2004, 2008 Bertie Kingore

Published by PROFESSIONAL ASSOCIATES PUBLISHING

Printed in the United States of America
ISBN: 0-9716233-3-3

ACKNOWLEDGEMENTS

I am indebted to our three sons for continually sharing their personal perceptions of growing up gifted. As emerging adults, their reflections regarding their learning needs and school experiences fuel my dedication to respond to the educational rights and needs of advanced and gifted children. I warmly thank again the teachers who differentiated instruction for them. S.Z., K.C., K.H., C.R., K.A., N.E., D.S., M.P., H.T., J.T., and J.R.: You are remembered with gratitude.

Two valued colleagues provide an empowering influence on my work in differentiation.
- Susan Winebrenner whose philosophy of inviting student to self-determine their degree of participation in differentiation is just right.
- Carol Ann Tomlinson whose concept of respectful work for all students permeates my teaching of students and work with teachers.

gratis

121486

TABLE OF CONTENTS

LIST OF REPRODUCIBLE FIGURES

INTRODUCTION

The cover is black and white because the impetus of this book is to simplify differentiation and to explain the process with *black and white* clarity. Simplifying differentiation enables more teachers to successfully implement an effective differentiation system which in turn benefits more students by having their individual needs respected.

It is black and white because differentiation is the yin and yang of skillful teaching. Differentiation poses the challenging, overwhelming, and at times negatively perceived task of appropriately responding to the diverse learning differences within a classroom. This challenge contrasts with the exciting, promising, fulfilling, and ultimately positive task of responding to students as individuals.

It is black and white to provide a stark reminder: it is time to initiate more effective and efficient differentiated instruction.

In working with wonderful teachers across the nation, the common thread of concern is *how to do it all*. Teachers want to differentiate. They certainly view it as important to their students, but they continue to experience frustration at the vastness of the task. *How-to* questions prevail. Management questions repeat themselves in district after district. Therefore, the focus of this book is to simplify

the implementation of differentiation to increase its practice. Specific aids and examples are included because teachers found them particularly beneficial to simplify the planning and preparation process of differentiated instruction.

Definitions are useful to understand reoccurring terminology in this book. *Readiness, learning profile,* and *interest* are used to accent our need to understanding how students vary as learners.

➡ *Readiness* is the information, concepts, and skills students demonstrate at the entry point of the learning experience.

➡ *Learning profile* is the combination of students' emotions, cultures, modality preferences, and intelligences that affect learning.

➡ *Interests* are topics, problems, and processes of personal relevance to students.

Most of the time, the term *readiness* is used instead of *ability*. I am concerned that we often do not know a student's actual ability. We are much more accurate in determining readiness; frequently what a student is able to demonstrate is readiness rather than ability. As a teacher, I worked with students of poverty and students with diverse backgrounds who performed at a lower-level of readiness yet had gifted potential when we could see beyond specific skill levels. Provide instructional services at the assessed readiness level while constantly observing and analyzing advanced potential. Expect students to escalate their learning.

Advanced, gifted, and *highly able* are used throughout the book.

➡ *Advanced* is the term used to denote learners whose needs exceed the basic curriculum yet are not identified as gifted learners. Advanced students need instructional services above the core curriculum to experience continuous learning.

➡ *Gifted* or *highly able* refers to students who perform in the highest ability range in the school. For our purposes, the terms are

Kingore, B. (2004). *Differentiation: Simplified, Realistic, and Effective*. Austin: Professional Associates Publishing.

used interchangeably to vary vocabulary. Gifted and highly able learners require pace and level acceleration in their instructional services to experience continuous learning.

Teacher tip...

The goal of this book is to provide teacher-useful and student-effective differentiation. These icons signal observations, suggestions, opinions, and insights from teachers regarding the differentiation of instruction in mixed-ability classrooms.

Think about it...

Throughout the book, this brain icon is used to invite the reader to reflect upon the content being addressed. Your responses and opinions are an important aspect of your continued growth in teaching as you make decisions about best practices for students.

Some educators may note that much of the book is applicable to the diverse needs and learning profiles of multiple populations. Since the thrust of the book is advanced and gifted students, one might mistakenly conclude that all learners need the same instruction or that all learners benefit from "gifted

instruction." A more appropriate implication is that all children can learn and deserve the challenge of learning at their highest potential. Raising the achievements of one population affects all and ultimately opens the door to even higher aspirations for advanced and gifted learners.

I continue to believe that the quality of the opportunities offered students determines the level of their responses. If we fail to ask high-level questions and provide students opportunities to engage in challenging tasks, we must be content with basic student responses instead of excellence. I know of no teacher who recommends a yearly goal of bringing students down to basic responses!

In a marvelous picture book entitled *Winnie the Witch* by Korky Paul and Valerie Thomas*, a witch lives in a black house with her black cat, Wilbur. Unfortunately, Wilbur's color blends in too well in the house and Winnie frequently trips over him. Her solution is to change his color to green and later to multiple shades so he is highly visible. The results are catastrophic to Wilbur. He is miserable. Because Winnie cares about Wilbur, she returns him to his original color and changes the color of the house instead!

At first, Winnie tries to make Wilbur change to fit her environment. But that does not work. Because she truly cares about him, she learns to change the environment so she can see him better.

Educators are changing the learning environment so they can see students' readiness levels, learning profiles, and interests more clearly. Through differentiated instruction, teachers customize levels of instruction to begin at students' levels of readiness and enable them to advance as far as they can. It is time to differentiate instruction through more simple, realistic, and effective means.

*Paul, K. & Thomas, V. (1987). *Winnie the witch.* New York: Kane/Miller Book Publishers.

Kingore, B. (2004). *Differentiation: Simplified, Realistic, and Effective.* Austin: Professional Associates Publishing.

DEVELOPING A BACKGROUND IN DIFFERENTIATION

Differentiation is a well known educational practice that is often talked about, sometimes not well understood, and frequently implemented ineffectively. Differentiation is difficult for some educators to implement because their own school experiences incorporated little differentiation. Differentiation strategies are also difficult for educators to learn about through classroom observation inasmuch as many aspects of differentiated instruction are not actively implemented in all classrooms. Hence, teachers may lack both a background of experiences and a system for learning what differentiation looks and sounds like when applied in a classroom. This chapter develops a background for understanding differentiation by considering what differentiated instruction intends, which instructional practices hinder or encourage differentiation, guidelines for establishing a learning atmosphere conducive to differentiation, and strategies that support differentiation.

WHAT IS AND IS NOT INTENDED IN DIFFERENTIATED INSTRUCTION

Differentiated instruction is designed to match the readiness levels of the students

Kingore, B. (2004). *Differentiation: Simplified, Realistic, and Effective.* Austin: Professional Associates Publishing.

in the classroom. Teachers customize instruction to learners' needs by adjusting the pace and level of instruction and varying the products of learning to reflect students' best ways to learn. Differentiated instruction recognizes and acts upon the reality that children learn differently. It is not a question of good or bad classrooms; it is not a question of which teachers are working harder. It is doing what is instructionally the right thing to do--beginning where students are and trying to take them as far as they can go in their learning. Without differentiation, Tomlinson warns us that classrooms swallow some learners and pinch others (1999). Figure 1.1 charts the elements of differentiation by comparing what differentiated instruction involves, what is intended in that instruction, and what is not intended.

Students are individuals. In a differentiated classroom, teachers perceive the differences that make students unique, not to distinguish one as better or less than another, but to form instructional objectives that effectively match each student.

Rather than whole-class instruction dominating, small groups of students frequently work together or with the teacher on different levels of concepts and skills. By instructing in flexible groups, the teacher is able to effectively vary the level and kinds of instructional materials as well as customize learning assignments--many of which directly respond to learners' interests.

Differentiation switches the instructional focus from competition among all students to a student competing with self. District-wide and class-wide competition focuses on:

- *How many students are behind,*
- *How far behind they are,*
- *How many are on level,* and
- *How many are ahead.*

That information drives accountability but does not effectively help children to succeed. In a differentiated classroom, accountability is acknowledged, yet the driving question for each student becomes:

How are you doing in relation to your readiness and potential, and what instructional intervention do I use to enable you to progress toward our learning goal?

Students are recognized for current levels of achievement and then challenged to strive toward their personal best. The intent is to enable them to experience success that motivates future effort.

Differentiated instruction personifies great teaching and what many great teachers aspire to do. Teachers want to differentiate instruction because they want to do what is best to enable students to be their best. Their instruction engages students as partners in learning who share the responsibility of being active participants in learning and assessing growth.

Teacher tip...

Be an enthusiastic coach in your classroom. Encouragement plays an important part in facilitating students' continual growth.

Kingore, B. (2004). *Differentiation: Simplified, Realistic, and Effective.* Austin: Professional Associates Publishing.

Figure 1.1:
THE ELEMENTS OF DIFFERENTIATION

Differentiated instruction involves:	Differentiated instruction is intended to:	Differentiated instruction is not intended to:
Student differences	Analyze students' readiness to determine instructional decisions.	Label students.
Instructional groupings	Flexibly grouping and regrouping students according to instructional objectives and in response to students' needs.	Primarily deliver Instruction in a whole-class group.
Materials and texts	Present multiple levels and kinds of learning materials.	Predominately use a single, grade-level text.
Learning assignments	Differentiate learning experiences to present respectful ways to learn. The contrast is in the depth and complexity of tasks.	Generally, assign the same learning task for all students to complete. The contrast is the degree of difficulty experienced by different students in response to the task.
Students' interests	Incorporate students' interests to increase their motivation to learn and to maximize individual potential.	Assess interests less often because the curriculum is predetermined.
Assessment and evaluation	Implement multifaceted, continual assessment to guide instructional decisions and focus students' learning goals. Evaluate and determine grades when required.	Predominately complete evaluations to produce grades in a grade book or scores on tests.
Excellence	Reflect students' personal best and the degree of individual growth from each learner's achievement level at the entry point of instruction.	Designate the students with the highest grades and achievements.
Standards	Integrate standards into the curriculum.	Teach standards as separate learning components.
Teachers' roles	Enable teachers to facilitate and coach students' learning. Customize instruction to seek ways for all students to succeed in learning.	Primarily provide direct instruction through delivering the curriculum only as designed by the texts.
Students' roles	Enable students to actively participate in learning, producing, and assessing own learning.	Require students to dutifully complete learning tasks designed for inclusion in the grade-level curriculum, regardless of individual readiness, learning profile, interests, or dispositions for learning.

Developing Background

Kingore, B. (2004). *Differentiation: Simplified, Realistic, and Effective.* Austin: Professional Associates Publishing.

INSTRUCTIONAL PRACTICES THAT HINDER DIFFERENTIATION

There are instructional practices and attitudes that hinder effective differentiation of instruction, particularly for advanced and gifted students. Reflect upon these obstacles to learning.

Negating student differences

I know everyone is not the same. But this is how I teach, and this is the curriculum I am supposed to teach.

Traditional assessment that results in gotcha

Gotcha is the result of the evaluation of a product or at the end of an instructional segment that rewards those who *got it,* penalizes those who did not, and determines the deficiencies for all of the students: *You got an A, but look at what you did wrong here.* It is a deficiency-based model that discourages intrinsic motivation.

Covering content

I have so much information to cover this year, I don't have time to differentiate. Covering and learning may not be related. Some teachers think: *I taught a great lesson; therefore, the students understand it.* But those teachers may be deceiving themselves and giving students (especially our brightest and most perceptive students) the impression that they only need a surface awareness of content to get by.

Glass ceilings

A glass ceiling is an invisible barrier that limits how much some students are allowed to learn. Teachers with low expectations for students or those who limit students to grade-level content are infringing a glass ceiling upon students' potentials. Glass-ceiling statements include:

* *This is only _____ grade. We don't teach that yet.*
* *I am expected only to get you to this level.*
* *I only know enough to get you to this level.*
* *I only have enough materials to get you to this level.*

Enrichment as replacement tasks

Enrichment, as provided in some grade-level texts, may treadmill learning for many gifted students. Assigning these students more learning experiences at the same level they have already mastered does not extend their learning or interests.

Grade-bound materials

Limiting students to grade-level materials minimizes opportunities for more complex responses. Advanced and gifted students need access to an abundance of beyond grade-level materials in order to expedite learning.

Excessive whole-class instruction or mixed-ability cooperative learning

Whole-class instruction or mixed-ability cooperative learning groups aim concepts and skills at the middle range of abilities for students in the class; hence, overuse limits opportunities for advanced and gifted students to accelerate learning at their level of readiness.

Limited differentiation training

Teachers are hindered in implementing differentiation when they have limited training or when the complexity of the training remains at an introductory level.

Time

Most teachers express frustration about not having time to get everything accomplished. Schedule rigidity is another negative time element as students seldom have a large block of time to pursue the uninterrupted research or study upon which many highly-able students thrive.

Attitudes

> TEACHER:
>
> *I need to spend my time with the students who really need me. That gifted kid already knows enough without my help.*
>
> *I need to spend my time with the students who may not pass the test. That gifted kid already knows enough to pass.*

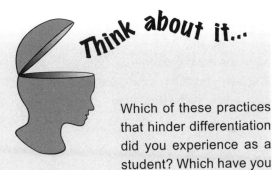

Which of these practices that hinder differentiation did you experience as a student? Which have you observed as an educator? What is your plan to overcome these obstacles to learning?

Never continue practicing with students anything that negatively affected your own learning.

INSTRUCTIONAL PRACTICES THAT ENCOURAGE DIFFERENTIATION

Certain instructional practices encourage differentiated instruction, particularly for advanced and gifted students. These practices compliment teachers' goal to instruct each learner at an optimum level.

Responding to learner differences

Recognize students' differences not to label them but to enable them to enter learning opportunities at the most appropriate level of challenge to foster their successes. When teachers respond to learner differences, a variety of learning methods and levels permeate the classroom learning environment.

Authentic assessment [1]

Authentic assessment occurs in learning environments as instruction and learning intersect. It is continuous and diagnostic as it enables teachers to respond to students' needs and enables learners to develop and refine their skills.

Students' self-assessments [1]

Self-assessment encourages students to increase their responsibility for learning and their motivation to excel. Metacognitive devices for student reflection, interest inventories, goal setting, and rubrics for students' self-assessments provide standards for evaluation instead of mere opinions.

Differentiation strategies that respond to students' learning needs [2]

Respond to students' learning needs and readiness levels by incorporating strategies such as curriculum compacting and tiered instruction to integrate concepts and skills

[1]See Chapter 9: Assessment Strategies that Impact Differentiation
[2]See Chapter 2: Instructional Strategies that Impact Differentiation

Kingore, B. (2004). *Differentiation: Simplified, Realistic, and Effective.* Austin: Professional Associates Publishing.

Developing Background

across discipline areas. These strategies enable teachers to differentiate the pace and level of instruction.

Clearly developed scope and sequence

A clearly developed scope and sequence is part of a curriculum map that enables acceleration and curriculum compacting to be readily implemented. It provides direction to guide students' incorporation of needed concepts and skills as they pursue independent study beyond grade level.

Replacement tasks determined by interests and readiness

Replacement tasks are necessary when preassessment identifies students who have mastered the concepts and skills in the next learning segment. These tasks need to be personally relevant, interesting, and involve vibrant learning possibilities. Students benefit from teacher facilitation as they make interest-based choices of products and processes.

Environments rich in materials

The purpose of school should be to set the idea that there is a book side to everything.

--Robert Frost

Students benefit from access to a wide range of kinds and levels of materials within the classroom. Teachers, however, also need an abundant source of resources in order to expedite their plan for differentiation.

Grouping options and applications [1]

Grouping is the cornerstone supporting differentiation. Flexible grouping responds to students' diversity by recognizing that no single group placement matches all of a child's cognitive or affective needs. Group placements are flexible and varied according to students' need and the demands of the learning experience.

Efficient management and organization [2]

Effective differentiation requires organization and management techniques that limit the intensity of teacher preparation. Differentiated instruction enriches learning experiences, efficiently uses instructional time, and promotes students' independence and responsibility. It necessitates that students learn how to work responsibly and productively in small groups while the teacher is engaged with other learners.

Integrated learning instead of isolated skill-teaching [3]

Isolated skills are harder to learn, more difficult to retain, and therefore, more time-consuming to teach. Concepts and skills are best learned when they are integrated, interactive, and interesting.

[1]See Chapter 5: Grouping to Enhance Differentiation
[2]See Chapter 6: Management Strategies that Impact Differentiation
[3]See Chapter 10: Integrating Learning Standards

Kingore, B. (2004). *Differentiation: Simplified, Realistic, and Effective.* Austin: Professional Associates Publishing.

Attitudes

> *Differentiating instruction is important to my students' success. Let's work together to facilitate this process one step at a time.*

The instructional practices that encourage differentiation need development and exemplification. The remaining chapters of this book provide information, techniques, and examples integrating these aspects of differentiated instruction.

GUIDELINES FOR AN ATMOSPHERE CONDUCIVE TO DIFFERENTIATION

Differentiated instruction is most effective when implemented school-wide. However, it is of value if only one or a small number of classrooms initiate differentiation inasmuch as the students in those classrooms benefit. Several guidelines follow to help provide a school-wide or classroom atmosphere conducive to differentiation.

Promote success for all students as they learn important information in different ways.

Success for all students requires teachers to vary the complexity of questions and tasks in response to students' readiness and learning style. Differentiation requires a varied duration of learning activities to respond to students' appropriate pace of instruction. It honors the diversity of students' responses by using open-ended tasks that invite multiple correct approaches and responses instead of a single correct answer.

Encourage respect, responsibility, ownership, and pride.

All students are respected and valued for who they are and what they can become. They are challenged to take responsibility for their learning so they experience ownership and pride in how they change and develop as learners.

Allow students to polish and refine their craft.

Teachers build upon what students are learning to do well as they help students develop and extend a solid foundation of needed concepts and skills. Rather than only delineating deficiencies, errors are analyzed to plan learning goals and approaches.

Recognize where each student begins, and enable each to experience as much progress as possible.

A focus on growth instead of only achievement enables students to succeed at multiple levels. The attitude becomes: *This is where you are. Let's see how far you can progress in your learning*. With highly-able students, the indication of success expands beyond the level of accomplishment to include the degree of change as a learner. Gifted students must demonstrate continued learning rather than merely receive high grades.

Invite challenge and complexity in both thought and production.

Challenge students toward more complex thinking and responses rather than simple-correct answers. Inquiry at high-levels of thinking and a rich variety of multi-level materials and resources prompt this complexity. Without complexity, gifted minds are less likely to remain actively engaged.

Kingore, B. (2004). *Differentiation: Simplified, Realistic, and Effective.* Austin: Professional Associates Publishing.

Developing Background

A primary child was asked why she did not like reading at school although she was such an avid reader at home. She explained: 'But at school I haven't read anything I didn't already know!'

Integrate high-order thinking, including the encouragement of abstract thinking and symbolism.

Increase high-level thinking and abstract thinking by incorporating symbolic relationships and visual symbols into lessons. For example, a student develops symbols for each key element in a given topic or creates symbols representing each main character in a novel.

Involve students in planning and organizing learning.

Ownership is increased and analytical thinking is engaged as students plan and organize aspects of their learning. Student-planned Adventure Trips that explore learning in and out of the school environment are an expanded example of students' ownership in learning.*

Extend students from consumers to producers.

Much of traditional education is based upon students as consumers completing the learning tasks prepared by teachers. To increase depth of understanding and more consistent applications of high-level thinking, students must become producers and decision-makers who produce the applications and examples that demonstrate learning.

STRATEGIES THAT SUPPORT DIFFERENTIATION

Several strategies are not considered differentiation strategies yet support the process so effectively they need to be mentioned. Mentors and buddies, student-managed portfolios, problem-based learning, workshop classrooms, and vertical teaming are examples of current practices that support differentiated instruction.

MENTORS AND BUDDIES

Teachers of gifted students actively seek individuals with expertise in a student's area of intense interest in order to expand that learner's opportunities for information and experiences beyond the curriculum. At the secondary level, mentors are typically adult experts in the field who interact with the student while relating the content, methodology, activities, and feelings involved with the profession. Approach community service groups as resources when seeking potential adult mentors.

While adult experts are also an asset at the elementary level, older students in the same building provide another resource for extending children's opportunities for advanced information. Appendix A: Buddies, provides information about using older students to assist and challenge younger students.

The use of mentors and buddies increases differentiation opportunities by providing the individual attention teachers so desire for their students. This strategy is particularly valid for advanced learners when the one-on-one interaction allows highly-able children access to materials and concepts beyond grade level so they may extend their learning and achieve at their individual levels of readiness.

---

*George Betts and Jolene Kercher's Autonomous Learner Model (1999) includes Adventure Trips and several other investigations requiring students to plan and organize learning.

Kingore, B. (2004). *Differentiation: Simplified, Realistic, and Effective.* Austin: Professional Associates Publishing.

STUDENT-MANAGED PORTFOLIOS

A portfolio is a systematic collection of student work selected largely by that student to provide information about the student's attitudes, motivation, levels of achievements, and growth over time (Kingore, 1999). It offers a concrete record of the development of students' talents and achievements during a year or more. In classrooms where all students develop portfolios, the portfolio process enables each student to be noticed for the level of products produced, and in this manner, increases inclusion instead of exclusion by providing multiple opportunities for children from every population to demonstrate talents and gifted potential. An effective portfolio system allows schools to honor the diversity of students and discover the strengths of each learner.

Portfolios that have the greatest educational value are student-managed and organized. Students learn to periodically select examples of their work that document agreed-upon criteria and then to file that work in the back of their portfolio so it approximates a chronological order and clarifies their growth over time. *How are you developing as a learner?* is the more appropriate question for differentiated instruction as it focuses on personal growth. *What is your best work?* is much less effective as it leads students to focus on grades instead of learning. Specifically, gifted students could have all *A* products and not have substantially advanced as a learner. Increasing emphasis on students' reflections and self-assessments is one of the advantages of portfolios.

Values of Portfolios for Advanced and Gifted Students

♦ Products can be assessed to assure that a level of depth and complexity appropriate for advanced-level students is reached,

thereby documenting differentiation and learning standards.
♦ Products can demonstrate and document all areas of giftedness.
♦ The portfolio helps teachers view students as individuals in light of their individual responses and selections.
♦ The portfolio can be shared with the parents or other professionals to document the growth and achievements of the gifted students.
♦ Portfolios provide examples of superior work for students to share among themselves as models to challenge ever-increasing levels of excellence.
♦ When most effective, portfolios allow learners with high-potential to, in essence, nominate themselves as gifted through their work and level of responses over time.

Portfolios do not support gifted potentials, however, when the learning opportunities offered students are limited to a collection of grade-level tasks. The quality of the learning opportunity and the potential of the learner determines the level of that person's response. Only to the degree that portfolios document students' highest levels of performance on a wide array of challenging tasks can the portfolio process substantiate giftedness.

WORKSHOP CLASSROOMS

Reading, writing, and math workshops provide an authentic purpose for the development of academic skills. Just as professionals seek assistance and interaction with other professionals, students work together to create, edit, and/or reflect upon each other's original work. Based upon individual needs, the workshops accent content, process, and product, and they are structured to ensure continued growth for all learners. Schedules are flexible and include periods of time for students' to engage in uninterrupted reading, writing, and

Kingore, B. (2004). *Differentiation: Simplified, Realistic, and Effective.* Austin: Professional Associates Publishing.

computing as well as time for pairs or trios of students to share, debrief, and conference among themselves or with the teacher.

The teacher continually assesses through observation and models appropriate work behaviors as needed. These assessments lead teachers to conduct brief, often rather informal mini-lessons to address the observed needs of one or a small number of students. The students' responsibilities accent continued progress through applications of academic logs, goal setting, self-assessment, and organizing portfolios of products that reflect their developing levels of expertise.

VERTICAL TEAMING

Vertical teaming is an administrative communication across elementary, intermediate, middle, and high schools serving the same population of students. Not typically considered a differentiation strategy, nonetheless, vertical teaming enables communication regarding students' whose needs exceed their grade placement in one or more disciplines. It allows decisions about placing students for instruction in grades levels and buildings according to readiness level rather than age level. Hence, vertical team communication can establish grouping solutions across grade levels or even between schools. It is an economical component in differentiated instruction for highly-able learners, as it only necessitates an adaptation of the regular school program.* Loveless (1998) stated that within-class and cross-grade ability grouping are both supported by research.

Olivia is an example of a student who benefitted from vertical teaming decisions based upon student needs. When beginning fifth grade, her third, fourth, and fifth grade math teachers advocated for advanced place-

ment for her in math. Test results confirmed her math readiness exceeded eighth grade concepts and computations. Her maturity and eagerness to learn led her parents and the school personnel to concur that advanced math placement was required. She was placed in an accelerated eighth grade math section for one period a day and succeeded with distinction. The rest of the day she worked in her fifth grade placement. She had the benefit of age-grouping for many of her learning needs and advanced placement to nurture her gifted potential in math. The next year, she continued advanced math placement in high school and then worked with a college math professor who mentored her passion for math.

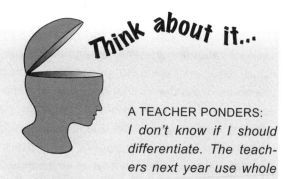

Think about it...

A TEACHER PONDERS:
I don't know if I should differentiate. The teachers next year use whole class instruction. Maybe I should get my class ready for that.

A parable

As a mother of three sons, I learn that there will be a devastating famine the next year. What is my best reaction for my children? Should I begin to cut back on their food supply so they become accustomed to less and less? Or, should I insure that this year they have the most nurturing ingredients within my power to supply to enrich their reserve?

I have the power to determine decisions about their nutrition this year. I am not in control of their future.

*Refer to Roger's (1998) synthesis of research on acceleration for depth of information regarding the affective and cognitive ramifications of advanced placements.

Kingore, B. (2004). *Differentiation: Simplified, Realistic, and Effective.* Austin: Professional Associates Publishing.

INSTRUCTIONAL STRATEGIES THAT IMPACT DIFFERENTIATION

Caring about the education of your students isn't enough. Teachers need tools-- practical and effective strategies that we can use with confidence and success, such as:

Curriculum Compacting, Flexible Grouping, Learning Centers, Open-Ended Tasks, Preassessment, Product Options, Research and Independent Study, Students as Producers, Students' Self-Assessment, Thinking and Inquiry, and Tiered Instruction.

GIFTED STRATEGIES VERSUS DIFFERENTIATION STRATEGIES

ADMINISTRATOR:
I want all my teachers trained in gifted strategies. They're good for all learners.

Before further discussion of strategies, we need to pause and question the term *gifted strategies.* What most educators are referring to should more accurately be called *differentiation strategies.* Decidedly, differentiation strategies are relevant for all learners. Conversely, serious misinterpretations result from referring to gifted strategies as being good for all learners; doing so blurs our understanding of the needs of special populations and contradicts the educational best practice of tailoring instruction to respond to students' learning differences. Gifted students, like other special populations, have instructional needs that are different than the instructional needs of regular learners.

Instruction in many mixed-ability classrooms is based upon what is most appropriate for the learning needs of on-grade-level students. Advanced and gifted learners, like other

Instructional Strategies

Kingore, B. (2004). *Differentiation: Simplified, Realistic, and Effective.* Austin: Professional Associates Publishing.

learners with special needs, require changes in the pace and level of that curriculum. In order to experience continuous learning, gifted students require an accelerated pace of instruction using advanced content.*

DIFFERENTIATION STRATEGIES

Differentiation strategies help teachers create classroom environments in which all students:
-- are respected participants
  -- with opportunities to engage in learning important concepts and skills
    -- at an appropriate pace and degree of challenge
      -- through interesting learning tasks that reflect their learning profiles.
The teacher brings to a successfully differentiated classroom the constructive attitude of approaching teaching as if each student was a family member: *What would I want my child to experience?*

Twelve differentiation strategies are presented in this chapter to help enable teachers to more specifically consider how to differentiate their instruction. While there are numerous strategies that relate to differentiation, the strategies developed here are selected as ones frequently implemented for their direct impact on differentiation. The strategies are presented in alphabetical order to avoid implying a hierarchy of value. Each strategy has a place in dynamic learning environments. The success of each depends upon the needs of the students, the teaching style and skill of the instructor, and the objectives of the educators making instructional decisions in response to state or district learning standards.

The strategies of differentiation are interdependent. Specifically, differentiation is not viable without flexible groups. Flexible groups based on readiness are impossible without assessment. Compacting and tiering instruction can not succeed without assessment and flexible groupings. Open-ended tasks flow into research and independent study. And so it continues across the strategies. Hence, it is imperative to understand each strategy to enable its integration into the whole.

RATING THE COMPLEXITY OF IMPLEMENTING DIFFERENTIATION STRATEGIES

Figure 2.1: Differentiation Strategies is a rating form to analyze the strategic implementation of differentiation strategies in your teaching. Rate the complexity of each strategy's implementation based upon your experiences in the classroom. A *1* rating indicates that implementing those strategies is more simple and less intensive than the other strategies being analyzed. (The rating relates to implementation and does not imply that the strategy itself is simple or less valued.) A *2* rating signifies that these valued strategies are in the middle-range of implementation complexity. A *3* rating denotes that these important strategies are needed but that implementation is more complex and intensive than any of the others.

When you have completed your ratings on Figure 2.1, review your results to celebrate your successful implementations and motivate your differentiation goals. By analyzing your current degree of instructional differentiation you can plan your future growth.

One element affecting the ease or complexity of implementing a strategy is decidedly the degree and types of experiences that teachers have had with it. In general, teachers score a 3 rating to the strategies with which they have had the least experience. For

---

*Chapter 4: Understanding and Accommodating Advanced Potential elaborates the needs of advanced and gifted learners in the classroom.

Kingore, B. (2004). *Differentiation: Simplified, Realistic, and Effective.* Austin: Professional Associates Publishing.

Figure 2.1:
DIFFERENTIATION STRATEGIES

Rate your implementation of the following differentiation strategies from 1 to 3. Then, list applications of each strategy practiced in your classroom.			
	1 ←	**2** →	**3**
	Simple implementation; used with confidence; can readily explain and demonstrate this strategy to other educators	Some implementation complexity; generally understand the strategy; need to refine management and organization to aid application	Complex, sophisticated implementation; intensive preparation; more information and training is needed
	Curriculum compacting	APPLICATIONS	
	Flexible grouping		
	Learning centers or stations		
	Learning centers (student produced)		
	Open-ended tasks		
	Preassessment		
	Product options		
	Research and independent study		
	Students as producers		
	Students' self-assessments		
	Thinking and inquiry		
	Tiered instruction		

Kingore, B. (2004). *Differentiation: Simplified, Realistic, and Effective.* Austin: Professional Associates Publishing.

Instructional Strategies

example, few teachers experienced curriculum compacting or tiered instruction during their own learning as students attending the grade level that they now teach. Furthermore, many teachers have indicated that they had little or no training in these strategies during their college studies. It is certainly more difficult for teachers to successfully implement a differentiation strategy with which they have little or no experience, particularly if they are not around other teachers who successfully model these strategies. Each strategy on Figure 2.1 is discussed in the remainder of this chapter.

CURRICULUM COMPACTING

Compacting is an instructional pacing strategy designed to eliminate further instruction in mastered curriculum and streamline content to a pace commensurate with students' readiness. Advanced students familiar with a topic can demonstrate mastery on a pre-assessment before instruction begins. These students require substantiation of what they know and replacement opportunities for continued learning instead of redundant assignments. Compacting is appropriate for advanced and gifted learners because it affords students who demonstrate high levels of achievement the time to pursue personally relevant differentiated activities and continue their learning.

Researchers document the need for curriculum compacting as a differentiation strategy for gifted students. As much as 50 percent of the current grade-level curriculum could be eliminated for these students without lowering achievement test results (Reis et al., 1992).

Written Documentation. Document each student exhibiting readiness for compacting. Include the scored preassessment used to determine mastery and a completed curriculum compacting form. Figure 2.2 is a variation of the concept originated by Joseph Renzulli and Linda Smith (1978)[1]. This documentation should be signed, dated, and contain the following basic information.

1. The learning standards, concepts, and skills mastered and verified by the pre-assessment of this segment of instruction
2. Any learning standards, concepts, and skills which may still need to be learned
3. Recommended replacement tasks of interest to the student for extension and acceleration in that subject area

The Learning Contract, Reading Contract,[2] and Proposal for a Replacement Task in Chapter 6 are additional methods that integrate with compacting and aid the organization of the process. Place the emphasis on student record keeping rather than add to teachers' paper management tasks.

Figure 2.2:
CURRICULUM COMPACTING

STUDENT *Anthony*   DATE *September 10*
TEACHER *Ms. Donaldson*
SUBJECT AREA/TOPIC *History*

Demonstrated mastery	Documentation:
Standards: • *Points of reference in US history* • *Compare political, economic, and social perspectives of conflicts* Concepts and skills: • *Reading and interpreting text* • *Drawing conclusions based on analysis of the Civil War period*	*Preassessment: End of unit benchmark test --Grade: 98*
Needs for further instruction:	**Procedures and resources:**
Increase in-depth information about political figures significant to the time period. *Explore what motivated the selected historical figures.*	*Sept. 10 - 14:* *Independent study* *Sept. 15 - 16* *Meet with class for discussion and quiz* *Sept. 17 - 24* *Complete independent study*
Replacement tasks:	**Resources:**
Read nonfiction and biographies *Develop a first-person oral presentation. The class will interview you as the historical figure you select.*	*Library* *Internet* *Historical society* *Reading Contract*

Kingore, B. (2004). *Differentiation: Simplified, Realistic, and Effective.* Austin: Professional Associates Publishing.

[1]For additional forms and elaboration, see Reis, Burns, and Renzulli (1992) or Winebrenner (2001).
[2]The Reading Contract example in Chapter 6: Management Strategies that Impact Differentiation elaborates the replacement task evolving from this Curriculum Compacting example.

Kingore, B. (2004). *Differentiation: Simplified, Realistic, and Effective.* Austin: Professional Associates Publishing.

Figure 2.2:
CURRICULUM COMPACTING

STUDENT _____   DATE _____

TEACHER _____

SUBJECT AREA/TOPIC _____

Demonstrated mastery Standards: Concepts and skills:	**Documentation:**
Needs for further instruction:	**Procedures and resources:**
Replacement tasks:	**Resources:**

Kingore, B. (2004). *Differentiation: Simplified, Realistic, and Effective.* Austin: Professional Associates Publishing.

FLEXIBLE GROUPING

Flexible grouping responds to students' diversity by recognizing that no single group placement matches all of a student's needs. Hence, with this strategy, teachers initiate short-term grouping and regrouping of students in response to instructional objectives, the demands of the task, and students' needs. It is in stark contrast to more stagnant grouping procedures in which students remain in the same group for most of the year or receive whole-group instruction for most of the school day.

Flexible grouping *is not* stagnant. The groups do not remain constant nor expect everyone to learn in the same way. *It is* flexible and varied working arrangements and group make-ups that are characterized by continual shifting according to instructional objectives and students' readiness levels.

Flexible grouping is a vital component of differentiation. Without flexible grouping, differentiation is unlikely to occur to any substantial degree. Since it is viewed in this book as the cornerstone that supports differentiation, Chapter 5 develops the options and applications of this strategy.

LEARNING CENTERS OR STATIONS*

A learning center or station is a physical area of the classroom that is organized with various materials and learning experiences for specific instructional purposes. Centers may be year-round centers, such as writing and research centers, or they may be topical and change periodically. Stations differ from centers inasmuch as different stations are established that relate to one concept or skill and provide varied experiences in the parts of that whole. An example is math stations for division that provide practice at one station while other stations accent computer applications of division, problem solving, and strategy investigations.

Centers are popular with many students because they incorporate diverse ways to learn away from students' usual desks or table areas. Provide appropriate materials in centers to enable students to explore and work independent of teacher direction. The focus is on practice, mastery, or extension of concepts and skills.

Some educators debate whether centers are social or learning-based. Perhaps there should be no debate, as both are readily incorporated. School is a place for learning together. When more than one student is in a center, socialization is invited in the context of learning discussions rather than just social exchanges.

The most productive centers involve open-ended inquiry rather than simple activities. Centers that challenge advanced learners need to include complex tiered activities and beyond-grade-level resources--particularly an ample variety of non-fiction materials.

Guidelines for Instructionally Vibrant Centers

- Focus on important learning outcomes integral to your curriculum. Ensure that students are not just *doing activities*.
- Document standards by posting a laminated list of learning standards and marking the ones integrated in the current center tasks.
- Promote high-level thinking responses instead of simple-correct answers and matching tasks.
- Post a rubric that defines quality work and positive work behaviors.
- Include a range of interactive activities and learning tasks that appeal to the diverse learning profiles and readiness levels of the students.

*Centers are addressed briefly in Chapter 5: Grouping to Enhance Differentiation as a flexible small-group application and in Chapter 8: Tiered Instruction with an example of a tiered learning center.

Kingore, B. (2004). *Differentiation: Simplified, Realistic, and Effective.* Austin: Professional Associates Publishing.

- Provide clear directions. In some classes, it may be advisable to develop step-by-step procedures and checklists that students use to monitor their progress.
- Promote students' organization by including boxes, in and out bins, task cards on metal rings, or folders. *A place for everything and everything in its place.*
- Develop routines for participating in centers so students understand expected behaviors, what to do, where to go, and how long to stay.
- Promote students' record keeping through a centers log in which they record the tasks they engage in and self-assess the quality of their work. Using Figure 2.3, each log would contain one copy of the title and rubric card with multiple copies of the third card to respond to multiple centers.
- Motivate quality responses to center tasks by including a cork or wipe-off board for students to post their work for others' review rather than only produce more papers for the teacher to grade.

LEARNING CENTERS (STUDENT-DEVELOPED)

One outcome of students' working in learning centers is the experience they gain in the process and products of centers. This experience enable students to progress toward creating their own centers. When centers are a significant component of differentiation, include one area of the classroom solely for student-developed centers that change as different students create additional products. Motivate students to develop centers as products of their interest-based research and study. This application provides an authentic audience for the research products and enables peers to participate in the student's learning.

Student-developed centers should accent in-depth content and interpretation

rather than flashy production. Many simple presentation formats are possible so that even young students can experience the satisfaction of creating a center for another student's learning. All student centers need to include: a visual aid or graphic listing one or more essential questions of the research, the materials related to the center, clear directions for how to use the materials, and answer keys when needed.

Simple Center Products

- Audio tapes. The student narrates and records a tape of an informative book about the topic, adding stops on the tape to give interpretations, elaborate, and explain points.
- Poster board collage. The visual-verbal student makes a collage of drawings and cut-out illustrations, symbols, and words significant to the topic. During center time, the student is in the center to elaborate and discuss any item of information that another child selects on the collage.
- Flap books. The student writes an essential question on the outside of the flap. The flap is lifted to reveal the answer and ref-

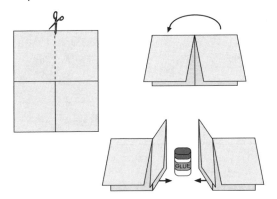

erences to materials located in the center with more information or illustrations about that question.
- Scavenger hunt. The student writes six to ten descriptive cards that lead the reader from one resource in the center to another in search of components of the final answer to an essential question.
- Trivia game. The student develops a set of cards with questions and detailed

Kingore, B. (2004). *Differentiation: Simplified, Realistic, and Effective.* Austin: Professional Associates Publishing.

Figure 2.3: CENTERS LOG AND RUBRIC

_____'s

Centers Log

DATE STARTED _____

DATE FINISHED _____

Rubric   DATE _____

Below Standard	**C**	**B**	**A**
I did not follow the directions. I did not work.	I worked but did not finish. I used some of my own ideas. I tried to help. I helped clean. My work has accurate information.	My work is complete. I used only my own ideas. I helped others. I helped clean. My work is accurate and informative.	My work is complete and carefully done. I used original ideas. I encouraged and helped others. I helped clean. My work is well developed, detailed,

---

CENTER _____ DATE _____

What I did:

What I learned:

Kingore, B. (2004). *Differentiation: Simplified, Realistic, and Effective.* Austin: Professional Associates Publishing.

responses about the research topic. The cards are organized into a trivia game for two other students to play. To add to the fun in playing, the students negotiates with the teacher to develop silly (*You get to tell two jokes.*) or serious awards for the winner (*You win 15 minutes of computer or drawing time.*).

More Sophisticated Center Products

* Power point™ presentation. Many research topics can be organized into a power point™ presentation to run in a center.
* Digital photographs. Some research topics lend themselves to a photo essay with photographs and large index cards containing explanations. *A Categorization of Community Flora* and *A Presentation of Local Historical Buildings* are two examples of students' research choices.
* Debate. Two to four students collaboratively research an issue or ethical concern. During center time, they present their information in the form of a debate in which two or more viewpoints are presented.

OPEN-ENDED TASKS

Open-ended tasks are flexible learning activities. The tasks are determined by teachers. The responses are as individual as the students. Open-ended does not imply that quality is not important or that any response is acceptable. Rather, these tasks signal that there is more than one way to approach the task and that more than one correct response is possible. When one correct response emerges, the challenge for students is to build upon that response and develop additional possibilities. Hence, open-ended activities replace worksheet activities that require little thinking with tasks that encourage active participation and challenge students to generate new responses.*

These learning experiences use multiple formats to scaffold diverse responses from students. The objective of these tasks is to celebrate diversity in thinking by encouraging students to respond with multiple correct ideas at different levels of complexity and understanding. These tasks are important in mixed-ability classrooms as they recognize many levels of success instead of focus on simple right or wrong answers. They become the tip of the differentiation iceberg when used to jump-start students' diverse responses.

This strategy is particularly relevant for young and special-need learners when the open-ended tasks are planned to elicit brief responses that demonstrate reasoning. I think of these responses as accenting the head not the hand. The intent is to challenge students to spend several minutes of high-level thinking that is translated into a product that may involve minimal writing.

These learning experiences are particularly relevant for advanced or gifted students who prefer to generalize and organize information in unique ways as they exhibit a depth of understanding beyond that of their age-mates. Use open-ended tasks to direct students' organization of information and serve as springboards for discussing and writing more extensively about a topic.

Many open-ended tasks are in the form of graphic organizers, such as Venn diagrams; they prompt understanding of relationships through a visual representation of information. As an example of a learning experience using a open-ended task, organize a Venn diagram on a bulletin board. Use stapled yarn or a marker to form a diagram on the light-colored background of the board. Students complete index cards and post responses in each appropriate section. The board might be used for one topic or become a year-around board that focuses learning for

---

*Several of the guidelines listed in Guidelines for Instructionally Vibrant Centers in this chapter are equally applicable as guidelines for open-ended tasks.

Kingore, B. (2004). *Differentiation: Simplified, Realistic, and Effective.* Austin: Professional Associates Publishing.

every topic. It is a concrete way for students and visitors to view the progression of the students' thinking and acquisition of understanding. Vary the shape of the diagram to maintain visual appeal. Overlapping any two outlines creates a potential Venn.

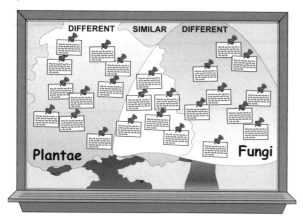

PREASSESSMENT

Preassessment is vital to match instruction to students' readiness.[1] Information from preassessments:

-- guides teachers' preparation of student-appropriate instruction,

-- responds to the pace and level needs of students, and

--accommodates students' learning profiles.

Teachers can not compact curriculum, develop tiered assignments, or flexibly group students by readiness or interests without information gained through preassessments. Hence, preassessment is an enabling strategy--it enables teachers to make informed decisions about students' learning which in turn enable students to continue learning.

The goal of preassessment is to accurately identify students' current levels of learning and determine the modifications needed for the next stage of learning. Preassessments generate information regarding students' interests, learning profiles, and achievement levels. Teachers access information about students' interests and learning profiles through interviews, informal discussions, and surveys.[2] They access information about achievement levels through multiple formats in addition to tests so all students have opportunities to display levels of understanding. Many learning experiences appropriate to students' learning profiles can also be used as preassessment tools.

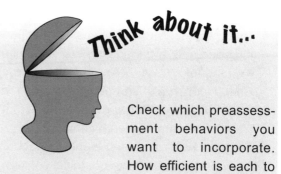

Check which preassessment behaviors you want to incorporate. How efficient is each to use? What kinds of information might each reveal? How valid is that information in relation to your teaching objectives?

• Reviewing portfolios and products from prior learning experiences
• Using the tests accompanying published grade-level materials as pretests instead of only at the end of a segment of instruction
• Interpreting observations of students in learning situations, such as performance tasks or activities
• Reviewing skills and concepts
• Discussing concepts and skills
• Reviewing students' independent reading of fiction and nonfiction materials
• Interpreting students' self-assessments
• Categorizing information from students' interest inventories
• Others

---

[1]Preassessment is a major contributing factor to the success of differentiation. Chapter 9 develops grading recommendations for preassessment, techniques to increase the instructional value of preassessment, and examples of simple, informative preassessment tools in addition to testing.

[2]*Assessment* (Kingore, 2005) includes examples of interest inventories that incorporate art sketches instead of only words to relate students' preferences.

Kingore, B. (2004). *Differentiation: Simplified, Realistic, and Effective.* Austin: Professional Associates Publishing.

PRODUCT OPTIONS

Products are what students create to demonstrate and extend what they learned as a result of content and process.

Well-designed product assignments motivate learners and result in products that document learning. To actively engage more students more of the time, classroom learning tasks need variety in the types of products assigned. Teachers strive to incorporate balanced offerings of products in order to encourage students to demonstrate their best ways of learning and to validate the significance of all modalities and intelligences.

Students vary so dramatically in their strengths, needs, and best ways to learn that determining lists of appropriate product options at varying degrees of complexity seems a daunting task. To increase the efficiency of that preparation, begin or continue creating a list of products applicable to the curriculum. Reflect upon the developing list, and ponder which product options:

- Are most appropriate for the students.
- Are most applicable to the content.
- Involve students in applying and transferring acquired skills.
- Promote the greatest depth and complexity of content.
- Have diagnostic value.
- Are respectful, equitable work.
- Promote students' success.
- Stem from authentic problems and audiences.
- Are more enjoyable to facilitate.

As product options are decided, organize the products in alphabetical order for quick reference. Then, customize those selections to students' specific learning needs and preferences by coding each product to the modalities and intelligences students primarily use when completing or sharing the product.

Appendix B: Product Options for Differentiated Instruction begins with a lengthy list of products to skim as a visual checklist to guide selection of the most appropriate product options for students. (I have frequently condensed the list into a reasonable number of offerings. However, teachers repeatedly comment that the expanded length prompted their thinking more effectively. Hence, a lengthy list is included for teachers to skim; it is by no means intended as a recommendation of quantity in your product variety! Product options are more typically a short list.) The product options list is followed with a Product Grid as one example of a format for organizing products to match students' learning modalities and multiple intelligences.

Teachers question: *How do we determine grades when students are completing different products?* Product options for students do affect grading procedures. Seldom is an answer-key as effective as a rubric when different products are involved to demonstrate learning. Chapter 9 provides several evaluation techniques and examples.

Think about it...

While matching product options to students' needs is paramount, the reality is that teachers do at times consider products which they most enjoy and avoid products they find unappealing. If not practiced at the expense of students, your personal preferences are also appropriate and may exude an enthusiasm that is contagious.

*Chapter 8 includes examples of formats for organizing product options for tiering instruction.

Kingore, B. (2004). *Differentiation: Simplified, Realistic, and Effective.* Austin: Professional Associates Publishing.

RESEARCH AND INDEPENDENT STUDY*

Research and independent study require a personal interpretation and response rather than merely reporting information already in print. It develops from students' interests and responds to the unanswered questions typical of highly-able learners. High-level thinking is continual as students evaluate their process and results, often cycling back to reconsider data. Rather than be viewed as a formal research-paper process for only secondary students, independent research has no prescribed product. The product is determined by the student as an authentic extension of the research. Research and independent study should begin in kindergarten and never stop because they are driven by curiosity.

Research and independent study contrast with teacher-guided or teacher-directed projects in which students are asked to research information and grow in knowledge by reporting or recording what is already known. This teacher-guided research is valuable to enable children to learn the skills of research and habits of mind that later affect more self-directed research. Guided research frequently becomes personally interesting, as when students research aspects of their lives: *What happened the day you were born?*

Research and independent study build upon the research and independent working skills acquired through teacher-guided studies. It is more personal and requires more open-endedness than when teacher-directed.

Research and independent study is:

- Student-interest based. The topic or problem is personally relevant to the student.
- Student-directed. The focus is on student production, original problem solutions, and the student's determination of authentic audiences for the results.

- Student-controlled parameters. In addition to determining the product of the research, students also determine the way to approach the problem and the time line for the investigation. Optimally, no predetermined closure date is imposed as real research develops its own length of pursuit. However, reality usually dictates some system of progress checks, and authentic audiences may affect the time frame.
- Investigations of real problems. Researchers are challenged to reach new conclusions as they discover and interpret knowledge. The ultimate challenge for researchers is to add new information, ideas, or products to the field of study.
- Dependent upon skills. It is a vehicle for continued development of sophisticated skills in research, reasoning, technology, communication, and self-directed learning.
- An ongoing replacement task for students who pretest beyond the planned curriculum.

Some adults assume that young children can not conduct research because they are too inexperienced to produce new information. In a real sense, this is true. Yet primary

Teacher tip...

Gifted students and creative thinkers may investigate more than one topic or problem simultaneously. Some have multiple investigative questions that detail their special interests and passions.

---

*Research and independent study is addressed briefly in Chapter 5 as a flexible small-group application because research can be conducted in small groups when more than one student shares a common interest.

Kingore, B. (2004). *Differentiation: Simplified, Realistic, and Effective.* Austin: Professional Associates Publishing.

children are among the most curious and driven to solve problems. Respond to that enthusiasm with opportunities to pursue their interests in research. A student's creation of new information through research must be considered within the context of the learner's age and experience. Something that is learned information for a secondary student may be a newly researched insight for a primary child.

Independent research begins with a student's interest and progresses to questioning, investigating, and product development. Empower the student with the idea that is it admirable to wonder and ask questions. Support that idea by modeling respect for questions.

> *What do you observe?*
> *What do you wonder?*
> *What makes you curious?*
> *What might it be?*
> *What could you investigate?*

Students can skim the list of thinking skills (Figure 2.7) to prompt their high-level thinking and formation of essential questions to focus their investigation. In some schools, students post their questions in the classroom, library, or a class online form to pique other students' interests and reactions.

Think about it...

How can you be certain you are encouraging real investigations instead of guiding their reporting of information? One test is students' intrinsic motivation. Real researchers feel impelled to investigate, to find out how it turns out. You do not have to prod their continuance.

STUDENTS AS PRODUCERS

In 1977, Joseph Renzulli, in discussing his Type III Enrichment, stated that youngsters must become investigators with a producer's rather than consumer's attitude. He advocated investigations of real problems with learners engaged in adding new knowledge, ideas, or products to the field of study. This simple idea balloons beyond students-as-researchers into a way of thinking about instructional planning. How much could or should students be constructing for themselves instead of merely responding to the teacher's planning?

In most classrooms, students are consumers using up the tasks teachers prepare. To increase depth of understanding, students must become producers as often as possible, producing the applications and examples that demonstrate learning. Students must have the responsibility of structuring most of the parameters of the task; if a teacher lays out all of the parameters, the student is more likely to perform as a consumer. When students generate responses, high-level thinking is exhibited, multiple skills and concepts are integrated, and a wider diversity of products result. The process readily incorporates different learning styles, making instruction responsive to learner profiles.

The strategy of students becoming producers flows from students' experiences with open-ended tasks. Those experiences prepare students to expect diverse responses. A difference between open-ended tasks and students as producers, however, is the degree of teacher-centered versus student-centered responsibility. Open-ended tasks are determined and driven by teachers. When students are producers, the teacher determines the content area as well as which concepts and skills to integrate, but does not determine the format of the response. The teacher facilitates students' progress, but does not exactly dictate the parameters of the process. The student-

Kingore, B. (2004). *Differentiation: Simplified, Realistic, and Effective.* Austin: Professional Associates Publishing.

centered decisions related to organizing and managing the process are part of students' development as producers. The ways to respond are as individual as the students.

Many students can become producers; but advanced and gifted students particularly need to become producers. After learning experiences are introduced through teacher-directed instruction, students work independently or in small teams to produce original ideas, new relationships, or products related to the content. The open-ended nature of the process challenges students to analyze, synthesize, and evaluate as they work. Student-developed learning centers discussed earlier in this chapter are an example of students as producers.

Opportunities abound for students as producers once we open our thinking to the possibilities. For example, Ms. Forbes, a kindergarten teacher, was working with her young ones in phonics instruction. To engage them in letter-sound relationships for *S,* she had a large sock on her hand that she named Sammy the Snake. Sammy slithered into the sack, brought out items beginning with *S,* and the children made the sound as she wrote the words on the board. After the successful lesson, one of her gifted readers said to her: *I'm wondering what you'll do for X.* Clearly, he had analyzed her objective of making the lesson very concrete for developing learners. His statement implied that he thought that would be rather hard to do for *X*! That moment illustrates a missed opportunity for a student to become a producer in the classroom. It would have been interesting to ask him to produce that lesson for *X* in order to elicit his perception of the task and how his gifted mind would approach it.

Computations in math provide multiple examples for students to become producers. Consider a typical multiple-choice test item:

73 X 14 =
A. 922   B. 912   C. 1012   D. 1022

Now, consider the following three ways to alter that process by requiring students to become math producers instead of math consumers.

1. The problem is 73 X 14. Show four ways to solve it.
2. Write and illustrate a word story problem that involves multiplying 73 X 14 for its solution. Explain your problem.
3. You have a variety of manipulatives, including unifix cubes, balance scales, blocks, buttons, a number line, calculator, and graph paper. You are teaching a second grader about multiplication. Which materials do you want to use? Demonstrate what you will do.

When students are producers, they provide evidence of understanding beyond factual knowledge. Students exhibit increased mental engagement, and students who are mentally engaged are seldom bored.

STUDENTS' SELF-ASSESSMENTS

Motivation to achieve increases when students are partners in assessment. Students should routinely analyze their achievements and works-in-progress to monitor their changes as learners and set goals for continued achievements. In this manner, assessment is a collaborative task in which each stake-holder provides feedback.

Rubrics are effective self-assessment tools when they:
- Reflect the most significant elements related to success in a learning task.
- Enable students and teachers to accurately and consistently identify the student's level of competency.
- Encourage students' reflection and high-expectations.
- Are shared with students prior to beginning the task so they know the characteristics of quality work.

Kingore, B. (2004). *Differentiation: Simplified, Realistic, and Effective.* Austin: Professional Associates Publishing.

Three self-assessment rubrics are shared as examples: Learning Characteristics, Reading Assignment and Response, and Problem Solving. Figure 2.4: Learning Characteristics requires little writing yet accents reflection as students and the teacher analyze work habits and learning behaviors.* Using different colors, the student and the teacher each mark the same copy of the form for comparison. (It is useful in a parent conference to ask parents to complete a copy of this form and then compare their perceptions with the teacher's and students' responses.)

Teachers use self-assessment rubrics, such as Figure 2.5: Reading Assignment and Response, to clarify the importance of a learning experience and to increase students' involvement in the task. (Mr. Perez, a secondary teacher, reported that his class was better prepared and more purposefully read assignments when using that rubric. Their attentive reading enlivened the class discussions of the content, and students commented that they enjoyed the class more.) Teachers use self-assessment rubrics, such as Figure 2.6: Problem Solving, to enable students to analyze their current level of understanding and focus their goals for continued learning.

Each of the following self-assessment rubrics encourages students' self-analysis. The assessments model some of the many different formats for rubrics, such as a checklist, letter grades, and holistic number ratings. Understand that holistic number ratings could be easily converted to letter grades when preferred by replacing *4-3-2-1-0* with *A-B-C-D-F*.

THINKING AND INQUIRY

All students are natural thinkers who bring with them many of the thinking tools they need to reason effectively. However, the unschooled mind is a mixed bag of sharp and fuzzy thinking, of ignorant and sound knowledge, of open-mindedness and prejudice (Paul, 1995). Teachers must help students converge thinking into reasoning and problem solving.

Teachers use questioning techniques to structure and focus students' high-level thinking. The synthesis of thinking skills in Figure 2.7 enables teachers to guide students into reasoning and problem solving as they explore multiple contents. These thinking skills mirror the high-level responses expected with many state learning standards. To enhance a lesson, use these thinking skills as a checklist-- skim over it to activate thinking of potential topic connections. Which of the thinking skills might effectively weave into the discussion to lift complexity or which might prompt higher problem-solving tasks for students in a particular learning context?

Incorporating selected thinking skills into the curriculum requires students to understand and apply information rather than only memorize and repeat it. High-level thinking is more engaging as it invites students to interpret and relate to the content rather than only *know* the content. Predict how students' level of involvement and thinking might elevate during a discussion of the Gettysburg Address if the teacher peppers the discussion with opportunities for inference, classification, and comparative reasoning.

- What does Lincoln seem to assume in this speech?
- Which traits of Lincoln led him to say: *The world will little note or long remember what we say here...*

*The content of the Learning Characteristics rubric parallels the positive work behaviors developed in Chapter 6: Management Strategies that Impact Differentiation.

Kingore, B. (2004). *Differentiation: Simplified, Realistic, and Effective.* Austin: Professional Associates Publishing.

Figure 2.4:
LEARNING CHARACTERISTICS

STUDENT _____   DATE _____

TEACHER _____   DATE _____

	Consistently	Sometimes	Not Yet
Work and Study Habits			
Stays on task			
Manages time well			
Organizes work			
Uses multiple, appropriate resources			
Reorganizes and returns materials			
Sets goals for self			
Seeks help when needed			
Does not call undue attention to self			
Completes quality work			
Persistence			
Shows patience			
Self-monitors and checks own work			
Edits and revises work			
Is willing to try something new			
Accepts responsibility for own learning			
Social Skills			
Communicates diplomatically			
Works cooperatively			
Listens attentively			
Helps others as needed			
Encourages others			
Respects others' ideas and property			
Works and interacts with others quietly			

A goal for my continued learning is:

Kingore, B. (2004). *Differentiation: Simplified, Realistic, and Effective.* Austin: Professional Associates Publishing.

READING ASSIGNMENT AND RESPONSE

NAME _____   DATE _____

On the back of this form, write a response to your reading by completing these four prompts:

1. *I noticed*   **2. *I feel***   **3. *I relate***   **4. *I question***

Your response is due on the day the reading is due. Grade your work by checking your proficiency level for each criterion and determining the total grade you earned.

GRADE	CONTENT	ORGANIZATION	COMPREHENSION
F	❏ There is no response.	❏ The organization is inadequate for the task.	❏ No comprehension is demonstrated.
D	❏ The ideas are insignificant or inaccurate.	❏ The writing is unclear and hard to follow.	❏ Support is needed to clarify understanding.
C	❏ The content is valid but sparse with little depth or elaboration.	❏ Some organizing is evident, but the response wanders.	❏ A beginning level of understanding is reflected.
B	❏ The content covers the topic well and is well developed	❏ The response is generally well organized and sequenced.	❏ Adequate understanding is reflected with appropriate detail and vocabulary.
A	❏ The content is in-depth with complex information and concepts.	❏ The written response is well organized and sequenced to communicate ideas effectively.	❏ Precise vocabulary, supportive ideas, and concept relationships demonstrate a thorough understanding.

Total grade for this assignment: _____

Comments:

Kingore, B. (2004). *Differentiation: Simplified, Realistic, and Effective.* Austin: Professional Associates Publishing.

Figure 2.6:
PROBLEM SOLVING

NAME _____ DATE _____

ASSIGNMENT _____

GRADE

4	The work is accurate, well organized, complete, and explicit. Appropriate strategies are applied to yield a valid solution. Precise vocabulary enhances and clarifies the process. • I knew what to do, what operations to use, and how to solve this problem. • My strategy worked; the solution makes sense and is easy to follow.
3	The problem is appropriately solved. Minor errors produce some confusion, but sufficient details are included to clarify the process and explain the results. • I checked my solution, and it makes sense. • I know what the problem is about, and I think I can explain most of it.
2	The solution is incomplete. There are gaps, major errors, or misinterpretations which obstruct a valid solution process. • I tried a strategy, but it didn't work well for the whole problem.
1	The problem is attempted but the process is inadequate and an appropriate solution is not reached. • I tried several things, but nothing worked. • I don't know what else to do.
0	It is blank, the meaning is unclear, or it is different than the assignment. • I'm not sure what the problem is or what to do.

Next problem-solving goal:

Comments:

Kingore, B. (2004). *Differentiation: Simplified, Realistic, and Effective.* Austin: Professional Associates Publishing.

- Role play a conversation between two Confederate leaders responding to Lincoln's speech.

High-level thinking is not limited to secondary students. Special-need students of all ages may share insightful responses to thinking prompts when invited to respond only in their strongest modalities. Young learners lack depth of experience but freely exhibit high-level thinking when prompted with selected thinking skills, such as comparative reasoning, classification and inquiry.

- *What patterns does the Itsy Bitsy Spider show us? Which ones can we act out?*
- *How is the Itsy Bitsy Spider's behavior like something you do?*
- *What characteristics does the spider demonstrate?*
- *What question would you ask it?*

All students need to be exposed to learning experiences that encourage them to think and process information at high levels. However, it is appropriate for advanced-level students and imperative for gifted students to spend the majority of their time experiencing the challenge of opportunities for in-depth, complex, and abstract thinking. Rather than only rely on the teacher's high-level prompting, advanced and gifted students need to be challenged to develop their own high-level questions to pose to themselves and to one another in response to content and to extend their learning.

Thinking skills prompt high-level responses when:

- Teachers incorporate selected thinking skills into the content being studied and employ those skills to increase the challenge level of a lesson provided in a text.
- Teams of teachers use the thinking skills as prompts when brainstorming curriculum-related high-level questions and tasks.

- Teachers use the thinking skills to generate test questions that require high-level thinking and reasoning instead of simple responses.*
- Small groups of students prepare content-related questions that incorporate the thinking skills. Later, the groups pose and respond to each others' questions during a class discussion.
- Students use the thinking skills as a checklist to help them formulate essential questions that guide their independent studies in their areas of interests.
- Students incorporate the thinking skills into a demonstration or a center they prepare to prompt the interactions and higher-level reasoning of their classmates.

Think about it...

Sometimes you do not have an abundance of time. *What can I possibly do in a brief period to incorporate higher-level thinking?* Try this three-minute technique. Use the thinking skills list (Figure 2.7) as a brainstorming prompt with a small team of colleagues. Set a timer for three minutes and challenge yourselves to generate as many high-level, curriculum-related applications as possible. Then, reflect upon the ideas, and develop those with promise.

*Several question triggers based upon these thinking skills are shared in Chapter 9.

Kingore, B. (2004). *Differentiation: Simplified, Realistic, and Effective.* Austin: Professional Associates Publishing.

Figure 2.7:

THINKING SKILLS*

*Thinking skills are **interdependent and rarely used independently** of one another.*

CLASSIFICATION
- Analyze attributes or characteristics
- Categorize
- Identify ambiguity

COMPARATIVE REASONING
- Differentiate similarities and differences
- Distinguish reality and fantasy or fact and fiction
- Determine sequence
- Determine cause and effect
- Identify patterns
- Develop analogies
- Distinguish point of view

INQUIRY
- Formulate questions
- Pose unknowns

INFERENCE
- Hypothesize
- Predict
- Assume

SYNTHESIS
- Conclude
- Generalize
- Think deductively
- Think inductively

EVALUATIVE REASONING
- Determine relevancy
- Substantiate
- Establish and apply judgmental criteria
- Rank or prioritize
- Interpret

TIERED INSTRUCTION

Tiered instruction enables teachers to ensure that students with different learning needs and different levels of readiness successfully work at varying degrees of complexity with the same essential concepts and skills. In mixed-ability classrooms, learning standards are more effectively integrated into the curriculum when incorporated at different levels of complexity through tiered tasks.

Instruction can be tiered by content (the complexity of what students learn), process (how students learn), and products (how they present their learning). Based upon preassessments, the teacher varies the complexity of an activity into several layers of difficulty and then matches each appropriate version to students' levels of readiness. The intent is to ensure that all students explore ideas at a level that builds upon what they already know and facilitates their continued learning.

Most teachers have little or no experience with tiered instruction. To them, it is an overwhelming strategy that appears to be a preparation and management nightmare. Since teachers ask so many questions about tiered instruction, Chapter 8 develops the guidelines, procedures, and multiple applications of this strategy.

Think about it...

Review the ratings that you recorded on Figure 2.1. Celebrate your *1* ratings and let your *2* and *3* ratings structure your action plan for continued growth in effective differentiation. Be aware of what is working and then move forward to enhance your differentiation of instruction.

*Synthesized from the work of Stiggins, 2001; Kaplan & Cannon, 2000; Paul, 1995.

Kingore, B. (2004). *Differentiation: Simplified, Realistic, and Effective.* Austin: Professional Associates Publishing.

CAN DO! SUCCESS-FILLED DIFFERENTIATION

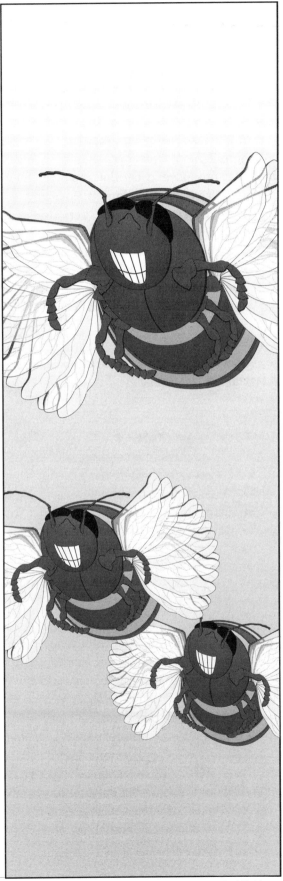

Whether you think you can or whether you think you can't, you're probably right.

--Henry Ford

Differentiating instruction invites educators to rethink traditional educational practices based upon a prior time when students were more similar in background and readiness. Educators today must embrace differentiated instruction for their students and assume a confident attitude that they can organize and manage this instruction. Marilyn Vos Savant (1997) offers an applicable analogy. Before limiting themselves in what they think they can do, educators should consider the bumblebee. The bumblebee is an aerodynamically unsound, little creature whose body is far too large, his wings are far too small, and he has hair instead of feathers. Judging his qualifications on paper, we would have to say that he could not possibly fly. But the bumblebee just moves his wings and flies merrily away! Differentiation can seem far too large an order if one considers only one teacher trying to support the diverse learning needs of so many students. It would seem that our wings would be too small to support the task. However, when educators band together with productive

Kingore, B. (2004). *Differentiation: Simplified, Realistic, and Effective.* Austin: Professional Associates Publishing.

ideas and solutions and then involve students in the responsibility as well as the benefits, differentiated instruction can fly!

▮ IMPLEMENTING DIFFERENTIATION ▮

Review the ratings that you recorded on Figure 2.1 in the previous chapter to reflect your background and current implementation of each differentiation strategy. For comparison, I rate the complexity of each strategy's implementation based upon:

1) A synthesis of the reactions shared by teachers I train and interact with who work in mixed-ability classrooms and special population classrooms across the nation, and

2) The differentiation practices I have observed in classrooms. The results of this synthesis follows.

Rated 1
Simple to implement
- ➥ Flexible grouping
- ➥ Open-ended tasks
- ➥ Students as producers
- ➥ Thinking and inquiry

Rated 2
Middle range of implementation complexity is required
- ➥ Learning centers or stations
- ➥ Student-developed centers
- ➥ Preassessment
- ➥ Product options
- ➥ Research and independent study
- ➥ Students as producers
- ➥ Students' self-assessments

Rated 3
Intensive, sophisticated implementation is required
- ➥ Curriculum compacting
- ➥ Tiered instruction

My personal and subjective implementation rating is intended to illustrate that most teachers do not consider differentiation simple or complete. Great teachers, like great artists, are never done in their quest for excellence. Be aware of which differentiation strategies are effectively implemented in your classroom or school and then move forward to enhance continued differentiation of instruction. The following steps sequence the implementation process.

Figure 3.1:
STEPS IN IMPLEMENTING DIFFERENTIATION

1. Analyze your differentiation.
2. Celebrate your success!
3. Develop an action plan.
4. Implement an additional strategy.
5. Network with other teachers.
6. Allow time.
7. Reflect.
8. Celebrate success, and progress to another strategy.

Initiate differentiation by analyzing the differentiation strategies implemented in your instruction. Recognize and celebrate your successes first! Acknowledge all that you have accomplished toward differentiating

Kingore, B. (2004). *Differentiation: Simplified, Realistic, and Effective.* Austin: Professional Associates Publishing.

instruction in your classroom. This validation step is important as teachers do not stop often enough to note what they are doing well.

After reviewing your accomplishments, develop an action plan to increase the effectiveness of differentiation. Analyze which strategies best address the students' needs and your instructional preferences. Prioritize which additional strategies might augment current differentiation practices. Focus on adding one strategy at a time to your repertoire rather than trying to do everything.

Select an additional strategy to implement. Learn more about this strategy by reading and attending conferences or inservice opportunities that address the strategy. Consider forming book clubs among faculty or a grade team to explore information.* As you investigate a strategy, analyze parts of the whole, and plan one part to initiate. If preferred, pilot the new strategy with one student or a small group rather than beginning with class-wide implementation.

Network with other teachers to brainstorm application ideas. Support groups of two or more teachers can meet regularly to share attempts and successes. Incorporate peer coaching between teachers as you discuss problems and share solutions. Extend and customize the process to your style and students' needs.

Allow time for you and your class to become comfortable with the strategy and the applications you implement. Educational practices that are valuable take real time and development. Make adjustments and problem solve as needed. Revisit the resources you found helpful, and compare your current status with the information gained from your reading and discussion. As confidence follows

your success, add another part or further applications of the strategy.

Over time, reflect upon what you have learned and accomplished with your differentiation practices. Elicit feedback and suggestions from students. Communicate with other teachers to share application ideas and prompt continued development.

Celebrate another success as you establish a comfort zone with the strategy. Acknowledge your professional growth and the benefits it brings to your students. Then, revisit your action plan, and progress to another strategy.

Be not afraid of going slowly.

Be afraid only of standing still.

SIMPLIFY THE PROCESS

Simplify the process of differentiating instruction by beginning with the strategies that are simpler to implement. There is little rationale for focusing on the most complex strategy and then experiencing frustration that prevents continuation. Cultivate success-filled experiences with differentiation by initially using strategies that are simpler to implement and then building upon those experiences to increase differentiation effectiveness. The ultimate goal may be compacting and tiered instruction, but first simplify the process by implementing other strategies that develop your repertoire and expertise. The following are possible components of simpler-to-implement differentiated instruction.

---

*Several excellent resources are listed in the references of this book. Additionally, a video staff development package enables professionals to see applications. *At work in the differentiated classroom* is a valuable video with the accompanying Facilitator's Guide developed by Carol Ann Tomlinson (2001, Alexandria, VA: ASCD).

Kingore, B. (2004). *Differentiation: Simplified, Realistic, and Effective.* Austin: Professional Associates Publishing.

Model for Success

To enable maximum learning and increased independence, the teacher initially teaches students how to complete a learning experience or product. Students can not be expected to work independently when they are uncertain how to complete the work successfully. The process must be modeled and the students experience success with each part of the whole before they can proceed by themselves. Hence, learning experiences and products are introduced in teacher-directed instruction.

Students also benefit from teacher assistance to learn how to identify the important information and the relationships among the concepts. Deciding what information is important and how to organize the data is a vital process that requires active involvement, increases learning, and helps students construct meaning.

Open-Ended Learning Experiences

Flexible, open-ended, multipurpose learning experiences are effective choices for initiating differentiation of instruction. Open-ended learning experiences are the tip of the differentiation iceberg. They do not fully address the pace and level needs of gifted students, but they do invite diversity of responses. Since more than one correct answer is possible, students construct their own solutions rather than simply reinvent ours. The open-ended tasks support respect for each learner's thinking rather than one correct response and all others wrong. Students get the sense that there are many ways to be right as they increase their comfort for risking divergent responses.

Open-ended problems remove the ceiling from tasks so participants can operate at higher levels. The results are layers of simple to more complex responses from students.

◆ Incorporate opportunities for multiple intelligences and learning styles. The subparts and open-ended nature of these learning experiences provide many ways for different styles and intelligences to be validated.

◆ Increase active participation by having students write responses before sharing their ideas in class. Announce: *Take one minute and write which points you think are most important before we share ideas;* or announce: *Write your best solution, and then, we will compare with each other.*

◆ Occasionally, change the work location. Move to the cafeteria to extend possibilities through expanded space. Go outside to stimulate different senses.

◆ As advanced student complete open-ended tasks, challenge them to include one or more elements of abstract thinking, complexity, or depth to extend learning.

Teachers repeatedly use open-ended learning experiences, such as the Venn diagram and concept mapping. Brainwriting is another open-ended task for simple implementation.* It is an effect way to focus thinking about a topic as it is introduced or to synthesize information toward the end of instruction.

➡ **Brainwriting***

Each person in a group of four or five students makes a copy of a brainwriting sheet. To make the sheet, students fold a blank piece of paper into quadrants, open it, and draw a square in the middle where the quadrants intersect. On the sheet, each student writes the topic in the square and labels each of the quadrants: nouns, categories, relationships, and symbols. One student makes an extra sheet to place in the middle of the table. In the spaces provided, students then begin writing various words and

---

*Adapted from Shade and Garrett. (2002). *Laughing Matters: Using Humor in Classroom Activities*. Austin: Professional Associates Publishing.

Kingore, B. (2004). *Differentiation: Simplified, Realistic, and Effective*. Austin: Professional Associates Publishing.

phrases that represent ideas relevant to the topic being studied. After completing two ideas, a student puts that sheet in the middle, takes a different sheet from the middle, adds two different words, and then exchanges again. Students do this for three to five minutes or until all sheets are filled. Then, as a whole group, they compare and contrast the related information.

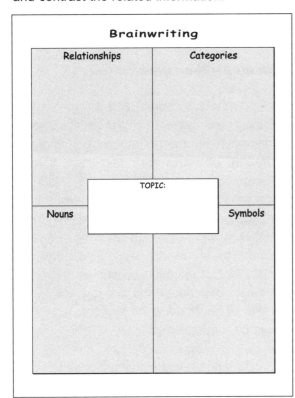

Flexible Grouping

Master teachers realize that whole class instruction is more limited in its ability to respond to individual learning needs and actively engage students. Therefore, differentiation focuses on learning in flexible, small groups. When students work in flexible groups, communication and negotiation become critical so that learning experiences and products accurately represent both content and the perspective of each student.

Whenever possible within your instructional objectives, keep group size small. Groups of two to four require more students to

be on task. Groups of five or more often result in some students doing most of the work.

Students-Led Inquiry

Students should learn to pose questions that stem from their interests and prompt their further learning. To encourage this behavior, teachers devise activities that require students to formulate, prioritize, and categorize questions. For example, instruct small groups of students to brainstorm 10 or more questions applicable to a specific topic. Next, students prioritize their questions from the most to least essential, and determine the criteria that guided their ranking. In the ensuing discussion, some students realize that certain kinds of questions promote simple answers or less thinking than intended, that some questions are too general, or that a wider variety of types of questions would be more beneficial. Prioritizing and categorizing helps students focus on essential instead of detail questions. This experience increases students' effectiveness in planning their independent studies or developing interview questions.

Students as Producers

Following multiple experiences with open-ended learning tasks and student-led inquiry, encourage many students to evolve into producers. Producers build upon the learning experiences and problem-solving opportunities provided by the teacher and begin to construct their own applications. Students demonstrate high levels of learning when they move from consumers responding to assignments, to producers constructing their own ideas, relationships, and products. Because students generate their own examples, a wider variety of responses at different levels of understanding and complexity result than when teachers produce the problems or examples for students to answer. Moving students to producers also increases personal relevance as students determine more aspects

Kingore, B. (2004). *Differentiation: Simplified, Realistic, and Effective.* Austin: Professional Associates Publishing.

of the product and demonstrate their best ways to learn.

The following examples illustrate a few ways to involve students as producers who integrate concepts and skills. In each case, the students must assume responsibility for the parameters of the task rather than follow a teacher-designed plan.

♦ Instead of merely answering the questions prepared by the teacher or embedded within the text, students create the questions to pose to classmates during discussions. Their questions must be concept-based and demonstrate understanding rather than simple detail. Students further prepare for discussions by listing the components of the correct answer they expect from classmates.

♦ Students plan their procedure and teach a mastered concept to one other person who then is able to demonstrate understanding. (Caution: Keep instructional objectives in mind. The intent is to substantiate understanding, not to engage students as part-time tutors.)

♦ Students plan, develop, and complete a project that integrates that skill with other learned skills.

♦ Students produce an original example that applies the targeted skills to another content area.

♦ Students produce an original example that extends the skills beyond the original lesson.

♦ After interpreting the information in its original text form, students graphically represent the concept or develop symbols to demonstrate relationships within the content.

Teachers often experience frustration feeling that students needs and the demands of teaching are so great there will never be enough time. Begin seeking ways to save time in preparation and instruction. A few ideas follow. Network with other teachers to share additional suggestions. Many minutes of the school-day can be used differently.

Save preparation time

Without compromising learning effectiveness, seek ways to minimize the intense preparation time that can accompany differentiation. The objective is to maximize student learning, not overwhelm teachers. Minimize preparation by using open-ended, multipurpose learning experiences that integrate with clear objectives and lead to student learning. Minimize by increasing student responsibility and student preparation. When we view students as independent and capable, we model the idea of never doing for students what they should do for themselves.

Spend energy in instruction rather than mere decoration. Look at the classroom through students' eyes. Which elements in the environment stimulate learning and which are more decorative than learning-driven? Bulletin boards, for example, should reflect effective learning experiences rather than become a statement of interior-design. A student-prepared bulletin board may lack the sophisticated design of an adult's board yet more effectively promote students' as productive, valued learners.

Use the following ideas to build upon and prompt your decisions of appropriate ways to save preparation time.

♦ Provide blank paper. Blank paper saves time because the teacher does not have to

*After interpreting the information in its original text form, students graphically represent the information or concept or develop symbols to demonstrate relationships within the content.

Kingore, B. (2004). *Differentiation: Simplified, Realistic, and Effective.* Austin: Professional Associates Publishing.

run copies of anything. Furthermore, high-level responses may be prompted more effectively by blank paper than fill-in-the-blank paper.

1. Column analysis. Students fold blank paper into columns on which to organize information. The paper can be folded into two, three, four, or more columns to organize areas on which to record comparisons of species, math operations, historical events, characters, polygons, and many other items. Students fold the paper, label each column at the top, and proceed to analyze and organize data. Paper folded for column analysis is also useful to record survey information for graphing.

2. Four-box fold. Continuing the technique used for brainwriting earlier in this chapter, fold a paper in half and then in half again to form quadrants. Students draw an oval in the middle at the intersection of the quadrants. In the oval, they write the topic; in each quadrant they write a label by which to organize the topic, such as any of the following: attributes, needs, problems, solutions, nouns, verbs, people, places, categories, relationships, or symbols.

♦ Promote students' record keeping and management. Even young students can record results of learning experiences to accent their personal growth over time. Additionally, if a student is absent, provide carbon paper for another student to use when taking notes so a copy is ready when the absent student returns. (Carbon paper is available at most office supply stores.)

♦ Repeatedly use graphic organizers. They require minimum preparation time and can be used multiple times. They invite students to:

• Visually represent abstract concepts and relationships,

• Illustrate and explain relationships found in textual material,

• Prepare and organize oral presentations and demonstrations, and

• Organize ideas before writing.

Organizers also assist students with limited vocabulary in expressing relationships graphically instead of only through written or verbal communication.

Save Instruction Time

♦ Use open-ended learning experiences more than once. After the initial experience, using open-ended learning tasks again saves instruction time. Since students already know how to proceed, the teacher does not need to use instructional time to explain.

♦ Use the overhead more effectively for group sharing. When students work in groups producing components that will be shared later by the whole class, provide each group an overhead writing pen and

Teacher tip...

One time-saving plus is a wide range of biographies and autobiographies in the classroom. It is relatively simple to get an abundant supply from the library, and many students are drawn to them to read as replacement tasks. Advanced students are intrigued with the lives of *real* people. For some, the biographies are life models for their interests.

Kingore, B. (2004). *Differentiation: Simplified, Realistic, and Effective.* Austin: Professional Associates Publishing.

one or more strips cut from blank overhead transparencies. As each group completes their ideas, they write them on a strip. When it is time for the whole class to participate, the strips are easily positioned on the overhead for all to read with no additional time spent in recopying. Another advantage of this technique is that the strips can be repositioned as hierarchical or sequencing decisions are made.

♦ Instruction time is saved when students are better prepared before working in a group with the teacher. Encourage students to use scrap paper as a planning sheet at their desks before they participate in a group or class discussion. This sloppy-copy encourages more students to actively think and organize their ideas before the discussion begins. (The focus is on thinking and the quality of ideas rather than writing conventions.)

♦ Save instruction time by avoiding needless interruptions. Negotiate as many classroom decisions as appropriate with your students. Post those decisions or produce a classroom pledge for all to sign as agreement to appropriate behaviors when working independently, in groups, or at learning stations.

GUIDELINES FOR DIFFERENTIATED LEARNING EXPERIENCES

�± Avoid trying to differentiate what was not effective in the first place.

↱ Recognize, respect, and respond to learner differences as learning experiences are planned.

↱ Vary the types of learning experiences so different kinds of learning styles and intelligences can be observed, identified, and then acted upon in lesson planning.

↱ Promote high-level thinking and responses. Challenge students to continually analyze and synthesize as they work to construct solutions. Also, encourage multiple responses from students instead of stopping discussion after only one response. Occasionally, follow up multiple responses by involving students in ranking the list of generated ideas based on effectiveness or some other pertinent criterion.

↱ Encourage complexity and challenge. Provide tasks that involve varying levels of difficulty and incorporate appropriate levels of challenge to account for individual readiness levels.

↱ Support student interest and choice. Provide multiple opportunities for students to choose topics to study, products to develop, and an array of extensions to enhance their learning.

↱ Promote content integration. Selected learning experiences should allow students to connect prior knowledge and new information rather than stress isolated skills. Select interesting activities with multiple opportunities for integration and application of concepts and skills. Busy teachers do not have time for activities that are merely fun to do. The goal is for every task to engage students and expand their content understanding.

↱ Require active involvement in learning. Select learning experiences designed to actively engage students' minds and bodies in learning. Students who are mentally engaged are seldom bored; active involvement increases their learning and personal connections to the content. The goal is for most of the students to be actively engaged most of the time.

↱ Continually share criteria for success and high achievement with students. Clearly

Kingore, B. (2004). *Differentiation: Simplified, Realistic, and Effective.* Austin: Professional Associates Publishing.

established criteria are communicated to the students in advance of the learning experience and used for self or collaborative evaluation. Some examples of criteria include: complexity of content or solution, accuracy and depth of information, quality, group cooperation, evidence of understanding, appearance, originality, integration of skills, organization, time management, applications of technology, and presentation.

needs through your implementation of specific strategies that correlate to instructional needs.

My Dutch mother always said: *What you're not up on, you're down on!* This adage is certainly true for parents' attitude about their child's classroom learning environment. The more we share information with parents, the more they have confidence that we care about their child's learning and that we know how to differentiate instruction toward maximizing their child's potential.

PARENTS ASK ABOUT DIFFERENTIATION

Parents sometimes ask a teacher or an administrator: *What are you doing for my gifted child?* Briefly explain to them what differentiation is and how it impacts instruction in your mixed-ability class. Then, use the differentiation strategies you rated as *1* to guide your response to those parents (Figure 2.1 in the previous chapter). Inform them of your current practices and your future goals in differentiation.

To more specifically address the learning needs of your highly-able learners, consider the information in Figure 3.2 that matches differentiation strategies to the instructional needs of these students. While each differentiation strategy may be applicable to advanced and gifted learners, the strategies are marked to indicate which are most likely to enhance specific pacing and level needs. You know your students! When talking with a parent, point out the pacing and level needs of that student and then explain how you are addressing those

CONSIDER
The Swans and The Ducks

To ensure success-filled differentiation, it is valuable to network with other professionals who also want to differentiate instruction. Change is often more comfortable when approached with others. Seek the swans. Swans are teachers who want beautiful learning opportunities to develop for students. They are teachers who share your passion for teaching and are ready to stretch out their necks to differentiate instruction. Swans respect and respond to the diversity of students.

Avoid the ducks-- they don't give a quack and only try to peck down your enthusiasm. They peck away at each new idea as soon as it is proposed. They are intimidated by change and prefer the drone zone of all teachers teaching the same way, on the same page, at the same time. Ducks negate diversity.

Kingore, B. (2004). *Differentiation: Simplified, Realistic, and Effective*. Austin: Professional Associates Publishing.

Figure 3.2:
DIFFERENTIATION STRATEGIES MATCHED TO INSTRUCTIONAL NEEDS

While any strategy may be applicable to advanced and gifted learners, the strategies checked are those most likely to enhance each specific instructional need.

PACE		LEVEL			
ACCELERATED RATE OF INSTRUCTION	MINIMUM REPETITION	ADVANCED CONTENT	HIGH DEGREE OF COMPLEXITY AND ABSTRACTION	IN-DEPTH STUDY	
✓	✓	✓			Curriculum compacting
✓	✓	✓	✓	✓	Flexible grouping by similar-readiness levels
		✓	✓	✓	Flexible grouping by interests
		✓	✓	✓	Learning centers or stations (student-developed)
✓	✓	✓	✓		Learning centers or stations (teacher-developed)
		✓	✓		Open-ended tasks
✓	✓	✓	✓	✓	Preassessment
		✓	✓	✓	Product options
✓	✓	✓	✓	✓	Research and independent study
		✓	✓	✓	Students as producers
		✓	✓	✓	Students' self-assessments
		✓	✓	✓	Thinking and inquiry
		✓	✓		Tiered instruction

Kingore, B. (2004). *Differentiation: Simplified, Realistic, and Effective.* Austin: Professional Associates Publishing.

UNDERSTANDING AND ACCOMMODATING ADVANCED POTENTIAL

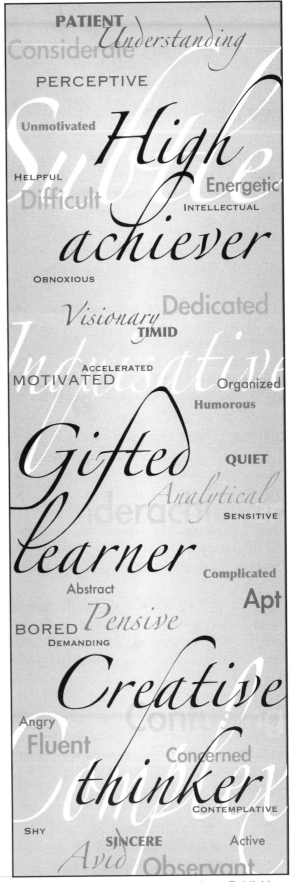

Understanding the instructional needs of advanced and gifted learners is the precursor to appropriately responding to those needs. Figure 4.1 succinctly represents how the learning needs of these students differ from all other wonderful students. This simplified explanation can help defuse cries of elitism and build perceptions of advanced and gifted students who deserve to continue learning at an appropriate level of instruction.

Figure 4.1:
INSTRUCTIONAL NEEDS OF ADVANCED AND GIFTED LEARNERS

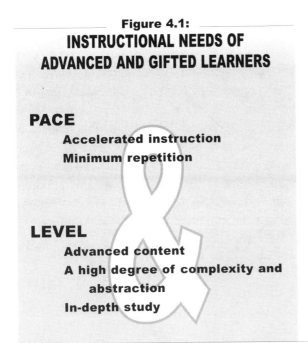

PACE
- Accelerated instruction
- Minimum repetition

LEVEL
- Advanced content
- A high degree of complexity and abstraction
- In-depth study

Kingore, B. (2004). *Differentiation: Simplified, Realistic, and Effective.* Austin: Professional Associates Publishing.

In order to enable advanced and gifted students to experience continuous learning, an accelerated pace of instruction is required. Specifically, these students learn with minimum repetition and require fewer guided-practice experiences. Therefore, they need to progress through curriculum at a more rapid pace. To enable this pacing adjustment, initiate preassessments to document previous mastery of content. Based upon that assessment, adapt instruction to streamline content at a pace commensurate with their learning profile. Without accelerated pacing, gifted students risk spending excessive class time waiting for other students to learn the content.

Advanced and gifted students also need adjustments in content levels. They seek advanced content that responds to their readiness levels. They require a higher degree of complexity and abstraction to remain mentally engaged in learning tasks. They desire an in-depth study of many topics instead of a surface overview. Characteristically, gifted students thrive on complexity, abstraction, and depth. They want to be specialists rather than generalists, particularly in their selected areas of interest. Without advanced levels of content, gifted students risk spending excessive class time revisiting concepts and skills they have already mastered, feeling that school is boring.

Educators are accustomed to instructional pacing and level changes for students with learning differences. Special education teachers develop individual education plans that specify pacing and level accommodations to expedite the learning of these special-needs students. Similarly, it is time to become more accustomed to pacing and level adjustments for advanced and gifted students who benefit from accelerated instructional pacing and the challenge of advanced content.

For most gifted students, both pace and level need to be addressed. As an example, a common response to students who demonstrate their gifted abilities through reading is to provide higher grade-level materials to challenge them. If these materials are texts or basals, a problem emerges: the adjustment only provides higher levels of materials, and hence, it is limited to an accommodation in level. The pace of instruction in those materials is still geared to the pacing needs of on-grade-level learners. Accommodations in both pace and level are often required.

An adage in gifted education posed the question: *What is the worst thing to do to gifted students?* The answer was: *Nothing!* Doing nothing perpetuated the myth that gifted children make it on their own. The obvious concern was that doing nothing to instruct gifted children denied them their right to learn. While doing nothing remains a viable concern, after multiple years teaching and working with teachers in mixed-ability classrooms, I believe the answer to that adage should be changed.

> *Q: What is the worst thing to do to gifted students?*
> *A: Make them learn at the pace and level of general education.*

Instruction that does not match their pace and level needs is damaging to advanced and gifted students' motivation to learn and their enjoyment of school. Ultimately, instruction that does not respond to pace and level encourages underachievement and results in advanced and gifted students who no longer have a disposition to learn. These students then choose to conform to the minimum that is required of them. The attitude becomes: *What's the minimum it takes to get the grade? That's what I'll do.*

Kingore, B. (2004). *Differentiation: Simplified, Realistic, and Effective.* Austin: Professional Associates Publishing.

WHAT'S GOOD FOR THE GIFTED IS GOOD FOR ALL STUDENTS?

A common idea expounded by some administrators and teachers is that all children are gifted; and if you treat all children as if they were gifted, they will achieve at a gifted level. That response is appreciated if it stems from high-expectations for all students. However, it oversimplifies the diversity of learners and suggests a one-way-fits-all attitude. To illustrate the fallacy of that attitude, consider the concept of pacing. Regular learners require repetition for mastery. That repetition is built into spiral curricula and materials. The exact number of repetitions depends upon factors such as the readiness of the learner, the concept-density of the material, and the match of instruction to learners' profiles. (Repetition does not necessarily imply isolated skills-driven worksheets. Great teachers artfully incorporate repetition needs through a creative diversity of learning experiences.) Conversely, educators and parents understand that gifted learners require minimum repetition for mastery and often seem to *get it* after a very small number of exposures. Indeed, some gifted children understand content the first time it is introduced at school or even have figured it out for themselves before the concept or skill is formally presented in a lesson.

Now, let's try to put into practice that idea of treating all children as if they were gifted so they can achieve at a gifted level. In response to pacing, the teacher in a mixed-ability classroom now adopts the concept of minimum repetitions because that instructional practice matches an instructional need of gifted learners. The teacher thinks: *I will use solid learning experiences, present that concept or skill briefly to my whole class, and move quickly forward.* Realistically, how is this class doing? Predictably, some students are responding positively and experiencing success; some students are a little unsure and concerned; and some students are over-whelmed, frustrated, and perceiving themselves as too dumb to learn. The idea of treating all children as if they were gifted is a fallacy that does not respond to sound educational practices or the diversities of learners. It is not equitable to present the same level of difficulty in the same manner to all students in a mixed-ability classroom.

Matching Classroom Instruction to Gifted Instructional Needs

Teachers want to enable students to learn. Yet, it is incredibly challenging to adapt curriculum to accommodate the diversity of students' needs. In mixed-ability classrooms, use these questions to guide instructional decisions.

♦ Is this an appropriate learning experience?

♦ Can all students do this?

♦ Should all students do this?

♦ Does this learning experience vary in complexity so students have opportunities to learn the same content level or extend learning beyond that level?

♦ Is this pace of instruction appropriate?

♦ Is this an appropriate learning experience? Obviously, the task needs to be appropriate to the social, emotional, and cognitive learning needs of the students.

♦ Can all students do this? If all students can do this, it is probably not rigorous enough to appropriately challenge advanced or gifted students.

♦ Should all students do this? If this learning experience is one that has potential to benefit all learners, teachers need to tier the complexity of the experience to correspond to students' readiness, learning profiles, interests, and dispositions for learning.

Kingore, B. (2004). *Differentiation: Simplified, Realistic, and Effective.* Austin: Professional Associates Publishing.

◆ Does this learning experience vary in complexity so students have opportunities to learn at the same content level or extend learning beyond that level?

Some students may need varied experiences that enrich learning of the same concepts. However, advanced and gifted students typically require opportunities to extend learning beyond level through advanced content and materials.

◆ Is this pace of instruction appropriate?

Students have different pacing needs. The goal is: *not too hot, not too cold, but just right.* Regular curriculum is paced too hot for students with fewer skills and too cold for students with advanced skills. It may be just right for some students in a mixed-ability classroom.

HIGH ACHIEVER, GIFTED LEARNER, CREATIVE THINKER

In this era of standards-driven education, legislators and educators continue to misinterpret high achievement as giftedness and creativity as fluffy extra. High-achieving students are noticed for their on-time, neat, well-developed, and correct learning products. Adults comment on these students' consistent high grades and note how well they acclimate to class procedures and discussions. Some adults assume these students are gifted because their school-appropriate behaviors and products surface above the typical responses of grade-level students.

Educators working with gifted learners and creative thinkers experience frustration trying to help other educators and legislators understand that while high achievers are valuable participants whose high-level modeling is desired in the classroom, they still learn differently from gifted learners and creative thinkers. When in environments where learners are respected, valued, and encouraged, gifted students' demonstrate complex, in-depth thinking with more abstract inferences and diverse perceptions than is typical of high achievers. Creative thinkers, when working in respectful learning environments, question the known, inject new possibilities, and make mental leaps that surpass the correct-answer-driven responses that are more typical of high achievers. Articulating the instructional implications of these learning differences is vital when we strive to differentiate instruction.

Szabos (1989) published a comparison of the bright child and the gifted learner that challenged me to re-examine the nature and needs of advanced students working at different levels of readiness Her comparison helps to delineate differences between bright and gifted, and it provides a useful format for discussions. However, some of the items listed in the comparison are questionable. For example, the gifted learner is credited with having wild, silly ideas. In reality, it is creative learners who exhibit the ideas often called wild or silly; not all gifted learners demonstrate that aspect of the creative process. As a second example of concern, Szabos lists bright children as enjoying straightforward, sequential presentations. This behavior seems more associated with learning preferences than with ability. Arguably, some gifted learners also enjoy straightforward, sequential presentations, but their questions and responses to such a presentation may dramatically differ from the questions and responses of bright children. As a final example, Szabos' comparison states that gifted learners prefer adults while bright children enjoy peers. This statement has negative connotations leading to the stereotype that gifted learners are so out of sync with society and have such poor social skills that they can only communicate with adults. In reality, gifted learners seek idea-mates rather than age-mates. They enjoy the company of peers when the peer group understands the shared ideas. In practice, gifted students often

Kingore, B. (2004). *Differentiation: Simplified, Realistic, and Effective.* Austin: Professional Associates Publishing.

Figure 4.2:

HIGH ACHIEVER, GIFTED LEARNER, CREATIVE THINKER

A High Achiever...	A Gifted Learner...	A Creative Thinker...
Remembers the answers.	Poses unforeseen questions.	Sees exceptions.
Is interested.	Is curious.	Wonders.
Is attentive.	Is selectively mentally engaged	Daydreams; may seem off task.
Generates advanced ideas.	Generates complex, abstract ideas.	Overflows with ideas, many of which will never be developed.
Works hard to achieve.	Knows without working hard.	Plays with ideas and concepts
Answers the questions in detail.	Ponders with depth and multiple perspectives.	Injects new possibilities.
Performs at the top of the group.	Is beyond the group.	Is in own group.
Responds with interest and opinions.	Exhibits feelings and opinions from multiple perspectives.	Shares bizarre, sometimes conflicting opinions.
Learns with ease.	Already knows.	Questions: What if...
Needs 6 to 8 repetitions to master.	Needs 1 to 3 repetitions to master.	Questions the need for mastery.
Comprehends at a high level.	Comprehends in-depth, complex ideas.	Abstracts beyond original ideas.
Enjoys the company of age peers.	Prefers the company of intellectual peers.	Prefers the company of creative peers but often works alone.
Understands complex, abstract humor.	Creates complex, abstract humor.	Relishes wild, off-the-wall humor.
Grasps the meaning.	Infers and connects concepts.	Makes mental leaps: Aha!
Completes assignments on time.	Initiates projects and extensions of assignments.	Initiates more projects than will ever be completed.
Is receptive.	Is intense.	Is independent and unconventional.
Is accurate and complete.	Is original and continually developing.	Is original, ever changing, and misunderstood.
Enjoys school often.	Enjoys self-directed learning.	Enjoys creating.
Absorbs information.	Manipulates information.	Improvises.
Is a technician with expertise in a field.	Is an expert, abstracting beyond the field.	Is an inventor and idea generator.
Memorizes well.	Guesses and infers well.	Creates and brainstorms well.
Is highly alert and observant.	Anticipates and relates observations.	Is intuitive.
Is pleased with own learning.	Is self-critical.	Is never finished with possibilities.
Gets A's.	May not be motivated by grades.	May not be motivated by grades.
Is able.	Is intellectual.	Is idiosyncratic.

Kingore, B. (2004). *Differentiation: Simplified, Realistic, and Effective.* Austin: Professional Associates Publishing.

seek interactions with adults because they assume the adult is more likely to have the background to discuss the content elevated by the student's interests.

Pondering several items on the original dichotomy, a three-way comparison of a high achiever, a gifted learner, and a creative thinker emerged (Figure 4.2). No column is necessarily mutually exclusive. For example, a high achiever might also be a creative learner, a gifted learner might also be a creative learner, a gifted learner might also be a high achiever, or a student might be all three. The characteristics are not intended to imply that the value of any column is greater than another. All children are equally valuable by nature of being human. High achievers, gifted learners, and creative thinkers (in any combination) should be equally valued in the classroom and in life.

This three-column analysis evolved over several years while working with students representing each of these groups co-existing in many classrooms. I have invited hundreds of teachers and students to review and discuss the items. The resulting three-column comparison is proposed for reflection. Stimulating discussion rather than fostering agreement is the goal.

These students and teachers found the following cartoons helpful in understanding the comparison since high achievers, gifted learners, and creative learners co-exist in many classrooms. In the first cartoon, the teacher announces an assignment, and the high achiever quickly tries to determine what the teacher most wants so he can please and satisfy the teacher's intentions: *What do you really want?* The gifted learner ponders what to do that would most interest her as she continues learning: *What I would like to do is...* Simultaneously, the creative learner's mind begins to race with a myriad of diverse and varied possibilities that could be explored: *What about...*

Figure 4.3: Response to an Assignment

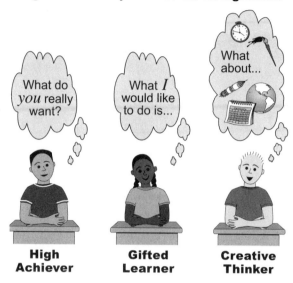

Later, in the second cartoon, the teacher poses a question to the class. The high achiever is delighted because he knows the answer and continues to be in control of high achievement: *Oh, I know that answer!* The gifted learner considers multiple nuances and alternative perspectives: *The question could mean...* or *It might suggest...* or *Another way to say that is...* or *Yah, but...* The creative learner is still obsessed with the seemingly endless possibilities of the earlier assignment, concentrating so much on his ideas that he completely misses the teacher's question: *What...?*

Figure 4.4: Response to a Question

Kingore, B. (2004). *Differentiation: Simplified, Realistic, and Effective.* Austin: Professional Associates Publishing.

Consider sharing this three-way comparison with gifted students to elicit their perceptions and stimulate discussion. Then, share those results with a wider audience of individuals concerned about the education of all learners. The information might clarify or extend understanding among administrators, teachers, parents, and students of the marvelous similarities and diversities of high achievers, gifted learners, and creative thinkers.

IMPLICATIONS FOR INSTRUCTING HIGH ACHIEVERS, GIFTED LEARNERS, AND CREATIVE THINKERS

Articulating the differences among the three categories of high achievers, gifted learners, and creative thinkers challenges educators to constructively address appropriate educational services for each. Factors affecting educational services include concerns related to knowledge versus understanding, mastery, evaluation, flexible grouping, and attentive behavior versus learning.

Knowledge Versus Understanding

Shepard (1997) provides a classic illustration of the differences between knowledge and understanding. When presented with the following problem, 86 percent of students completed it correctly:

4 x 3 =
A. 9   B. 12   C. 15   D. 18

Then, students were confronted with the problem in a concept-based form.

Which goes with:

XXXX   A. 3 x 4 =
XXXX   B. 3 + 4 =
XXXX   C. 3 x 12 =

With the second problem, only 55 percent of those same students answered correctly. For many, rote learning (the first problem) did not transfer to conceptual understanding of the mathematics involved (second problem). Students can know things but not understand them. Ultimately, life-long learning resides in understanding.

The current skills-intensive emphasis in many classrooms increases the danger of fostering knowledge more than understanding. Gifted learners and creative thinkers are left with few opportunities to satisfy their needs for in-depth development of complex, abstract concepts and relationships.

Mastery

Mastery--a buzzword associated with high-stakes testing--is an extension of the dilemma of knowledge versus understanding. Concerned educators question whether mastery is the ultimate educational goal for many students: *Is mastery a goal or merely a pathway?* Creative thinkers learn more when they use basic knowledge as a springboard to expand possibilities rather than as an end in itself. Gifted learners typically require fewer repetitions to reach mastery; hence, they should spend minimal time on these exercises and be challenged instead with essential questions that embellish mastery and lead to enduring understandings (Wiggins & McTighe, 1999).

There are two ways of knowing (Stiggins, 2001). To be a master of knowledge, students can memorize it or know where to find it when needed. Since it is obvious that the library and internet hold more than our brains, both ways of knowing provide an excellent basis for successful problem solving, particularly when the problems involve essential questions instead of simple correct answers. If the goal of education extends beyond mastery or passing standardized tests, then both ways of knowing must be acknowledged and valued. We know, and students understand, that the world does not operate solely on memorized information. (Of course, to enable our students to escalate beyond mastery, we ourselves must develop expertise in the disciplines we teach. Stiggins cautions that we must be pre-

Kingore, B. (2004). *Differentiation: Simplified, Realistic, and Effective.* Austin: Professional Associates Publishing.

pared to share with students the concepts, generalizations, and theories that hold facts together (2001).)

Evaluation

Inasmuch as evaluation drives instruction in this era of high-stakes testing, the rubrics used in many classrooms need overhauling to increase their emphasis on content. If high-level problem solving and depth of content are paramount to instruction, then these levels must also be established as evaluation criteria. Gifted learners need a high level of content and a faster pace of instruction to continue learning. Use rubrics that honor diverse learning profiles and challenge advanced learners to escalate their understanding of concepts and skills. Avoid rubrics that stress procedures over depth or focus on grade-level content instead of acceleration. Creative thinkers flow outside the box and approach problems in a diverse fashion. It is integral to the advanced achievement of these students that rubrics incorporate criteria descriptions inviting creative adaptations, innovative approaches, and extensions of content rather than only simple correct answers and behaviors. Criteria for abstract thinking, complexity, and content depth that invite the integration of creativity in beyond grade-level responses are shared as a component of performance assessment in Chapter 7. Other rubrics, such as one for oral presentations that stress depth and complexity rather than only performance behaviors, may be found in Chapter 9.

Flexible Grouping

While whole-class instruction dominates many classrooms, it is clear that employing only one grouping option for the majority of instruction is an inappropriate response to learners' differences. Flexible grouping is a necessity in a differentiated learning environment. Without flexible grouping practices, advanced and gifted students'

needs for an accelerated pace, advanced level, and compacted curriculum are not adequately addressed.

Gifted and creative students need to work in a variety of grouping options. Gifted and creative students must at times work:

♦ **Individually** to avoid compromising what they can accomplish. Working independently enables them to pursue individual interests and investigate essential, unanswered question using beyond-grade-level materials and technology.

♦ **In small, similar-readiness groups** to honor their needs for idea mates and creativity mates rather than only age mates. Working in similar-readiness groups can: engage abstract and complex thinking, prompt construction of symbolic relationships, encourage use of sophisticated vocabulary specific to a field, and provide learning opportunities that are not limited to grade-level concepts or materials.

♦ **In small, mixed-readiness groups** when a teacher's objectives are either group-building or having high-ability students assist students with fewer skills to complete a group learning task or product. This option is inappropriate if overused or applied in place of other learning opportunities for gifted and creative students.

♦ **In whole class settings.** This option is most viable when everyone in the class has about the same schema for the content and needs the same or nearly the same level of information. Teachers should evaluate the appropriateness of whole-class grouping by observing the degree of active, on-task engagement exhibited by each member of the class. When some or many students are not mentally engaged, whole-class instruction is seat-time rather than learning enhanced.

Kingore, B. (2004). *Differentiation: Simplified, Realistic, and Effective.* Austin: Professional Associates Publishing.

In mixed-ability classroom, teachers wisely modulate among all of the grouping options. There are several instructional agendas to consider, so their decisions about grouping are based upon content goals, the needs of students, and classroom management procedures. However, when the intent is to address the accelerated instructional pacing and the more complex content-level needs of advanced and gifted learners, these students need to work with similar-readiness groups or work individually.

Research studies support the positive effects of flexible grouping with gifted students (Gentry, 1999; Loveless, 1998; Rogers, 1998). Tailor instruction to specifically address grouping options that escalate advanced and gifted students' learning. Realize that ultimately the effectiveness of any grouping decision depends upon the quality of the learning opportunities presented to students. Presenting grade-level content in a small group of advanced learners is not sufficient to promote their higher levels of learning.

Attentive Behavior Versus Learning

Many years ago, Paul Torrance (1970) mused that teachers are more concerned with what students appear to be than who they are. Typically, high achievers are attentive learners. They acclimate well to class procedures and are appreciated for the school-appropriate behaviors they model. Conversely, some creative thinkers and gifted learners are criticized for their off-task behaviors. Instead of focusing on what they are doing, ponder why they are doing it. Creative thinkers are attentive when learning opportunities invite original thinking. Gifted learners are attentive when concepts and skills are at their advanced readiness levels. Inattentive, off-task behaviors are more likely when classes stress the same level of learning standards as the ultimate goal for all students regardless of readiness or learning profile. Students' attentive, on-task behaviors

are not the learning goal; they are the result of respectful tasks designed for students at their appropriate pace and level of instruction.

Schools' planned curricula and learning environments have fostered and perhaps suggest a preference for responding to the instructional needs of high achievers--noticed for their neat, well-developed assignments. Hence, the first step is to clarify and extend understanding of the similarities and differences among high achievers, gifted learners, and creative thinkers. This understanding then challenges educators to provide services that potentially match the paces, levels, and learning profiles of these students. We truly can educate rather than give lip-service to serving gifted learners and creative thinkers. Perhaps the ultimate goal of education is not to teach students what we know but to teach them to understand conceptually and pose essential questions that escalate continuous growth and understanding. In addition to *accurate and complete*, it is time to envision *original and continually developing* as desired education outcomes for students. All children deserve the right to learn at their highest level or readiness--even the gifted.

Teacher tip...

Provide books with gifted and creative characters. We all need books with characters to whom we can relate. As creative and gifted students read stories involving characters who respond with innovative, advanced behaviors, they benefit from vicarious substantiation that others think and feel the way they do.

COMMUNICATING WITH PARENTS

Many educators say that all parents think their child is gifted. Parents are not trained in gifted education and have a specialized perspective. Thus, some parents underestimate children's abilities, and others overestimate them, as when parents' egos supersede their child's needs. Nonetheless, their insight to their child's at-home demonstrations of learning heighten our understandings of the child's instructional needs.

1. Increase the credibility of how parents advocate for their child. Encourage parents to support their perceptions of their child's abilities by organizing and sharing with the school a small set of the child's products that illustrate observed characteristics. A portfolio of six to eight items can document the degree of depth and complexity in the child's work outside of school (Kingore, 2001).

2. Provide information to parents so they can be active partners with schools in supporting the education of their children. Consider sharing with parents a copy of the high-achiever, gifted learner, and creative thinker comparison as a discussion prompt. Parents might be encouraged to share and discuss the comparison with their gifted children to elicit their perspectives.

3. Focus conversations about a child's instructional needs in a classroom with Figure 3.2. When conferencing with parents, refer to the chart to accent the match between the child's instructional needs and the differentiation strategies in practice in the learning environment.

4. Ensure the parent that school personnel understand that the gifted are not all packaged the same. The gifted represent varied *packages* of strengths, needs, and dispositions, including twice-exceptional students, learners from diverse cultures, children from poverty, perfectionist students, learners with physical impairments, students with behavior problems, and children with gifted potential who have had little opportunity to accelerate academic skills. Be a resource provider to guide parents' search for specific information about the special needs of their gifted child.*

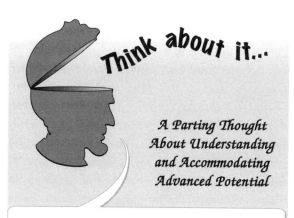

Think about it...

A Parting Thought About Understanding and Accommodating Advanced Potential

Abraham Lincoln once said:
It is true that you may fool all of the people some of the time;
You can even fool some of the people all of the time;
But you can't fool all of the people all of the time.

(With apologies to Abraham Lincoln)

Some of the gifted curriculum
        all kids can and should do.
Perhaps *much* of the gifted curriculum
        many kids can do.
But if *all* of the kids can successfully do
        all of the gifted curriculum
        all of the time...
It's not rigorous enough!

*It is beyond the scope of this book to appropriately address the special populations of the gifted. The Special Populations, Early Childhood, and Parent & Community divisions of the National Association for Gifted Children are rich resources. They can be located at: <http://www.nagc.org>

Kingore, B. (2004). *Differentiation: Simplified, Realistic, and Effective.* Austin: Professional Associates Publishing.

GROUPING TO ENHANCE DIFFERENTIATION

Grouping is the cornerstone that supports differentiation. Providing an optimal learning environment for all students becomes a daunting task without flexible grouping. Pettig (2000) stresses that regardless of whether the differentiation is based upon student readiness, interests, or needs, the dynamic flow of grouping and regrouping is one of the foundations of differentiated instruction. Without implementing strategic grouping practices, students' needs for appropriate pace, level, and compacting are not addressed; and assessment, rather than substantially affecting instruction, only serves to determine grades.

Today's grouping practices accent flexible groups rather than the stagnate grouping procedures in which students are given whole-group instruction or placed in the same group for all or most of the school year. Flexible grouping is the practice of short-term grouping and regrouping students in response to different learning objectives and students' needs. We now know that individuals learn best when involved in a variety of group placements that respond to their diagnosed affective and cognitive needs as well as the instructional objectives of the teacher.

Kingore, B. (2004). *Differentiation: Simplified, Realistic, and Effective.* Austin: Professional Associates Publishing.

FLEXIBLE GROUPING

Flexible grouping responds to students' diversity by recognizing that no single group placement matches all of a child's needs. To avoid the stigma of labeling children by ability, group placements should be varied according to students' needs and the demands of the task.

The word *fluid* is the best description for flexible groups. Working arrangements are fluid and include whole class learning, pairs-trios-quads, student-selected groups, teacher-selected groups, and random groups. The fluid composition of groups is characterized by continual regrouping of students according to skill, readiness, acceleration, cooperative task, interest, learning style, or socialization. In any week, a student may work independently, join one group for a specific purpose, and then participate in other groups to accomplish different objectives. Hence, a student's group placement is fluid rather than fixed.

Group size is another variable that is relative to students' need and the conditions of the task. At times, teachers organize a group of six to ten students to provide a rich pool of diverse ideas and content backgrounds. At other times, teachers create a group of four or five students so the instructional focus can be more specific and increase attention to individual needs and ideas. Teachers also consider noise and management issues to determine group size. In general, smaller groups encourage a larger percentage of students to be task committed. Groups of pairs or trios frequently increase students' active engagement in a learning task and may provide a more accurate assessment of results.

Decisions about group options and students' placements within groups must be based upon instructional objectives, the needs of students, and classroom management procedures. To be effective, groups require clear directions and the appropriate support necessary to ensure that students know how to work successfully in each group placement (Tomlinson, et al, 2002).

Some of the most frequently used classroom grouping options are:

- **Whole class instruction,**
- **Mixed-readiness (heterogeneous) small groups,**
- **Similar-readiness (homogeneous) small groups, and**
- **Individual work.**

Consider the values of this variety of options. Accepting that no group arrangement is totally perfect for instruction, it is useful to analyze the advantages and disadvantages of each option. The format of Figure 5.1. invites educators to record reactions to the four grouping options. Working alone or with a team of colleagues, respond to each of the eight areas with your classroom experiences and insights. Then, analyze and reflect upon your reactions. *What relationships or patterns do you observe? What conclusions can you draw regarding grouping to maximize learning opportunities?* Whether faculties, instructional teams, or individuals complete this exercise, it becomes clear that no single grouping option is perfect for all of the students all of the time.

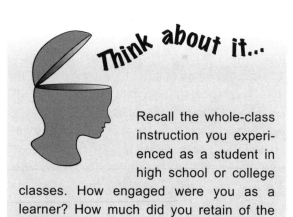

Think about it...

Recall the whole-class instruction you experienced as a student in high school or college classes. How engaged were you as a learner? How much did you retain of the information presented during whole-class instruction?

Kingore, B. (2004). *Differentiation: Simplified, Realistic, and Effective.* Austin: Professional Associates Publishing.

Figure 5.1: FLEXIBLE GROUPING OPTIONS

Advantages	*Disadvantages*
Whole-class instruction	
Mixed-readiness small groups	
Similar-readiness small groups	
Individual work	

Kingore, B. (2004). *Differentiation: Simplified, Realistic, and Effective.* Austin: Professional Associates Publishing.

FLEXIBLE GROUPING OPTIONS

1. Whole Class

What is it?

Whole class instruction is viable when everyone in the class has about the same schema for the content and needs the same or nearly the same level of information.

What does it accent?

Whole class instruction accents the affective domain, group building, and continuity of information.

What are the advantages and disadvantages?

Whole class instruction has the advantage of students learning to accept and listen to everyone in class. It is more effective for the introduction of information and is less labor intensive for teachers to present material to the whole class at the same time. However, the disadvantages are that some students are less mentally engaged, the pace and level of instruction may be inappropriate for some, and a few students' correct answers mislead the teacher to assume every student has mastery.

What are some implementation guidelines?

The litmus test of whole-class instruction is the degree of active, on-task engagement exhibited by each member of the group during the learning task. The following learning experiences are defensible examples of whole class grouping in a differentiated classroom.

* Introducing information and materials
* Reading aloud to the class to share literature and information
* Involving the class in choral reading, creative dramatics, and role playing
* Providing affective-domain experiences
* Conducting group-building tasks and discussions
* Sharing the products and ideas that result from learning tasks
* Directing closure tasks

2. Mixed-Readiness Groups
(Heterogeneous)

What is it?

High-, middle-, and lower-readiness students work together in one group. The high-readiness students typically assist students with fewer skills to complete a group learning task or product.

What does it accent?

Work in mixed-readiness groups accents grade-level content, social skills, group building, process skills, and grade-level products.

What are the advantages and disadvantages?

Mixed-readiness small groups have advantages such as the modeling of leadership and ideas, students helping each other, and the perception of equal expectations seeming more fair. Disadvantages of these groups, however, include the concerns that the learning tasks are usually geared to the middle-range of the class' readiness levels so more students can succeed. Thus, these group experiences are less appropriate for some at-risk and most advanced students. There also is the reoccurring problem of some students doing too much or too little of the task.

What are some implementation guidelines?

The teacher places a mixed-range of students in a group to assist one another. The intent is to develop or practice the skills of collaboration. In reality, the objective is often peer-tutoring.

Cooperative learning is a frequently used application of mixed-readiness groups. Typically, the entire class is simultaneously involved in cooperative learning groups as the teacher facilitates the process. In most cases, the teacher determines the cooperative groups. At times, however, students may self-select groups.

Kingore, B. (2004). *Differentiation: Simplified, Realistic, and Effective.* Austin: Professional Associates Publishing.

FLEXIBLE GROUPING OPTIONS

3. Similar-Readiness Groups
(Homogeneous)

What is it?

Students assessed at similar readiness levels work together, participating in instruction at the pace and level most appropriate to the group.

What does it accent?

It accents preassessment; instruction responding to preassessment through content, process, and product; and interaction skills.

What are the advantages and disadvantages?

Advantages of similar-readiness small groups are that instructional pacing and complexity can match student's readiness level and that students are more prepared to use the same materials and learn at a similar level. As disadvantages, however, some adults worry that groups of students with less skills lack high role models. Furthermore, similar-readiness groups are not considered politically correct from some adults' perspectives and could result in labeling students if overused or misused.

What are some implementation guidelines?

Similar-readiness groupings allow students to learn at their appropriate pace and level. The learning materials and tasks can be more specifically suited to each group's readiness. Avoid having one group complete fun projects as another completes skill sheets. The intent is to level the learning field as all students engage in interesting work.

Many teachers observe new leadership emerging when students work in similar-readiness groups. Some quieter students are more comfortable sharing ideas in these groups.

Membership in these groups varies in different content areas. For example, a student with fewer skills in math may excel in another content area and need to work with students demonstrating advanced skills in that content.

4. Individual Work

What is it?

Students work, usually seated at their own desks or table areas, to complete content-related activities and materials that focus on practice, mastery, or extension of specific skills and concepts.

What does it accent?

Individual work accents content, process, product, individual differences, and assessment.

What are the advantages and disadvantages?

Having students work individually has the potential advantages of matching students' pace and level while allowing for individual responses and more accurate assessments. However, individual work fails to align with students' pace and level when all students are to complete the same assignment. The disadvantages of individual work are that less motivated learners may be off-task, it can be isolating if overused, and it is more labor intensive for teachers as assigning different learning experiences for students requires more preparation work and grading.

What are some implementation guidelines?

Assignments need to be varied among students to match their readiness and learning profiles. While individual assignments differ, all individual work must be interesting and respectful of students' self-concepts.

The entire class can complete different individual assignments or tasks at the same time, some students can work individually while others are engaged in direct teacher instruction, and still others work in different flexible group applications.

Kingore, B. (2004). *Differentiation: Simplified, Realistic, and Effective.* Austin: Professional Associates Publishing.

FLEXIBLE SMALL-GROUP APPLICATIONS*

It is clear that employing only one grouping option for the majority of instruction is a flawed practice. The reasonable conclusion is to modulate among the options to maximize learning opportunities for all students with the objective of off-setting the disadvantages of one grouping option with the advantages of another. Teachers using a variety of groupings are able to observe a student in those various settings and gain a more accurate understanding of the whole child. Students who participate in a variety of groupings encounter different social and learning contexts to influence their development of self as they experience learning successes and challenges.

Once the need for a balance of grouping options is acknowledged, the next step is to consider the variety of flexible, small-group applications in differentiated classrooms and determine which to employ in your instruction. Begin by reviewing the grouping applications currently organized in your classroom. The format of Figure 5.2 invites you to rate your frequency of use of ten small, flexible group applications on a scale of one to five, with one being *never use* and five being *frequently use*. Also, add and rate any additional applications not included on this list. Then, mark which small grouping option(s) that application illustrates: mixed-readiness small group, similar-readiness small group, or individual work.

Reflect upon your responses. In what ways do your applications respond to the diverse learning profiles of your students? How effectively do your responses modulate among grouping applications and options to maximize learning opportunities for all students? How consistently are similar-readiness groups and individual work used to match advanced students' pace and level? How can

teachers in one grade level or across grade levels work together to cooperatively use these flexible-grouping applications?

To clarify implementation choices, a brief overview of each small-group application in a differentiated classroom considers four questions:

1. *What is it?*
2. *What does it accent?*
3. *When is it most effective for advanced and gifted students?*
4. *What are some implementation guidelines?*

CENTER OR LEARNING STATION

What is it?

A center or learning station is a designated area of a classroom where students go to work with an organized set of content-related activities and materials that focus on practice, mastery, or extension of specific skills and understandings.

What does it accent?

It accents content, product, and process skills, particularly student interactions and communications.

---

*Chapter 6 addresses related grouping issues, such as positive work behaviors, how to assign students to groups, and how to encourage students' task commitment and productivity.

Kingore, B. (2004). *Differentiation: Simplified, Realistic, and Effective.* Austin: Professional Associates Publishing.

Figure 5.2:
FLEXIBLE SMALL-GROUP APPLICATIONS

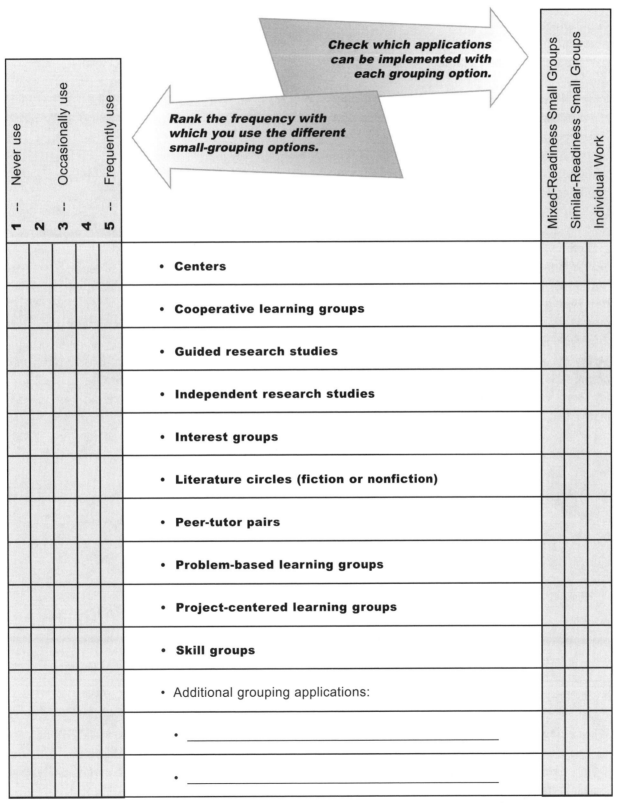

Check which applications can be implemented with each grouping option.

Rank the frequency with which you use the different small-grouping options.

						Mixed-Readiness Small Groups	Similar-Readiness Small Groups	Individual Work
1 -- Never use	2 --	3 -- Occasionally use	4 --	5 -- Frequently use				
					• **Centers**			
					• **Cooperative learning groups**			
					• **Guided research studies**			
					• **Independent research studies**			
					• **Interest groups**			
					• **Literature circles (fiction or nonfiction)**			
					• **Peer-tutor pairs**			
					• **Problem-based learning groups**			
					• **Project-centered learning groups**			
					• **Skill groups**			
					• Additional grouping applications:			
					• _____			
					• _____			

Kingore, B. (2004). *Differentiation: Simplified, Realistic, and Effective.* Austin: Professional Associates Publishing.

When is it most effective for advanced and gifted students?

A center that challenges advanced learners needs to include beyond-grade-level resources and tiered activities that provide opportunities for complexity and depth. One outcome is to motivate students to develop centers as products from their research.

What are some implementation guidelines?

The activities in centers must be instructionally valuable, focus on important learning goals, and encourage high-level thinking rather than simple right answers or matching tasks. Document the learning objectives and skills incorporated in the center by posting a laminated list of learning standards and checking the ones employed in the current center tasks. Avoid fragmented activities that may look attractive but do not relate to content. Avoid matching tasks and folder games that are so quickly and easily completed that they minimize students' thinking and encourage short attention spans. Evaluate all types of commercially developed lessons and materials for those that integrate with your content and instruction. With today's diversity of learners, centers are sound vehicles for providing learning tasks that incorporate multiple ways to learn. Content-related discussions among learners are encouraged.

When is it most effective for advanced and gifted students?

When mixed-readiness learning tasks are used, they should focus on group building techniques rather than skill development or content highly-able students already know. When gifted students have likely mastered the intended content in a cooperative learning task, place them together as a group to complete a more complex cooperative learning task. This adjustment allows them to practice the desired social interaction behaviors and continue their learning. They are also more likely to demonstrate positive attitudes about cooperative learning.

What are some implementation guidelines?

Realize that cooperative tasks typically aim at a middle-of-the-class readiness level and thus do not meet the learning needs of above-average or limited-skill learners. Some gifted students do not like frequent participation in mixed-readiness cooperative groups because they perceive an attitude from other students of "You know it, you do it, we'll just copy it." When advanced students work in their own cooperative group, other leaders emerge in the heterogeneous groups (Gentry, 1999; Schunk, 1987).

COOPERATIVE LEARNING

What is it?

Cooperative learning is the educational practice of heterogeneously grouping one high-ability, one low-ability, and two or three middle-level students to complete a learning task and practice effective social interaction behaviors.

What does it accent?

Cooperative learning accents social skills, process, mixed-readiness groups, and students-helping-students.

Think about it...

As a student, what did you experience in a group task when you were the person with the highest skills or most task commitment? How did you feel?

Kingore, B. (2004). *Differentiation: Simplified, Realistic, and Effective.* Austin: Professional Associates Publishing.

GUIDED RESEARCH STUDY

What is it?

A guided research study can add depth and interest to a classroom topic as it teaches the skills that are prerequisites to more independent study. To teach research skills, incorporate technology, and develop the habits required in self-directed learning, the teacher assigns students a topic for research or provides students a list of topic choices. The teacher typically determines the parameters of the task, including completion dates.

What does it accent?

Guided research studies accent content, product, and process skills, particularly high-level thinking, research skills, technology, and life-long learning skills.

When is it most effective for advanced and gifted students?

Guided research is most applicable with young gifted students or with advanced and gifted students who need to learn research skills and increase their ability to pursue learning tasks independently. Aim the research study to match these students' advanced reading ability and encourage independent reading of multiple, above grade-level sources of information.

What are some implementation guidelines?

The study might be completed individually or in similar-readiness small groups that encourage students to discuss the process and product. The product may be in the form of a research paper or multiple other open-ended formats that allow students to demonstrate their learning. Different product options respond to the diverse learning profiles of students and may encourage continued student interest in the research. Predetermine an audience for the results to provide students with reasons to develop high-level responses and provide effective closure.

INDEPENDENT RESEARCH STUDY

What is it?

An independent research study invites students to pursue their passions for extensive knowledge and understanding in self-selected areas of study. Students most often work individually, but it can also be completed in small, interest-based groups. Independent research evolves from personal interests, building upon the research and independent work skills acquired through prior experiences and teacher-guided research studies. Independent research studies differ from interest groups and projects in that the studies are more student-centered, student-directed, open-ended, and can be long-term.

What does it accent?

It accents content, product, individual differences, interests, and process skills, particularly high-level thinking, research skills, technology, and life-long learning skills.

When is it most effective for advanced and gifted students?

Independent research studies are an effective replacement task for students who pretest beyond the planned curriculum. The essence of research makes it vital that these students self-determine and pursue the topics and products that reflect their passions for learning. Gifted students require access to beyond grade-level resources and benefit from interactions with experts in the field. Their research should culminate in a format to communicate the information to an audience.

What are some implementation guidelines?

An interest inventory or interview and an assessment of an individual student's content readiness provide information regarding the student's research interests and readiness for independence. Rather than directly determine the scope, sequence, and final product of the study, the teacher's main role is as a facilitator who confers with the learners as they

Kingore, B. (2004). *Differentiation: Simplified, Realistic, and Effective.* Austin: Professional Associates Publishing.

Grouping to Enhance Differentiation

develop intriguing, essential questions. The teacher guides the students' applications of sophisticated research processes and supports their pursuit of advanced concepts. Learning contracts and proposals, such as those shared in Chapter 6, are useful for helping students focus their process and product decisions. The assistance of a librarian, media specialist, experts in the field, or special populations teacher such as a gifted specialist can be invaluable in helping make independent research successful.

INTEREST GROUP

What is it?

Within a topic, a teacher categorizes different subtopics for students to study and share with the class. An interest group forms to pursue more extensive information than the entire class might need to learn about a topic or aspect of a topic. Interest groups differ from independent research studies in that the interest group topics are more teacher-structured and the process is short-term.

What does it accent?

It accents content, product, students' interests, and process skills, particularly student communications and research skills.

When is it most effective for advanced and gifted students?

Interest groups can be effective for a group of advanced students or mixed-readiness level students when they share a common interest that motivates them to extend their learning. When an interest is strong, students may develop a more extensive background in that one area. Thus, students who typically demonstrate diverse ranges of skills and concept developments can come together on a more level learning field as they pursue this common interest.

What are some implementation guidelines?

As the teacher shares different subtopic choices, several students who are interested in one subtopic form a short-term group to collaboratively learn about the subject. Sometimes the process prompts independent research studies in which students continue the specialization through research over a longer period of time. The assistance of a librarian, media specialist, or special populations teacher such as a gifted specialist can be valuable assets in this process.

LITERATURE CIRCLE (FICTION OR NONFICTION)

What is it?

Literature Circles are informal, interest-based, flexible groups that change with each book students read. Their purpose is to augment the regular reading program, build upon students' interests, and encourage a love of reading.

What does it accent?

It accents content, students' interests, and process skills, particularly high-level thinking and student communications.

Teacher tip...

Incorporate an abundance of nonfiction materials in classrooms. A common request from advanced students to librarians is: *Do you have any books about _____?* Advanced and gifted students enjoy great literature but also want more complex information about their areas of interest.

Kingore, B. (2004). *Differentiation: Simplified, Realistic, and Effective.* Austin: Professional Associates Publishing.

When is it most effective for advanced and gifted students?

A Literature Circle provides groups of advanced students opportunities to read at their appropriate pace and level. This flexible group also encourages advanced readers to construct complex and abstract analyses with others who are prepared to think at that level. Inasmuch as gifted students are typically interested in nonfiction as well as fiction, the books available need to include biographies, autobiographies, and other interesting content-specific books. Provide a wide range of reading levels, including beyond grade-level materials.

What are some implementation guidelines?

The assistance of a librarian or media specialist can be invaluable in helping make this process successful. Provide multiple copies of books representing varying levels of complexity and appealing to diverse interests. Each student selects a book, and similar-readiness and mixed-readiness groups are formed by students reading the same book. The various groups read different books, books by the same author, or books around a common theme.

To maximize high-level thinking instead of round-robin reading, students read the material before meeting as a group. The focus is conversational as groups discuss story elements, inferences, opinions, personal connections, and extensions. The experience celebrates reading great books and sharing intriguing ideas with peers. The teacher facilitates the process, prompts content comparisons, motivates sharing across groups, and authentically assesses students' strengths and needs as well as possibilities for future book selections.

PEER-TUTOR PAIR

What is it?

Advanced students serve as tutors and peer coaches to ensure the success of struggling learners or help students with fewer skills learn, practice, or master a skill or process.

What does it accent?

It accents assessment, grade-level skills, mastery, grade-level content, and process.

When is it most effective for advanced and gifted students?

Be sensitive to the concern that advanced and gifted students are not learning at their appropriate rate and level when peer tutoring. Consider what to do to compensate for this concern. Peer tutoring is inappropriate if overused or used to replace other learning opportunities for advanced and gifted learners.

What are some implementation guidelines?

The teacher forms tutor pairs, matching high-readiness students with ones with fewer skills . Based upon assessment information, the teacher determines which skills need to be addressed and provides the materials for student tutor pairs to use. The focus is on students helping students. Carefully determined peer pairs can produce productive student interactions. The grouping can be of great benefit to teachers and to struggling students.

PROBLEM-BASED LEARNING

What is it?

Problem-based learning is an inductive teaching method in which the teacher presents students with an authentic problem that is less-structured, undefined, and complex. Students collaboratively investigate and solve the problem using their knowledge and understanding to apply consistent patterns of reasoning.

What does it accent?

It accents content, product, and process skills, particularly high-level thinking, research skills, and student communications.

When is it most effective for advanced and gifted students?

Advanced and gifted learners need to investigate problems that are often issue-based

Kingore, B. (2004). *Differentiation: Simplified, Realistic, and Effective.* Austin: Professional Associates Publishing.

and extend beyond grade-level. A wide-range of beyond grade-level resources allows more complex, in-depth solutions.

What are some implementation guidelines?

The teacher guides, facilitates, and coaches as students work on same, similar, or diverse problems. The students proceed to analyze the problem and pose solutions through variations of problem-solving steps, such as problem awareness, fact finding, problem definition, idea generation, solution finding, acceptance finding, implementation, and reflection. These open-ended problems invite active involvement and incorporate multiple modalities. The problems need to integrate content so students increase their learning and research skills as a result of completing these projects. Students respond most enthusiastically when the problem is personally relevant and authentic rather than contrived.

PROJECT-CENTERED GROUP

What is it?

The teacher presents students with a clearly-defined project or product assignment to complete collaboratively. In most class projects, the teacher directs the project by specifying the parameters, process, and time schedule of the task as all students work on the same or similar project.

What does it accent?

It accents content, product, and process skills, particularly student communications.

When is it most effective for advanced and gifted students?

Project-centered groups are most effective when advanced and gifted learners have some choice of projects or products and then are challenged to work beyond grade-level.

What are some implementation guidelines?

These teacher-determined projects are popular with many students and teachers because they are hands-on and motivate active involvement. The project must be instructionally valuable. Avoid just fun to do experiences by documenting the learning objectives and skills incorporated in the tasks. Learners should *increase their learning* as they complete these projects. Avoid expensive projects since spending money on school projects is inappropriate for many family budgets.

SKILL GROUP

What is it?

A skill group is a short-term group placement based upon diagnosed skill needs and composed of students with the same needs. Typically, the group is teacher-directed.

What does it accent?

It accents assessment, skills, process, and reteaching or acceleration.

When is it most effective for advanced and gifted students?

Advanced students benefit most when the objective is to accelerate advanced-level skills. If grade-level skills are needed, gifted students usually need minimum repetition and may exit the group before other students.

What are some implementation guidelines?

Based upon assessment information, the teacher determines which skills need to be addressed for specific groups of students, and then prepares materials that explore or develop those skills. A skill group works together for short-term mini-lessons and guided practice. Students are regrouped as they master the skill. For students with limited skills, the focus is most often on reteaching grade-level skills. For advanced and gifted learners, the focus should exceed grade level the majority of the time. Strive to avoid excessive revisiting of skills just because they are on the grade-level state test.

Kingore, B. (2004). *Differentiation: Simplified, Realistic, and Effective*. Austin: Professional Associates Publishing.

FLEXIBLE GROUPING WITH ADVANCED LEARNERS

Research studies support the positive effects of flexible grouping with highly able students within a classroom, among grade-level classrooms, across grade levels, throughout an entire school, or even between schools (Gentry, 1999; Loveless, 1998; Rogers, 1998). The rest of this chapter invites a more specific consideration of cluster grouping and other flexible grouping practices that influence the achievement of advanced students.

Revisit the exercise shared earlier in this chapter (Figure 5.1) to reconsider grouping options specific to the learning needs of advanced learners within a mixed-ability classroom. What are the advantages and disadvantages for highly-able students as they participate in whole class instruction, mixed-readiness small groups, similar-readiness small groups, or individual work? Your own responses are the ones that are important. However, Figure 5.3 shares some responses from other great teachers practicing effective instruction of advanced learners.

Similar to conclusions from the earlier exercise in flexible grouping for all students, each grouping option also has advantages and disadvantages for advanced students. Highly able learners need to experience different grouping options: sometimes working with others at different levels, sometimes working with those at a similar level, sometimes participating as a part of the whole class, and sometimes working alone.

It is obvious, however, that the accelerated instructional pacing and the more complex content-level needs of advanced learners are best met when they either work together with other advanced students or work individually. Highly able students exhibit more off-task behaviors and lower responses working in whole class or mixed-readiness groups when those groups are used frequently for instruction that does not match advanced students' learning needs.

Realize that ultimately, the effectiveness of any grouping decision depends upon the quality of the learning opportunity that is presented to students. For example, the grouping options of similar-readiness groups or individual work can not appropriately respond to students' instructional pacing and learning needs if the learning task requires too much or too little challenge.

INDIVIDUAL WORK
When is it most effective for advanced and gifted students?

Individual work is effective for highly able students when the assignments are at students' advanced readiness level and encourage in-depth and complex responses. Gifted students need continuous learning opportunities that are not limited to grade-level concepts, skills, or materials. The following are examples of potentially appropriate individual work experiences.

- Completing class assignments and compacted curriculum tasks
- Reading for enjoyment
- Writing in journals or learning logs
- Completing contracted independent studies
- Working with computer programs
- Completing a test or other evaluation task
- Pursuing an individual learning interests
- Continuing library research
- Study time

However, if gifted students are frequently expected to complete individual work while the rest of the students more frequently work with the teacher or with others, gifted students feel undervalued as learners and stand out as different from the rest of the class. Furthermore, gifted interpersonal learners miss interacting with peers in learning situations.

Kingore, B. (2004). *Differentiation: Simplified, Realistic, and Effective.* Austin: Professional Associates Publishing.

Figure 5.3: FLEXIBLE GROUPING WITH ADVANCED LEARNERS IN MIXED-ABILITY CLASSROOMS

Advantages	*Disadvantages*
Whole-class instruction	
Opportunity to accept, discuss, and listen to others' diverse perspectives. Useful for topic introduction, general directions, read alouds, closure, and group building.	Off-task behaviors may be demonstrated as level and pacing is more likely to be inappropriate. May be bored with content level. Less active engagement in learning.
Mixed-readiness small groups	
Advanced students can experience the satisfaction of helping less-skilled learners and modeling more complex ideas. May build confidence for advanced students as tasks require simpler skills.	Advanced learners infer that school is easy and boring. More likely to work below readiness level as tasks are typically set for the middle range of learners. Advanced learners may resent the responsibility of teaching others and wonder: *When it is our turn to learn?* They may be expected to do too much of the group's work. Can dominate.
Similar-readiness small groups	
Instruction can match pace and readiness levels. Above grade-level materials can be used so in-depth content is developed. Advanced students can challenge each other as they share expertise, use higher vocabulary, and incorporate more abstract or complex ideas.	Advanced students who are introspective, less verbally advanced, or less confident can be intimidated by the rest of the group. May result in labeling if overused.
Individual work	
Appropriate pace and level is possible. Individual interests and ideas can be pursued. Allows greater diversity of responses. Encourages greater depth and complexity in responses. Allows accurate evaluation.	Individual work can feel isolating if overused. A less-motivated advanced student may underachieve or exhibit a lack of task commitment.

Kingore, B. (2004). *Differentiation: Simplified, Realistic, and Effective.* Austin: Professional Associates Publishing.

SIMILAR-READINESS GROUPS
When are they most effective for advanced and gifted students?

Employing similar-readiness groups allows advanced students to learn at the accelerated pace and more complex level appropriate for their abilities and skills, use beyond grade-level materials, and often proceed with minimal repetition. The intent is to escalate their learning.

To minimize undo attention to gifted students, form similar-readiness groups of advanced students to work together while the rest of the class is also grouped in small groups. Most of the time, the varied readiness groups use different levels of content materials or pursue different concepts. At times, all groups could be engaged in a similar, open-ended task that encourages responses at different degrees of complexity. Grouping gifted students together while all small groups in the class complete the same level single-answer task may influence process but will not produce substantially higher levels of responses. Similar-readiness groups are most effective for gifted students when the content level and pace of instruction matches their readiness.

Gifted students benefit from learning together.

Teacher tip...

Get gifted students together. They have such a different intensity and level of insight when they spur each other on. They also use much higher vocabulary when working with other advanced learners.

CLUSTER GROUPING

Cluster grouping is a placement prototype that positively impacts opportunities for the continual learning and high achievement of advanced and gifted students. Based upon an analysis of student abilities throughout the entire grade level, identified gifted students are placed in one section of that grade level. This placement results in a cluster of students with similar readinesses learning together in a classroom. Ideally, five to eight gifted students are placed in a classroom with an otherwise mixed-ability student make-up. (If there are more than eight gifted students, two cluster classrooms may be formed.) The other grade-level classrooms are composed entirely of other mixed-ability students, including advanced students who demonstrate above-average skills but no identified gifted students. In these classes, the above-average students provide advanced-level ideas and skills that teachers want modeled to all students. Gentry's (1999) three-year study of cluster grouping in elementary schools documents that:

- New student role models and leaders emerge in classes with no gifted students,
- Cluster grouping positively affects the achievement levels of *all* students at any grade level using clustering, and
- The groupings provide numerous benefits to teachers.

Schuler (1997) also documents the positive achievement effect that cluster grouping has on all students.

Clustering responds to the fact that gifted students benefit from learning together and need to work with intellectual peers who have similar areas of strength (Kulik, 1992; Rogers, 1998). This prototype allows gifted students to interact and learn together part of the day while avoiding permanent and potentially negative grouping labels for other students. It also becomes a more realistic use of the

Kingore, B. (2004). *Differentiation: Simplified, Realistic, and Effective.* Austin: Professional Associates Publishing.

teacher's time and intent to match instruction to students' appropriate learning levels since there is a small group of students sharing the need for beyond grade-level instruction.

To ensure that the advanced learning needs of gifted students are met within the clustered class, the cluster is assigned a teacher who is trained in differentiating and compacting the curriculum for highly-able students.

The success of the cluster's response to gifted students' learning needs is directly related to the depth of training of the teacher and the availability of curriculum and materials that exceed grade-level.

The placement only provides the location for learning; advanced-level instruction must follow or the placement is only lip-service to gifted students' needs.

The achievement of gifted students is heightened when the teacher adjusts the curriculum to gifted students' aptitude levels and uses acceleration opportunities in tandem with this clustering strategy (Kulik, 1992; Rogers, 1998). Since several gifted students are clustered full-time in one room, a teacher can place them together in a group part of the day for more effective curriculum compacting. Accelerated pacing of instruction is employed, allowing students to learn at the pace and level most appropriate for their abilities and skills.

Cluster grouping supports flexible grouping practices by encouraging a variety of grouping arrangements. In response to different instructional objectives within the same clustered classroom, gifted students work together as a group, work with other students in small groups, work with the entire class, and work independently. Cluster grouping allows advanced and gifted students to learn together on a daily basis (because the research supports that they learn better in homogeneous groups) while students of all other ability levels are grouped heterogeneously (as research indicates is best for them) (Winebrenner & Brulles, 2008; Winebrenner & Devlin, 2001).

Cluster grouping deserves thoughtful consideration as a placement prototype for highly able students because it is an all-day solution to their readiness and peer needs. Resource or pull-in/out programs may provide excellent learning opportunities with a well-trained specialist but these programs typically serve students only part of the day or even part of the week. When the teacher of a cluster class is trained to properly differentiate and compact the curriculum for highly-able students, those students benefit from appropriate instruction all day in a learning environment that requires only minimal funds to support because it is simply a variation of the regular school program.

Think about it...

If parents question their child's placement and voice a preference to have their child placed in the cluster class, ask them to substantiate why that placement is more appropriate. Ask them to provide a portfolio of items documenting what their child does that can only be nurtured in a cluster class.

*Susan Winebrenner, a leading advocate for cluster grouping programs, uses her web site to organize a network of schools and districts currently using a cluster program. A visit to her site is an excellent way to access and interact with practitioners of this prototype.   <http://www.susanwinebrenner.com>

Kingore, B. (2004). *Differentiation: Simplified, Realistic, and Effective.* Austin: Professional Associates Publishing.

MANAGEMENT STRATEGIES THAT IMPACT DIFFERENTIATION

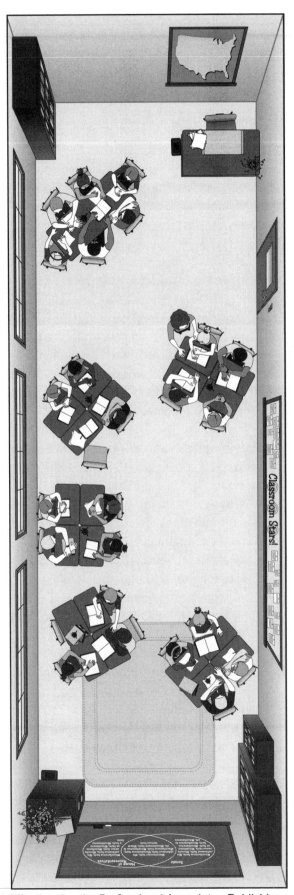

Differentiated instruction necessitates that students work independently on some learning tasks as the teacher engages other students in direct instruction. Realistically, all learners are not prepared to work independently in a productive manner. Some students have experienced little opportunity to learn productive work behaviors; others have attitudes and habits that can be counterproductive to working independently. Management strategies positively impact differentiation when they enable productive working behaviors in multiple settings. Effective teachers determine the behaviors that students can and should practice in their classes to promote responsibility for learning and to develop independent learning skills.

In a differentiated learning environment, students work in a variety of grouping configurations completing varied learning experiences to extend their learning. The goal is to implement management strategies that enable successful rather than stressful small group interactions. This chapter discusses how to manage small groups, develop positive work behaviors, and increase students' task commitment and productivity.

Kingore, B. (2004). *Differentiation: Simplified, Realistic, and Effective.* Austin: Professional Associates Publishing.

Management Strategies

MANAGING SMALL GROUPS

Before initiating small groups, it is wise to preplan in order to avoid potential problems. Experienced teachers focus on anticipating problems rather than reacting to them. Consider modeling and rehearsing with your class the routines you want to establish for small group work. Clearly established routines and procedures enable learning experiences to proceed more efficiently with fewer interruptions or conflicts.

PREPARE STUDENTS FOR THE TASK

Before initiating any small group assignments, prepare students with the parameters of the task so they know what is expected and which behaviors are desired. The following elements help prepare students for successful outcomes.

◆ Provide clearly developed directions, criteria, and expectations before the task begins.
  • Provide both verbal and written directions to eliminate confusion and reach diverse learning modalities.
  • Post or provide a copy of the directions for the group's ongoing reference.
  • Discuss the expectations for the group, and then, post a rubric that clarifies the levels of proficiency.

◆ Establish a reason for quality by announcing to students how the group's work will be shared with others. Select your preferred options from the list, *Provide Audiences for Students' Work,* in this chapter.

◆ Use signals that inform students when to begin and end tasks. Once established, signals save class time because fewer directions need to be verbalized. They are one factor that produces smoother, more quiet transitions.

Signal Examples
  • Some teachers use a remote control to activate a CD of music that is established as the signal piece. The same musical selection is used repeatedly so students know: *When you hear the music...*
  • Other teachers announce the behavior and then tell students when to proceed. This signal gives students a second to process the information before acting upon it. *In two seconds, you may quietly move into your group. (Pause.) Begin.*
  • In primary classrooms, teachers lead students in an oral countdown as a beginning and ending: *10,9,8,...*
  • When students rotate among tasks or centers, teachers can use the simple chant: *2-4-6-8, rotate.*

INITIATE NOISE CONTROL

◆ Concretely establish the desired range of volume. As a class, discuss a *productive buzz* of sound versus the roar of *chaos*. Role play the different levels of sound on a continuum from *preferred* to *out of control*. Noise problems tend to reoccur, so be prepared to revisit earlier discussions and role play again.

◆ Elicit students' ideas. Students may have more ownership in noise control efforts when they participate in establishing the parameters.

◆ Talk softly as much as possible. A soft voice often makes students listen more carefully. Conversely, as you increase your volume, so do others in the room.

◆ Use colored dots. Have sets of colored dots to place on desks as appropriate. A green dot signals students that they are working at a productive level. A yellow dot is a caution suggesting students need to adjust their noise level. A red dot signals that the group's noise level exceeds the appropriate level and requires immediate change. Practice positive reinforcement by using a majority of green dots as groups demonstrate the desired volume.

♦ *You can use anything you hear from another group.* A simple, yet amazingly effective device is to announce that students can use anything they over-hear. Since students typically do not want others stealing their ideas, the students tend to draw closer together and talk rather quietly as they plan and work together.

♦ Establish a signal for quiet. As a class, determine a simple signal to use when immediate attention or quiet is needed, such as when an announcement is made or a refocus of the task is required. Examples of effective signals include: hands raised and held in place, clap patterns, and *When you hear my voice, snap* [fingers snap one time]. Each signal is held or repeated until the desired level of quiet is reached.

LEARNING TASK OPTIONS
FOR STUDENTS

A TEACHER ASKS:
What are effective learning task options for the rest of the class when I'm working directly with a small group?

The answer to this question depends on the teacher's style and comfort zone as well as the ages, needs, and skills of the students. The physical size and organization of the classroom also influences which options are most viable. In all cases, promote quality and productivity by incorporating clearly

established expectations, positive work behaviors, and self-assessment tools for students. It is an asset when students have the flexibility to independently use the library to extend resources for their projects or learning tasks. The media specialist or librarian might briefly meet with the class to negotiate appropriate working behaviors for students when in the library without teacher guidance. The following ideas serve to prompt decisions regarding the best work options for students.

♦ Complete assignments from compacted curriculum or daily instruction.

♦ Pursue contracted independent work. Teachers incorporate learning contracts and reading contracts that provide parameters and self-assessment rubrics to promote quality. Several examples are provided in this chapter.

♦ Participate in flexible groups. Literature circles using non-fiction or fiction materials, peer-editing and -review teams, problem-based learning groups, and creative problem-solving through performance tasks are some of the grouping assignments that teachers successfully employ. The teacher determines the parameters for these groupings.

♦ Use computers. Students complete word processing tasks, conduct research-based searches, or use provided software programs to practice or extend their learning of concepts and skills.

♦ Participate in centers. Students work in centers that are teacher-prepared or student-developed areas of the classroom where integrated learning tasks are organized.

♦ Complete task cards. Task cards are independent learning tasks with self-contained directions so students can work without additional instruction. The cards are

Kingore, B. (2004). *Differentiation: Simplified, Realistic, and Effective.* Austin: Professional Associates Publishing.

teacher-produced to extend the current topic of study, or they can be commercially-produced sets that integrate with the learning objectives of the class. These tasks are completed at students' desks or in a designated area of the room.

◆ Conduct research and independent study. Students develop the parameters of the task to correspond to their interests and organizational plan. Learning contracts are typically incorporated to specify the guidelines negotiated between the teacher and student. Self-assessment rubrics for processes and products help promote quality. The assistance of a librarian or special populations teachers, such as a gifted specialist, can be invaluable in helping make this research option successful.

◆ Pursue project-centered learning. The teacher determines the parameters for individuals or small-group projects.

◆ Work with buddies or mentors. Older students or adults with expertise in an interest-area assist students who are pursuing and developing that interest.*

Think about it...

In addition to you, who else in your school could help provide challenging and appropriate instruction to advanced and gifted learners? How could each person help?

◆ Select from a set of *Now Whats!* Now Whats are previously taught and agreed upon alternatives for students to choose.
  • Games
  • Books (topic-related fiction or nonfiction)
  • Art
  • Conversations that are respectful to others' learning
  • Puzzles or other manipulatives
  • Learning tasks--simple and student-selected--that are readily applicable to multiple topics, such as Venn diagrams, acrostics, and alphabetical listings

◆ Propose a replacement task. A student develops a proposal for a replacement task and completes a form stating the parameters of the task to propose to the teacher (see Figure 6.7).

POSITIVE WORK BEHAVIORS

Determine the behaviors that students can and should practice to promote their responsibility for learning and to develop their independent learning skills. Then, clearly communicate those desired learning behaviors to students. State the behaviors in positive terms as much as possible, communicating what to do rather than what not to do. Furthermore, less may be best. Keep the list as brief as is appropriate to students' needs.

Figure 6.1 provides several questions posed to help focus and establish positive work behaviors in the classroom, particularly when the teacher is occupied instructing other students. Individually or with colleagues, respond to these and any other questions regarding the independent work behaviors important to the successful management of instruction and the application of flexible groupings. The time spent developing positive

---

*See Appendix A: Buddies: Older Students as Mentors and Collaborative Learners

Kingore, B. (2004). *Differentiation: Simplified, Realistic, and Effective.* Austin: Professional Associates Publishing.

work behaviors can result in increased student task-commitment and production.

Clarify which behaviors are nonnegotiable. For example, it is not debatable *if* clean up will occur, only *how* it will be completed. Once your priorities are determined, guide students in a discussion of the work behavior process and possibilities. Developing positive work behaviors with students avoids many potential behavior problems. Students feel more ownership when they participate in the process of establishing classroom expectations. When students are clearly aware of expectations--developed with fairness and respect--most can meet those expectations. Review your positive work behaviors over time, and discuss with students the changes to consider that might better promote learning.

When positive work behaviors are established, consider combining them into a contract for students who accept the responsibility that accompanies independent study or replacement tasks for previously mastered concepts and skills (Figure 6.4). Students, parents, and the teacher all sign the contract to communicate that everyone understands the expectations.

Teacher tip...

At times, you can not afford to be interrupted. Determine a device that reminds students not to interrupt you while it is in use. One middle school teacher has a *Do Not Disturb* sign that is placed by a small group he is teaching. One elementary teacher wears a tiara when she needs uninterrupted time with a student or group.

Figure 6.1:

ESTABLISHING A POSITIVE WORK ENVIRONMENT

- When may students work together?
  - ↪ How many may work together?
  - ↪ Which places in the room are most appropriate for small-group interaction?

- Which combinations of the following enable the most effective initial instruction?
  - ↪ Whole-class oral instructions
  - ↪ Posted written instructions
  - ↪ Rebus charts and instructions
  - ↪ Audiotaped instructions
  - ↪ Individuals or small groups meetings
  - ↪ Student Assistants (Figure 6.2)

- What are guidelines for noise levels?

- What are students to do if they need supplies or materials?

- When can students use special resources, such as computers or the library?

- What combination of options are available when help is needed from students working independently? How can time that is spent waiting for assistance not be wasted?
  - ↪ Signals for help (Figure 6.3)
  - ↪ Peer collaboration
  - ↪ Student Assistants (Figure 6.2)
  - ↪ Adult assistance in room from parents or teaching assistants

- What are students to do with completed products?

- What are students to do with work-in-progress that will be continued in the next class period?

- What clean up and reorganization responsibilities are required?

- Other questions

Kingore, B. (2004). *Differentiation: Simplified, Realistic, and Effective.* Austin: Professional Associates Publishing.

Figure 6.2:
STUDENT ASSISTANTS

Task Assistants

Task Assistants are students experienced with a specific learning task or product. Working with individuals or small groups, the assistant is recognized as one who can answer questions and provide help when needed. Consider laminating digital photographs of each student so you can post the Task Assistant's picture in a designated place in the classroom. The picture is a positive recognition and informs others of the identity of the assistant. Even students with fewer skills can meet with the teacher in advance to learn how to do a task and then serve as the assistant. All students need multiple opportunities to be task assistants.

Skill Assistants

Skill assistants are students prepared to help others with specific skills. When working with writing conventions, for example, skills such as the use of commas, capitalization, or specific spelling patterns are stapled to each pocket of a shoe bag or pocket chart. Students write their names on strips cut from index cards and put the name-strips in each specific skill pock-

et with which they believe they have ample understanding to help others. As students have a question about a skill, they search that skill pocket for the name of a peer available to help. This technique also motivates some students to master a skill as they enjoy being assistants with expertise in that skill.

Buddies

Buddies are students, usually from an older class, interacting to complete learning experiences with students who would otherwise lack the skills to accomplish that task (see Appendix A). For example, young gifted children often demonstrate advanced thinking ability, but their writing abilities are more typical of their age. When Buddies write the young children's dictation, the younger children can engage in more complex, in-depth explanations and see those ideas expressed in print. This is a valid way to differentiate learning experiences for advanced, special-need, and grade-level learners because the one-on-one interaction allows the children to proceed and achieve at their readiness levels.

Figure 6.3:
SIGNALS FOR ASSISTANCE

Provide students with a signal system to use when they need assistance. Signals are one device to defuse the problem of students interrupting the teacher or other students, and they can eliminate the time wasted when students raise their hand and wait. Signals also communicate when peers can seek a student's help or when that student is concentrating and can not be interrupted. Focus upon simple signals that students enjoy using rather than those that may embarrass students.

- Make cut-outs of hands that are green on one side and red on the other, and then laminate them. Students place the green side up when they are making progress and are available to give a hand to someone else; the red side communicates that they need assistance.
- Cut question marks out of construction paper, and laminate them. The question mark signals that there is a problem and invites the teacher or a student to stop and help.
- Students design a *Do Not Disturb* sign for their desk when they need uninterrupted concentration.

Kingore, B. (2004). *Differentiation: Simplified, Realistic, and Effective.* Austin: Professional Associates Publishing.

Figure 6.4:
CONTRACT FOR POSITIVE WORK BEHAVIORS

❏ I will follow these guidelines as I work individually or with others.

❏ I will stay on task and manage my time.

❏ Quality work is my goal.

❏ I will work and interact with others quietly.

❏ I will respect the opinions and property of others.

❏ I will do everything I can to help myself and others learn.

❏ I will do nothing to call undue attention to myself.

❏ I will self-assess my work process and product.

❏ I will place completed work in the place designated by my teacher.

❏ I will reorganize and return all materials and resources as I finish.

❏ _____

❏ _____

I agree to these guidelines, and understand I may participate in independent study or replacement activities only when these guidelines are followed.

STUDENT'S SIGNATURE _____ DATE _____

PARENT'S SIGNATURE _____ DATE _____

TEACHER'S SIGNATURE _____ DATE _____

Management Strategies

Kingore, B. (2004). *Differentiation: Simplified, Realistic, and Effective.* Austin: Professional Associates Publishing.

TASK COMMITMENT AND PRODUCTIVITY

Productive, task-committed students are an asset in every learning environment. Today's teachers have learned, however, not to expect all or even most of the students to enter a classroom with those commitments. Rather than expect students to have intrinsic motivation for high achievement, incorporate strategies that teach students to produce quality work. To increase task commitment and productivity:

• Define quality,
• Survey students' interests,
• Implement goal setting,
• Initiate management techniques that promote productivity and quality,
• Use learning contracts, and
• Provide audiences for students' work.

DEFINE QUALITY

Teach students to work toward quality. In past learning environments, students may have misconstrued that being correct, neat, and on time were the valued criteria. Guide students to understand that those attributes are important, but that quality is the target. Class time spent discussing and defining quality can increase students' commitment to excellence.

♦ Show examples of high-quality and lower-quality products to help students form more concrete targets.

♦ Develop a class list of students' Top Ten quality factors. Students will define and refine their thinking about quality as they establish the hierarchy of these factors from lowest to most valued.

♦ As a class, develop a rubric for quality. For example, the rubric might progress from *accurate information,* to *thoughtful information and details,* to *in-depth, clearly supported information.*

SURVEY STUDENTS' INTERESTS

Differentiated instruction recognizes and builds upon students' interests because students are more motivated to learn when their interests are incorporated. Advanced and gifted students will also develop elevated levels of expertise through their in-depth pursuit of topics of personal interest.

Figure 6.5 provides an alternative to the typical written interest inventory with a variation that appeals to your visual and spatial learners. To begin, students brainstorm what they are most interested in and want to learn more about at school. The students organize their interests into categories to list on the form and then draw multiple responses in each. Students can also add words or phrases, almost graffiti style, to clarify their choices. Suggest that advanced students create symbols for their interests instead of just drawing literal pictures. Explaining the symbols often invites students to discuss their inventories at greater length with each other.

Inform the students before they begin if you plan to display the inventories in the room for all to view. The inventories make an interesting and often visually-intriguing display for students to compare and contrast information; but students should know in advance how their work will be shared.

IMPLEMENT GOAL SETTING

Empower students to be active participants in their learning by encouraging them to review their work, assess its strengths, and determine potential areas or skills for growth and development. Students then set goals to accomplish those changes. The psychology of goal setting suggests that students are more likely to work toward achieving goals in which they feel ownership.

Kingore, B. (2004). *Differentiation: Simplified, Realistic, and Effective.* Austin: Professional Associates Publishing.

Figure 6.5:
LEARNING INTERESTS

At school, I am interested in learning more about:

Kingore, B. (2004). *Differentiation: Simplified, Realistic, and Effective.* Austin: Professional Associates Publishing.

Management Strategies

The Goal Setting Plan (Figure 6.6) is a format successfully used in many classrooms of upper elementary and secondary students. The potential value of this form is that it asks students to state a goal and then outline the specific steps to accomplish that goal. This planning is an important link to success for many students as it requires them to set up their own procedure to reach a goal. While five steps are indicated, there is no predetermined number of steps to reach a goal. Students should plan the number of steps most appropriate to reach their goal. At a later date, students revise their goal setting plan to reflect the status of their goal.

Additionally, as a simple goal setting technique, provide a copy of the rubric intended for evaluating the current learning task or product. Students begin the task by marking on their copy of the rubric the levels of proficiency they intend to attain.

INITIATE MANAGEMENT TECHNIQUES THAT PROMOTE PRODUCTIVITY AND QUALITY

While Guiding Only One Small Group

> A TEACHER ASKS:
> *What are effective management techniques to use when small groups work independently and I guide another small group?*

◆ Create smaller groups. Groups of two or three may exhibit more on-task behavior and less conflicts than larger groups.

◆ Communicate specific directions, expectations, and positive work behaviors.

◆ Provide clearly developed criteria and expectations before the task begins.

- **Checklists.** Some groups benefit from a checklist as a written record of the components of the process. Provide a checklist for students to mark as they complete parts of the entire task. This process helps them track their own progress and decreases the problem of students saying they are done when they have not completed the task.
- **Rubrics.** Refer to the posted copy of the task rubric. *According to our rubric, your productivity is earning a _____. Is that your intention?*

◆ Use contracts in which students negotiate objectives, positive work behaviors, and end products.

◆ Designate an audience for the work. Knowing how students' work will be shared, displayed, or published increases students' level of concern for excellence.

◆ Maintain focus on students' ownership and accountability. Don't do for them what they can do for themselves.

> TEACHER:
> *I'm pleased with one aspect of your group's work. What do you notice is going well?*
> [Pause for student response]
> *I'm also concerned about one aspect. What do you think it is? What suggestions can you make to correct the need?*

◆ Elicit students' ideas for aiding productivity.

◆ Provide a choice of products or tasks whenever feasible.* Choice is a powerful motivator. Suggest two or more options for products instead of requiring all groups to do the same thing. *What do you choose as your best way to demonstrate how much you have learned?*

---

*See Appendix B: Product Options for Differentiated Instruction

Kingore, B. (2004). *Differentiation: Simplified, Realistic, and Effective.* Austin: Professional Associates Publishing.

Figure 6.6:
GOAL SETTING PLAN

STUDENT _____   DATE _____

SUBJECT AREA/TOPIC _____

Goals:

Action Plan

1.

2.

3.

4.

5.

REFLECTION DATE _____

☐	☐	☐	☐
I did not try.	I did not fully accomplish my goal or carry out my plan correctly.	I followed through with my plan well, and my work reflects my effort.	I extended my own learning and exceeded my goal.

What I accomplished:

I feel _____ **about this accomplishment because:**

Kingore, B. (2004). *Differentiation: Simplified, Realistic, and Effective.* Austin: Professional Associates Publishing.

♦ Provide behavior choices. *If you choose to work alone rather than with your group, you must complete the entire project by yourself.*

♦ Incorporate the cooperative learning strategy of designating individual responsibilities within the group. Depending upon the task and the group, consider individual assignments for group members, such as recorder, materials gatherer, discussion director, and summarizer.

♦ Tape record groups. A startling and simple technique is to quietly place a tape recorder in the middle of an off-task group and announce: *I am recording your group today.* This technique produces an immediate surge of productivity.

♦ Announce: *Any group can choose to work together as long as you are productive. When not productive, I determine who may or may not remain in the group.*

♦ Involve groups in self assessment as a group consensus task.

♦ Write quick notes of problems to address when you finish your direct teaching with the current group. If violations occur that require a response, write yourself a quick note of the observed problem with the date and perhaps even the time recorded. A note signifies the need for a follow-up later in a private discussion with the student(s) instead of a public confrontation that breeds power struggles. (These notes will also be beneficial at teacher-parent conferences.) Recording the problem for later action prevents an interruption to instruction and saves the valuable time of the group with which you are working.

♦ Implement Student-Selected Time Out. Diffuse a problem by separating an irritated student from the group. The student can work alone or calm down for a few minutes and return to the group whenever ready. Giving students the power to control how long the time out lasts self-motivates improved behavior.

♦ Create a product bulletin board. It is a useful device for keeping track of students' work or progress. Students have immediate accountability for their work, and the class enjoys seeing what others have done. One glance at the bulletin board confirms that everyone is on target or signals who may need help. It is a more efficient assessment of progress than leafing through folders or stacks of papers, and it demonstrates to visitors the productivity of the class.

Bulletin Board: *Learning in Progress*
-- **Preparation.** On a bulletin board that is available all year, put a light colored backing on the board and add a border if you prefer. Then, staple different colors of construction paper or yarn to the board, dividing it into boxes--enough for the number of students you have in your class or in one section. Put one student's name in each box, and add a caption, such as *Learning in Progress.*
-- **Application.** As group-work ends, students use self-adhering plastic clips or push pins to organize and post their work with a status note attached. When work time begins again the next day or when it is time to hand in the work for evaluation, students take down their work and proceed.

STATUS NOTE
NAME _____ DATE _____
I accomplished this today:
This will be my next step:

Kingore, B. (2004). *Differentiation: Simplified, Realistic, and Effective.* Austin: Professional Associates Publishing.

While Facilitating Among All Groups

A TEACHER ASKS:
What are effective techniques to use when all students work in small groups while I facilitate among all of the groups?

Facilitating all students while the whole class works in small groups is a particularly effective management choice when the teacher wants to assess and more directly observe students at work in cooperative learning tasks, literature circles, performance tasks, and projects. The following are examples of techniques that promote students' productivity and quality.

♦ Writing notes while moving among the groups piques students' self-awareness. Students may ask: *What are you writing.* My most effective response is: *Things I need to remember about your work.* Students are not exactly sure what that means and usually get back on task quickly.

♦ Accent teacher proximity. Move near groups who need a reminder or refocus.

Teacher tip...

Call on all learners--including the gifted. Students raise their hands because they want to share information or have a question. No student should be ignored.

♦ Provide an assessment tool to each group before the task begins so they know the expectations. Involve groups in self assessment when the task is finished. When the self-assessment device is on target and well constructed, students are quite accurate in their assessment.

♦ Determine and announce before beginning the task a culminating activity in which all groups briefly share and compare the results of their work. This step provides students a reason to produce.

ELICIT STUDENT'S PROPOSALS FOR REPLACEMENT TASKS

One way to respond to the individual differences and interests of your students is to elicit their proposals for replacement tasks through a simple form such as Figure 6.7. Students perform at a higher level when they have some power of choice in their learning. *Choice* does not provide students with a license that *anything goes.* Rather, the proposal enables teachers and students to negotiate learning experiences which are appealing to the student and applicable to the desired learning outcomes.

This proposal format asks students to think about their priorities and then plan an appropriate project that is interesting to them but also applies related skills. Thus, the project is developed as a defensible learning experience rather than just fun. Students also plan and record a sequence for completing the project to self-guide their successes.

Students complete the form and then meet with the teacher to discuss and refine organization. Having students complete the proposal first requires them to organize their thoughts and enables a more productive use of time when the teacher and a student meet.

Management Strategies

Kingore, B. (2004). *Differentiation: Simplified, Realistic, and Effective.* Austin: Professional Associates Publishing.

Figure 6.7:
STUDENT PROPOSAL FOR A REPLACEMENT TASK

STUDENT _____   DATE _____

TEACHER _____

SUBJECT AREA/TOPIC _____

1. **What are you interested in doing?**

2. **How does this plan use your current skills and talents?**

3. **What important skills or information can you gain from this project?**

4. **What will be your final product?**

5. **What resources will you need, and how will you access them?**

6. **How may I or others help?**

7. **On the back of this page, sketch a time line or flow chart of your project showing dates and steps from the beginning to the completion of your work.**

Kingore, B. (2004). *Differentiation: Simplified, Realistic, and Effective*. Austin: Professional Associates Publishing.

USE LEARNING CONTRACTS

Learning contracts accent content, process, and product as they specify materials, concepts and skills, process procedures, and product options. They support differentiation by organizing students' responsibilities for replacement tasks and documenting the customized learning plan and process. Contracts provide opportunities for students to work independently with some freedom while maintaining the teacher's instructional objectives.

Learning contracts communicate what is expected and encourage students' responsibility for learning. They typically specify positive work behaviors to increase the likelihood that a student's behaviors are appropriate for the learning environment and the requirements of the learning tasks. Figure 6.8: Learning Contract and Figure 6.9: Reading Contract are included as examples to model possibilities.*

PROVIDE AUDIENCES FOR STUDENTS' WORK

Providing an audience for students' work increases their motivation to excel and reinforces the idea that what students do is valued by you and others. As another component toward motivating high achievement and excellence, propose multiple ways for students to share the results of their work. For maximum student benefit, involve students in determining the most appropriate or preferred audiences for their work.

Students can:

• Develop or extend a bulletin board or wall display with their work for others to respond.
• Post work outside the room to extend the audience.
• Publish work in class reports, class books, class newspapers, individual books, or school-wide anthologies.

Figure 6.8: LEARNING CONTRACT

Figure 6.9: READING CONTRACT

*Appendix B: Product Options for Differentiated Instruction is a possible resource when developing learning contracts. Student can self-select products or the teacher can facilitate selection by providing two to four appropriate product options for the student's selection.

Kingore, B. (2004). *Differentiation: Simplified, Realistic, and Effective.* Austin: Professional Associates Publishing.

Figure 6.8: LEARNING CONTRACT

The Student

I want to learn _____

_____

_____

I will use at least these resources.

- _____ - _____

- _____ - _____

My finished product will be _____

_____

I will present my product to _____

The Teacher

Subject areas: _____

Positive work behaviors:

- _____

- _____

- _____

- _____

Assessment criteria for the task:

- _____

- _____

- _____

- _____

To be completed by _____

STUDENT'S SIGNATURE _____

     DATE _____

TEACHER'S SIGNATURE _____

     DATE _____

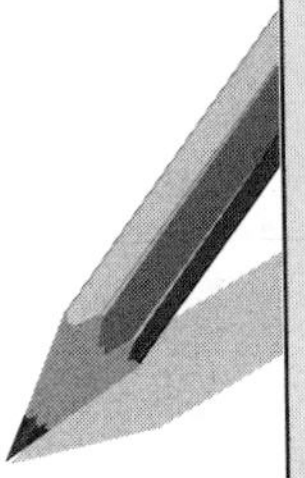

Kingore, B. (2004). *Differentiation: Simplified, Realistic, and Effective.* Austin: Professional Associates Publishing.

Figure 6.9:
READING CONTRACT

I will read _____

    by _____.

This book has _____ chapters or _____ pages.

This is my schedule for reading.

Sunday	Monday	Tuesday	Wednesday	Thursday	Friday	Saturday

This is what I will do while I read and the product I will complete.

_____

_____

_____

_____

The Teacher

Positive working behaviors:

- _____

- _____

- _____

Skills to incorporate:

- _____   • _____

- _____   • _____

STUDENT'S SIGNATURE _____

    DATE _____

TEACHER'S SIGNATURE _____

    DATE _____

Management Strategies

Kingore, B. (2004). *Differentiation: Simplified, Realistic, and Effective.* Austin: Professional Associates Publishing.

- Submit work to a national magazine that publishes students' work. A media specialist can help locate publications that accept students' work and determine what kinds of products each publication accepts.
- Demonstrate the process or share the work with a younger class of students.
- Demonstrate the process to a small group or whole class of peers.
- Share the work orally during whole-class discussions.
- Discuss the work with one to three classmates in a group for peer response.
- Share products with someone at home. Requesting a brief written response from whomever views the work may add even more importance to the process.
- Tape record researched information to place in a center or share at home.
- Produce a video to share in a center, in class, between classes, during education displays, and at parent nights.
- Share the work with other adults in the school. Arrange for the principal, assistant principal, fine-arts teacher, PE teacher, school office assistant, or other adults to come into the room and respond to students' work.
- Post work on the class website to prompt peer or adult responses.

Teacher tip...

Students are less motivated to produce when the only audience for their work is a teacher's grading pencil. Strive to provide a variety of audiences to give students more reasons to excel.

SCHEDULING SMALL GROUPS

Multiple flexible groupings of students are scheduled when the teacher wants to provide alternatives to whole-class instruction. While no single organization is decidedly superior, some grouping options are more conducive to escalating students' learning at appropriate levels and some may provide a better match to a teacher's specific learning objectives, style, and comfort zone. Scheduling is best based upon the common-sense observation that most students work more productively and appropriately when not engaged in the same type of task for an excessive period.

When considering options in scheduling, divide the class into smaller, flexible units instead of planning for the whole class to work on the same activity or assignment at the same time. Remember that flexibility in grouping is intended. Vary group memberships as objectives and tasks change.*

Figure 6.10 provides a variety of small-group options as scheduling examples. In each example, students participate in small groups that cycle through different scheduled learning experiences. Teachers can easily condense or extend the number of grouping options to suit time demands and their preferred classroom organization. Four groups are used here as an example.

Some teachers, trying to move from whole class instruction, begin with just two grouping options to simplify management. Most teachers then expand to multiple options--the variety is more motivating to students and provides more avenues for matching options to students' preferred ways to learn.

Students participate in each work option every day or over two or more days within short class periods. Teachers typically

*See Chapter 5: Grouping to Enhance Differentiation

Kingore, B. (2004). *Differentiation: Simplified, Realistic, and Effective.* Austin: Professional Associates Publishing.

schedule each group as a 15 to 30 minute segment. Therefore, at different times:

1. Students are directly instructed by the teacher in small groups, and
2. Students work without teacher instruction in small groups or independently.

In most classrooms, teachers direct the instruction of one small group while the other students are engaged in different learning configurations. The first five arrangements in Figure 6.10 model several scheduling options in which the groups rotate in and out of the teacher-directed group. The teacher prepares varying levels of complexity in each lesson and interacts with different groups of students, teaching a guided lesson of specific concepts and skills appropriate for those students' readiness.

At other times, teachers prefer for all students to simultaneously engage in small-group alternatives so the teacher can better assess and facilitate. This management choice is also effective when teaching small groups how to work well together. The last three arrangements in Figure 6.10 model that preference in which the teacher facilitates all of the students

as they work in small groups. Moving among the groups, the teacher typically coaches, problem solves, and writes notes or completes checklists assessing the strengths and needs demonstrated by the students. This assessment guides future group interactions. For example, a short-term skill group may be formed to reteach a skill or a similar-readiness group may be formed to accelerate their challenge level.

ASSIGNING STUDENTS TO SMALL GROUPS

Readiness-Based Groups

Initiate preassessments to determine students' readiness levels, and form groups based upon similar readiness of skills and content backgrounds.

Skill Groups

• Continuing assessment. Use continuing assessment during instruction to determine students who would benefit from reteaching, additional practice, or acceleration of skill levels.

Figure 6.10:
SCHEDULING SMALL GROUPS

Group 1   Group 2   Group 3   Group 4

(The teacher instructs one group at a time in these five scenarios.)

SCHEDULING SCENARIOS			
Teacher Directed	Independent Work	Independent Work	Independent Work
Teacher Directed	Independent Work	Computers	Research Task
Teacher Directed	Cooperative Group	Centers	Independent Work
Teacher Directed	Centers	Centers	Centers
Teacher Directed	Centers	Independent Work	Literature Circle

(The teacher facilitates and assesses among all groups in these three scenarios.)

Cooperative Learning	Cooperative Learning	Cooperative Learning	Cooperative Learning
Center A	Center B	Center C	Center D
Literature Circle	Literature Circle	Literature Circle	Literature Circle

Kingore, B. (2004). *Differentiation: Simplified, Realistic, and Effective.* Austin: Professional Associates Publishing.

Management Strategies

- Self nomination. Consider inviting students to self-nominate their participation in specific skill groups. Students are often aware of their needs and know when they would benefit from a skill group's focus.

Interest-Based Groups

Conduct interviews, interest inventories, or surveys. Then, use the information to form interest groups or post the results so students can identify others who share their interests.

Project-Centered or Problem-Based Groups

- Groups for problem-based or project-centered learning tasks can be randomly assigned when the objective is a mixed-readiness group experience or a cooperative learning task.
- When the objective is to match the group membership to specific requirements of the task, conduct interviews, interest inventories, or surveys and then combine that information with assessments of students' readiness levels to determine the most appropriate group placements.

Self-Selected Groups

- Students chose with whom they want to work. Control group size by specifying how many students may work in a group.
- Promote student choice and honor both interpersonal and intrapersonal learners by simply stating to the class as a learning task begins: *You may work by yourself or with one or two other people.* Students then begin the task individually or select other class members with whom to work.

Random Groupings

- Colored dots. Provide different colored dots to signify each group. The intent is for students to randomly select a dot and form a group with others selecting the same color.
- Number off. Determine the quantity of groups you want. That quantity determines the range of numbers used when numbering off. For example, for six groups, students number off one to six, and then those with the same number form a group.
- Text strips. Cut lines from different nursery rhymes, songs, poems, historical documents, and speeches into strips of print, and mix up the strips. Each student selects a strip and walks around quietly reciting the words to locate others with lines to the same piece. When the piece is complete, the group is formed.
- Categories. Use a variety of categories, such as colors of clothing, birth month, or favorite current movie to form groups. (Avoid categories that may be sensitive to some students, such as height or size. Also avoid categories that may inadvertently separate students by ethnicity, such as hair color.)

A PARTING REALITY CHECK...

Differentiation impacts classroom management as most students are more attentive and motivated to achieve when the level of instruction matches their readiness, needs, and learning profiles. However, some students have learned and continue to practice unproductive habits that impede learning in school environments. Additionally, some students' lives are so complex and stressful with financial strife, survival concerns, substance abuse, or health issues) that they exhibit inappropriate learning behaviors that they seemingly can not overcome. These needs and behaviors must be addressed so learning can follow. Counselors, previous teachers, administrators, and parents are all invaluable in understanding these needs and determining a plan for productive learning.

Kingore, B. (2004). *Differentiation: Simplified, Realistic, and Effective.* Austin: Professional Associates Publishing.

ELICITING ADVANCED ACHIEVEMENT

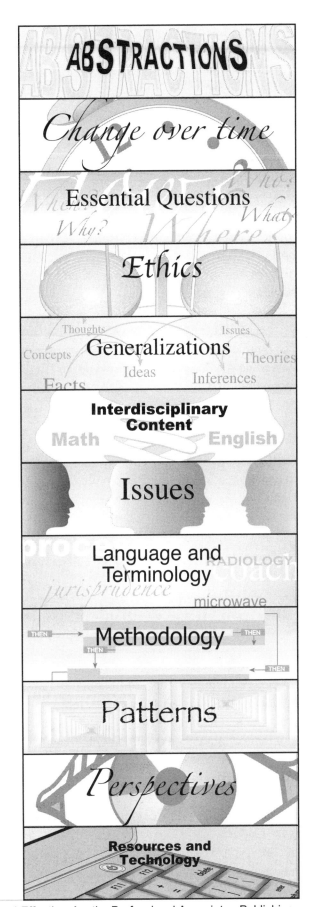

It is vital to respond to the educational diversity of all students' needs and readiness levels. Winebrenner counsels educators to accept the fact that students are at different levels in their learning and need constant opportunities to work at those various levels (2001). When we value and accept individual differences, we differentiate instruction and provide diverse levels of continued learning in response to different learners' readiness.

When instructing gifted students, differentiate curriculum *content, process,* and *products by deletion, extension,* and *addition.* Instruction that is differentiated for highly-able students must increase the complexity of the *content* as well as the *process* by which the students learn so that depth and breadth are demonstrated in the *products* by which they present their learning. To accomplish this elevated complexity, pretest students and then *delete* any known concepts and skills from the instruction. The time gained by that deletion makes it possible to respond to the students' interests and readiness levels by *extending* content with further development of existing concepts or *adding* content that is not in the regular curriculum.

Kingore, B. (2004). *Differentiation: Simplified, Realistic, and Effective.* Austin: Professional Associates Publishing.

In teacher training, I have learned to expect the following expression of concern from teachers of upper-elementary and secondary students: *My gifted students really don't want to work. I get better responses from my regular classes.* I then pose to them: *What might we do to elicit higher responses from these advanced students?* At that point, the answers became vague: *more high-level thinking, more focus, more abstract thinking, more dedication, more materials, more depth, more complexity, more technology...* When I probe for specific elaboration, most teachers discuss using Bloom's Taxonomy and then have nothing more to offer.

Educators want to elicit advanced achievement but are often in a quandary about how to do so. They lack a specific approach or technique to lift students' accomplishments. Teachers must first identify the specific elements of advanced achievements and high-level responses in order to elicit them. Identifying and defining elements of abstract thinking, complexity, and depth develop the terminology needed to differentiate curriculum for advanced and gifted students.

ELEMENTS OF ADVANCED ACHIEVEMENT: ABSTRACT THINKING, COMPLEXITY, AND DEPTH

To be applicable, these elements must be clear and understandable to educators and students. As I worked for several years with students and teachers to identify and integrate elements of advanced achievement, it became evident that some terminology relating to these elements did not communicate a specific direction for content integration. Some terms associated with complexity and depth were vague and caused confusion or decreased interest in the process. Additional elements emerged as significant when teachers analyzed that their objectives for gifted students included abstract thinking opportunities. They questioned how abstract thinking integrated into the elements of complexity. Together, we worked to synthesize classroom experiences with the work of curriculum leaders such as H. L. Erickson, S. Kaplan, J. McTighe, and G. Wiggins. Over time, a list of elements emerged that teachers could effectively use to escalate the complexity of both instruction and students' responses.

Teachers concluded that when they prompt more abstract thinking, complexity, and depth they are more likely to get the advanced achievement they expected. Gifted learners need opportunities for abstract thinking and complex content to stay mentally engaged in learning. They thrive on intellectual challenges and in-depth study rather than content generalities and overviews. In mixed-ability classrooms, providing that level of challenge for advanced students is difficult to manage while maintaining appropriate instruction for all other students. However, the process becomes manageable and effective when teachers clearly define and integrate the elements of abstract thinking, complexity, and depth to focus advanced levels of instruction and then teach students how to apply these elements to their studies. This technique requires less intensive teacher preparation and simplifies management issues as it develops students' independence and responsibility for continued learning.

These elements of abstract thinking, complexity, and depth are proposed in Figure 7.1 to stimulate teachers' decisions regarding students' needs in their disciplines or grade levels. Review the elements to determine which ones most relate to eliciting advanced levels of students' learning in your instruction. These elements are listed in alphabetical order so that a hierarchical value is not implied. The intent is for both critical and productive thinking to be subsumed in each rather than translate into separate elements.

Kingore, B. (2004). *Differentiation: Simplified, Realistic, and Effective.* Austin: Professional Associates Publishing.

Figure 7.1:
ABSTRACT THINKING, COMPLEXITY, AND DEPTH (ACD)
(Demonstrated beyond grade-level expectations)

Abstractions	Abstractions express symbolic or metaphorical responses beyond concrete data or experiences.
Change Over Time	Change Over Time explores the relationships of past, present, and future trends.
Essential Questions	Essential Questions address the significant, related questions that explore and interpret key ideas students must acquire to understand the topic.
Ethics	Ethics involve the perceived conflicts or dilemmas related to a topic, such as human rights, rules of conduct, environmental decisions, and moral principles.
Generalizations	Generalizations are the inferred ideas or principles that evolve from considering overarching meaning and relationships.
Interdisciplinary Content	Interdisciplinary content invites exploration of a topic across disciplines to encourage relationships and enrich the depth and breadth of understanding.
Issues	Issues are points in question, or matters of dispute, whose resolutions are significant to the public.
Language and Terminology	Language and Terminology involve the sophisticated words and specific vocabulary related to a profession or field of study.
Methodology	Methodology is procedural knowledge and the proficiently with which students carry out a process.
Patterns	Patterns identify the recurring events, attributes, behaviors, and ideas within a topic or event; students use that present information to predict future arrangements.
Perspectives	Perspectives involve the multiple viewpoints possible when people respond to ideas, events, or behaviors; students interpret what motivates points of view and opinions.
Resources and Technology	Resources and Technology encourage complexity when sophisticated, concept-dense resources are incorporated to embellish content beyond grade level.

Kingore, B. (2004). *Differentiation: Simplified, Realistic, and Effective.* Austin: Professional Associates Publishing.

These elements of advanced achievement must be demonstrated beyond the grade-level expectations to approach a level expected from highly able students. This advanced level of response requires exploration, interpretation, and development of relationships across contents rather than simple reporting of the content.

> *Integrating elements of abstract thinking, complexity, and depth avoids instruction based on advanced and gifted students doing more, working harder, or making less errors; the focus instead is on students thinking differently.*

Over time, teachers begin to refer to the elements as *ACD* to simplify communication as they explore multiple application possibilities. The objective is for teachers to clearly understand elements of advanced achievement and simplify their preparation and management of this differentiation. The first step is to define more specifically how each of these elements of abstract thinking, complexity, and depth relates to advanced achievement. The next step is to plan ways to use the elements to differentiate instruction by eliciting higher responses and developing students' independence and responsibility for continued learning.

Teacher tip...

Greater complexity with advanced content must be expected from gifted students. Settling for less breeds poor learning habits and counterproductive attitudes.

UNDERSTANDING THE ELEMENTS OF ABSTRACT THINKING, COMPLEXITY, AND DEPTH

ABSTRACTIONS

Abstract thinking infers beyond concrete data or realities and, at times, is intuitive. It poses and reconciles paradoxes and involves the application of symbols and metaphorical thought. Students represent ideas symbolically and theoretically as they demonstrate abstract thinking.

CHANGE OVER TIME

Most content areas focus on one aspect of time. History, for example, focuses on the past while most instruction focuses on conditions and events in the present. Change over time invites a pondering of past and present as a window to trends and future implications. Students consider the past, present, and future concepts with enduring value in an area of study as they analyze change over time.

ESSENTIAL QUESTIONS

Essential questions reflect the key ideas students must acquire to understand the topic. They are posed as questions to stimulate open-ended inquiry rather than propagate simple fact collection. These questions represent the heart of exploring and interpreting the big ideas indispensible to a topic but also related across topics. They raise significant, related inquiry that requires analysis and exemplification while feeding upon a vast background understanding. Students pose or consider essential questions such as:

*   How is observation crucial to scientific advancement?
*   What patterns influence story structure?
*   How is mathematics useful in daily life?

Kingore, B. (2004). *Differentiation: Simplified, Realistic, and Effective.* Austin: Professional Associates Publishing.

- What interrelationships are essential among the systems of the human body?
- Why does history seem to repeat itself?

ETHICS 4

Ethical concerns are revealed by the dilemmas or controversies related to a topic. Gifted students frequently have a heightened awareness of ethics and are driven to seek resolutions or action for change. Students weigh the ethical considerations and ramifications involving human rights, judgments, rules of conduct, environmental decisions, and moral principles.

Teacher tip...

Gifted children's moral awareness level and ethical concerns are often heightened. They love to discuss issues and philosophical topics that might not interest their age mates.

GENERALIZATIONS 5

Generalizations are inferred ideas or principles abstracted beyond particular facts or instances. They express understanding of relationships among data or principles. Gifted students interpret, extend, or create a generalization that is unexpected for the age of the learner. Generalizations evolve from considering overarching meaning and relationships.

INTERDISCIPLINARY CONTENT 6

Exploring the topic across two or more academic disciplines enriches the depth and breadth of students' understanding. Students consider what is happening in art, current events, social interactions, literature, and politics that influences information and thinking related to the topic. Ken Burns * PBS series on the U.S. Civil War illustrates the power of interdisciplinary content. He made history alive and personal for viewers when he included art, photographs, music, interviews, and personal letters from that period.

ISSUES 7

Issues are disputed aspects of a topic whose resolutions are significant to the public. Like ethics, gifted students respond passionately to issues involving survival, conflicts, politics, finances, and even nutrition. They seek the crux of the issue as they discuss its aspects.

LANGUAGE AND TERMINOLOGY 8

Language and terminology involve the use of more sophisticated words and specific vocabulary related to a field of study. In general, the more you know about a topic, the more specific the terminology you use when discussing it and the more you can elaborate to clarify the topic to others. Gifted students use language to explain abstract relationships through metaphorical responses.

METHODOLOGY 9

Methodology involves procedural knowledge and how proficiently students carry out a process. Sophisticated methodology is not always apparent in the product. Hence, the

*Burns, Ken, dir. *The Civil War*. PBS, 1999.

Kingore, B. (2004). *Differentiation: Simplified, Realistic, and Effective.* Austin: Professional Associates Publishing.

teacher or student are the only ones able to document when the methodology a student employs is an unexpected yet effective approach to the problem, such as reasoning in reverse. Methodology is also advanced when students extrapolate beyond the system of methods or procedural rules, as in the sciences.

PATTERNS

Patterns reveal the combinations of qualities or acts that form an arrangement. They identify recurring events, elements, behaviors, and ideas within a topic or event. (The order of events may themselves be a pattern.) Gifted students interpret, extend, or create unexpected patterns. Advanced applications of patterns evolve as students use a characteristic arrangement to model something new or beyond that pattern.

PERSPECTIVES

Perspectives involve the multiple or unique viewpoints possible when people respond to ideas, events, or behaviors. Students' backgrounds and readiness levels often lead them to different interpretations or reactions to the same event or idea as they view the relevant data and create a meaningful relationship. Gifted students also add breadth when they analyze what motivates other points of view and opinions.

RESOURCES AND TECHNOLOGY

Highly able students become fascinated at an early age with reference materials. They unexpectedly use sophisticated resources that are more concept-dense than resources typical of the grade level. As with methodology, a teacher or student is most privy to insights into the complexity of a student's resources and technological applications.

DIFFERENTIATING WITH ABSTRACT THINKING, COMPLEXITY, AND DEPTH

Applications of abstract thinking, complexity, and depth promote higher achievements from advanced and gifted students. The process of encouraging advanced achievement proceeds from teacher-directed to collaborative inquiry to autonomous student inquiry. Initially, teachers direct and model the incorporation of ACD into lessons for high levels of challenge. Next, teachers facilitate as they collaboratively work with students to integrate ACD in order to lift the rigor of a lesson or independent study. The ultimate goal is autonomous students, able to independently implement depth and breadth in their learning.

DIFFERENTIATING WITH ABSTRACT THINKING, COMPLEXITY, AND DEPTH

The teacher incorporates abstract thinking, complexity, and depth as criteria on rubrics.

The teacher refers to the elements to increase challenge through inquiry and tiering.

The teacher uses the elements to focus students' thinking and advanced investigations..
1. The teacher selects the elements.
2. The teacher and student collaboratively select the elements.

The students self-select elements to enhance their learning.

Kingore, B. (2004). *Differentiation: Simplified, Realistic, and Effective.* Austin: Professional Associates Publishing.

TEACHER-DIRECTED APPLICATIONS

Rubrics That Promote Advanced Achievements

Rubrics communicate a teacher's expectations of quality in a product or process. Increase abstract thinking, complexity, and depth by communicating these elements as criteria on the rubrics used for students' self-assessments and evaluations. When these elements are built into evaluative tools shared with students before a task begins, students have a clear message that abstract thinking, complexity, and depth are expected in their learning processes and products. A simple version of ACD as criteria on a rubric is shared in Chapter 9. A more complex version of these elements as rubric criteria is included in the performance assessment scoring guide that ends this chapter. We dare not expect consistent applications of abstract thinking, complexity, and depth if we do not include these criteria as guidelines to quality.

Increasing Challenge within a Lesson

To enhance challenge within a lesson, skim Figure 7.1 to activate your thinking of potential instructional connections. Select elements of ACD that have the potential to lift a general education lesson. Incorporating these elements enables teachers to increase rigor when prompting inquiry, tiering general education curricula, and eliciting students' high-level investigations and products.

➡ Prompting Inquiry

Use the elements of ACD to incorporate thinking skills and plan inquiry. Figure 7.2 correlates these elements to several possible thinking skill connections* and then includes triggers for questions that incorporate these elements. Refer to the elements and select relevant ones to prompt inquiry within a specific lesson. Notice

the significant number of thinking skills that integrate with each element. Complexity involves interdependent thinking skills.

➡ Tiering a lesson

Analyze a text book or general education lesson, and use the ACD elements to tier its complexity. Which elements have potential topic connections? Which might effectively weave into the discussion to lift complexity?

Teachers use ACD to structure and guide students' into complex thinking and reasoning as they explore multiple contents. Consider how complexity is elevated during a lesson about DNA research when Mr. Denamer provides sophisticated resources and technology opportunities and then enhances the discussion with essential questions, ethics, perspectives, and change over time.

- Pose five questions essential to this topic.
- Explore the topic from the perspectives of leaders in medicine, religion, and politics.
- Debate the appropriateness of genetically altered products in our daily lives.
- What ethical controversies are related to DNA research?
- Based upon the present status, forecast future trends in DNA research.

Ms. Ruiz uses hands-on activities with her primary children during math lessons. To demonstrate number sense, her children made books using sets of hole reinforcers. For each page, they drew a picture incorporating the reinforcers as part of the illustration and then wrote the pattern: *[number of] hole reinforcers can make a [thing]* . Children made books with pages illustrating the numbers one through twelve, even numbers through twenty, or base five through fifty.

Ms. Ruiz tiers the complexity of the math lesson with her primary gifted students by incorporating advanced opportunities in

---

*Chapter 2: Instructional Strategies that Impact Differentiation introduces these thinking skills in Figure 2.7.

Kingore, B. (2004). *Differentiation: Simplified, Realistic, and Effective.* Austin: Professional Associates Publishing.

Figure 7.2:
ABSTRACT THINKING, COMPLEXITY, AND DEPTH RELATED TO THINKING AND INQUIRY

Thinking skills are interdependent and rarely used independently of one another.

ELEMENTS	THINKING SKILLS	INQUIRY: QUESTION TRIGGERS
Abstractions	• Pose unknowns • Interpret • Generalize • Develop analogies • Hypothesize • Identify ambiguity • Think deductively and inductively	*Which symbols could represent ____?* *How is ____ like ____?* *What are the paradoxes?*
Change over time	• Hypothesize • Predict • Categorize • Determine sequence • Determine cause and effect • Rank or prioritize • Think deductively and inductively • Analyze attributes • Differentiate similarities and differences	*How has ____ changed over time?* *How has time affected ____?* *Based upon past actions, what are the future trends?*
Essential questions	• Formulate questions • Categorize • Pose unknowns • Analyze the attributes • Hypothesize • Identify ambiguity • Determine relevancy • Determine cause and effect • Rank or prioritize • Think deductively and inductively	*What three questions pose key concerns for this process?* *Which characteristics are most significant to ____'s survival?* *What information is indispensible to this topic?*
Ethics	• Determine relevancy • Conclude • Generalize • Identify point of view • Assume • Rank or prioritize • Think deductively and inductively • Interpret • Establish and apply judgement criteria • Identify ambiguity • Determine cause and effect • Substantiate	*Which moral assumptions are involved in this controversy?* *How has bias affected this discussion?* *What is your interpretation of that judgment?*
Generalizations	• Establish criteria • Identify ambiguity • Rank or prioritize • Think deductively and inductively • Substantiate • Differentiate similarities and differences • Interpret • Determine relevancy • Determine cause and effect	*What is the key relationship among these principles?* *What overarching meaning can be drawn from the examples?* *What is main point of this philosophy?*
Interdisciplinary content	• Formulate questions • Conclude • Generalize • Think deductively and inductively • Assume • Differentiate similarities and differences • Interpret • Determine cause and effect • Pose unknowns • Identify ambiguity • Determine relevancy	*How is this controversy expressed in other disciplines during that time period?* *What are common elements of these disciplines?* *Which events influenced this movement in art or literature?*

Category	Skills	Questions
Issues	• Formulate questions • Assume • Conclude • Think deductively and inductively • Identify ambiguity • Differentiate similarities and differences • Interpret • Distinguish viewpoint • Distinguish fact and fiction • Determine relevancy • Substantiate • Establish criteria	*What is the crux of this issue? Why is the resolution of this issue significant to the public? How relevant is this issue today?*
Language and terminology	• Develop analogies • Categorize • Differentiate similarities and differences • Interpret • Determine relevancy • Analyze the attributes or characteristics • Think deductively and inductively • Assume	*Which five words are most important to this topic? Which terms best describe this process? What terminology is significant to this field?*
Methodology	• Hypothesize • Predict • Assume • Conclude • Generalize • Interpret • Determine sequence • Determine relevancy • Think deductively and inductively	*How did methodology taint the results? Which method is most relevant? How would you describe the procedure?*
Patterns	• Formulate questions • Hypothesize • Assume • Think deductively and inductively • Categorize • Differentiate similarities and differences • Analyze attributes • Interpret • Determine cause and effect • Determine relevancy	*Based upon the pattern of the events, what can be forecasted regarding future actions? What is the implied mathematical rule? What are the reoccurring ideas?*
Perspectives	• Pose unknowns • Assume • Conclude • Generalize • Interpret • Categorize • Think deductively and inductively • Identify ambiguity • Differentiate similarities and differences • Determine relevancy • Distinguish reality and fantasy	*How does the perspective of another character affect that interpretation? What are the opposing viewpoints? Why might a scientist take offense at that conclusion?*
Resources and technology	• Formulate questions • Pose unknowns • Interpret • Hypothesize • Predict • Assume • Distinguish fact and fiction • Establish and apply judgement criteria • Identify ambiguity • Think deductively and inductively • Substantiate • Differentiate similarities and differences • Conclude • Determine the cause and effect • Generalize • Analyze the attributes or characteristics • Determine relevancy • Distinguish point of view • Categorize	*Which resources provide the most in-depth information? How is that resource biased? What advantages does technology offer when researching this topic?*

Eliciting Advanced Achievement

Kingore, B. (2004). *Differentiation: Simplified, Realistic, and Effective.* Austin: Professional Associates Publishing.

methodology and perspectives that challenge them to figure out how to organize a problem and learn that there is more than one way to solve a problem. She poses a question and a pattern. *How can you figure out how many hole reinforcers were used in your book?*

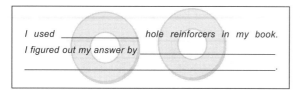

I used _____ hole reinforcers in my book.
I figured out my answer by _____
_____.

Eliciting Students' High-level Investigations and Products

Use the ACD elements to focus students' thinking and organize their investigations and products. For example, select elements applicable to a specific lesson or topic and propose those elements as the product assignment is discussed with students.

Rather than encourage simple fact gathering during a unit on biomes, Mr. Hanson

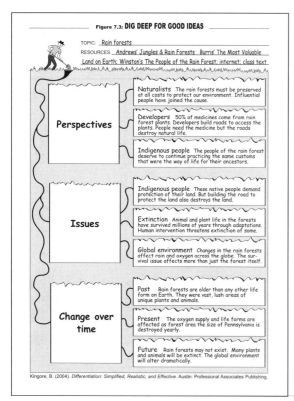

Figure 7.3: **DIG DEEP FOR GOOD IDEAS**

TOPIC: Rain forests
RESOURCES: Andrews' Jungles & Rain Forests; Burris' The Most Valuable Land on Earth; Winston's The People of the Rain Forest; internet; class text

Perspectives

Naturalists The rain forests must be preserved at all costs to protect our environment. Influential people have joined the cause.

Developers 50% of medicines come from rain forest plants. Developers build roads to access the plants. People need the medicine but the roads destroy natural life.

Indigenous people The people of the rain forest deserve to continue practicing the same customs that were the way of life for their ancestors.

Issues

Indigenous people These native people demand protection of their land. But building the road to protect the land also destroys the land.

Extinction Animal and plant life in the forests have survived millions of years through adaptations. Human intervention threatens extinction of some.

Global environment Changes in the rain forests affect rain and oxygen across the globe. The survival issue affects more than just the forest itself.

Change over time

Past Rain forests are older than any other life form on Earth. They were vast, lush areas of unique plants and animals.

Present The oxygen supply and life forms are affected as forest area the size of Pennsylvania is destroyed yearly.

Future Rain forests may not exist. Many plants and animals will be extinct. The global environment will alter dramatically.

Kingore, B. (2004). *Differentiation: Simplified, Realistic, and Effective.* Austin: Professional Associates Publishing.

selects specific elements to focus students' advanced responses and interpretations. All of his fourth-grade students read, discuss, and organize their acquired information on graphic organizers, such as Figure 7.3. As work proceeds, he challenges a small group of advanced students reading above grade-level materials to use the ACD elements of perspectives, issues, and change over time to guide their questioning and interpretations. Incorporating those elements escalates their thinking as they organize their acquired information about rain forests. Later, they use their information on the graphic organizer to plan an independent study.

COLLABORATIVE APPLICATIONS

With experience using ACD to organize students' content explorations, teachers begin to teach students to apply these elements to their studies by including students in the decision-making process of determining which elements relate to a specific topic. Collaboratively, as they discuss the content, the teacher and the students plan which elements to use to lift a learning task. The teacher may propose two or three elements to incorporate and then elicit the students' ideas for others to employ.

For example, Ms. Kung provides graphic organizers that her middle school students use to organize information and ideas gained from reading fiction before they engage in discussions or develop longer discourses. She encourages students to self-select the novels they want to read from a lengthy list of quality literature. After Beverly, a gifted student and creative thinker, has read approximately a third of her chosen book, Ms. Kung conferences with her briefly to discuss her progress and reactions. Because Beverly is interested in writing, Ms. Kung prompts her to think like an author and explore the rich language of the book. Beverly also selects *issues*

Figure 7.3: **DIG DEEP FOR GOOD IDEAS**

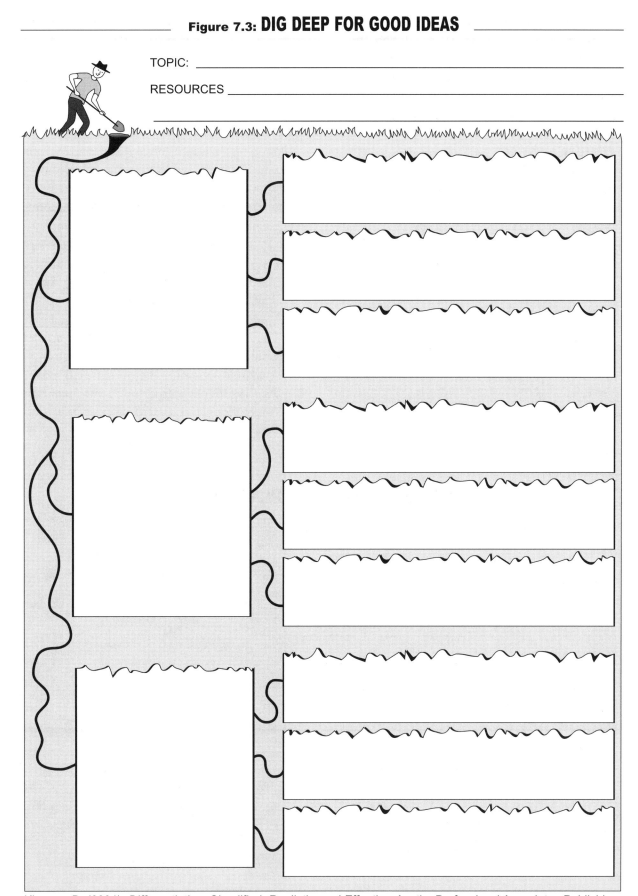

TOPIC: _____

RESOURCES _____

Kingore, B. (2004). *Differentiation: Simplified, Realistic, and Effective*. Austin: Professional Associates Publishing.

as an element she wants to consider. She then proceeds to finish the novel, pondering the language and issues inferred by the content that she will discuss later in a small-group literature circle. She uses a graphic organizer to record her notes that will guide her discussion.

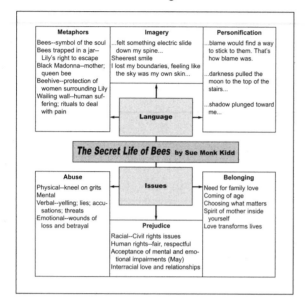

AUTONOMOUS STUDENT INQUIRY AND APPLICATIONS

The ultimate goal of differentiated instruction is to develop autonomous students able to more independently implement depth and breadth as they continue learning. Autonomous student inquiry and applications lead to students independently incorporating abstract thinking, complexity, and depth to promote their higher achievement levels. After successful applications with ACD, students are able to self-select elements to uplift the content challenge as they demonstrate independence and responsibility for continued learning. Three applications of student autonomy follow.

♦ Students have a copy of Figure 7.1 to analyze the elements for inclusion in assigned or self-selected learning tasks. As they investigate a topic, they skim the

---

Figure 7.4: ABSTRACT THINKING, COMPLEXITY, AND DEPTH

NAME _____

DATE _____

This is important because _____

_____

_____

_____

This work shows that I can _____

_____

_____

_____

Next time I want to _____

_____

_____

Check which elements are demonstrated within this product.

- **ABSTRACTIONS**
- **CHANGES OVER TIME**
- ESSENTIAL QUESTIONS
- ETHICS
- GENERALIZATIONS
- INTERDISCIPLINARY CONTENT
- ISSUES
- LANGUAGE AND TERMINOLOGY
- METHODOLOGY
- PATTERNS
- PERSPECTIVES
- RESOURCES AND TECHNOLOGY

Kingore, B. (2004). *Differentiation: Simplified, Realistic, and Effective*. Austin: Professional Associates Publishing.

elements to determine which ones enhance interpretations of information and uplift the content challenge. Students discuss their choices and ideas for continued learning with their teacher who facilitates the process.

♦ Students use Figure 7.2 to incorporate thinking skills and plan inquiry that prompts their research and independent studies. After brainstorming connections, students discuss potential questions and procedures with each other and the teacher to extend their ideas and plan resources.

♦ Students can also use portfolio captions to substantiate the complexity of their work. The elements of abstract thinking, complexity, and depth can be incorporated on the caption strips students use to organize a product for their portfolio (Figure 7.4). Advanced and gifted students independently complete these captions, checking the elements of ACD they applied in the replacement tasks and independent studies. In this way, students assume the responsibility of documenting their advanced achievements.

ASSESSMENT OF GIFTED-LEVEL ACHIEVEMENTS

For several years, districts and states have used performance assessments as part of their evaluation of learning standards. Performance assessments have two parts: a performance assignment and a set of scoring guides. Students complete the assignment under the watchful eye of an evaluator who observes their work and uses the scoring guides to judge the quality of achievement demonstrated (Stiggins, 2001). Performance assessments are frequently used to document statewide achievements in writing.

A promising application of performance standards is their use in evaluating the performance of students as an outcome of their participation in a gifted program. For example, the Texas Education Agency[1] under Ann Wink's direction in Gifted Education is engaged in a multiple-year pilot of performance standards for gifted students. These assignments are used near the end of the school year to evaluate students' advanced, innovative products and performances. Graduating gifted students also have opportunities to create products and performances of professional quality as part of their program services (TEA, 2003).

Building upon the use of performance assessment, consider the value of developing performance standards for use in classrooms where gifted students receive instruction. These standards could become a continuing assessment of the value-added factor of gifted services by addressing questions, such as: *How do processes and products demonstrated by gifted students differ from those of other students? How are gifted services affecting the outcome of gifted students' achievement?*

Thus, rather than being used only as a summative device to evaluate gifted students, the performance assessments can be used as formative information to document the achievements of gifted students throughout the year and clarify how their gifted performance is beyond core-curriculum responses. This application of performance assessment becomes instructionally useful by providing information to the teacher (potentially to students and parents) regarding the quality of demonstrated performance.

Dr. Diane Patin[2], Program Director for Encounters Gifted and Talented Program, advocates the continual use of performance assessments in instruction for advanced and

[1]The Texas Director of Gifted Education and may be reached at: <http://www.tea.state.tx.us/gted>
[2]The Encounters Gifted and Talented Program may be reached at: <http://www.aldine.k12.tx.us>

Kingore, B. (2004). *Differentiation: Simplified, Realistic, and Effective.* Austin: Professional Associates Publishing.

gifted students. Teachers responsible for instructing these students are trained in the process and then use their performance assessment scoring guides to assess product outcomes in their classrooms. The goal is to document how the products and performances of both their advanced and gifted students exceed core curriculum expectations. The information is used to impact instruction rather than to evaluate teacher or student effectiveness.

One example of a scoring guide for a performance assessment that delineates advanced-level and gifted-level achievements is shared in Figure 7.5. Based upon that assessment, some teachers conclude that the products they had considered suitable for gifted-level responses are actually more appropriate expectations for advanced students or high-achievers. The process challenges teachers to uplift opportunities, materials, and expectations for highly able students. Teachers generally concluded that products or performances devoid of ACD elements were unlikely to substantiate gifted-level achievements.

The greatest value of this application of performance assessment is to identify and describe specific elements of gifted-level products and achievements. Teachers need to understand what gifted-level performances look and sound like. When teachers more concretely understand these elements, they can incorporate increased complexity in their instruction, expand achievement expectations for highly able students, and more appropriately challenge gifted learners.

In programs responsible for responding to the instructional needs of gifted students, the curriculum must be evaluated for both concrete and abstract products. Concrete products are what students produce or demonstrate; abstract products are the more enduring and transferable outcomes of learning, including frameworks of knowledge, levels of understanding, problem-solving strategies,

habits of mind, dispositions for learning, values, and self-efficacy (Tomlinson et al, 2002). The application of abstract, complex, and in-depth products and processes increases the likelihood that instruction for advanced and gifted students does not only include the general school program provided to all students but expands beyond it.

When implementing performance assessment, the scoring rubric must be interpreted in light of the student's age and grade-level placement; complexity in a kindergarten product is vastly different from complexity in the products and responses of a middle-school student. Performance assessment challenges teachers to analyze students' products and reflect upon their own instruction. The results allow teachers to monitor and adjust their instruction in order to promote high-level achievement and enhance gifted students' successes.

Teacher tip...

When a child is advanced or gifted in reading, share with parents the responsibility for challenging the child. Suggest library visits and share resources that help parents know you are working with them to challenge their child. Remind parents that gifted children develop at an early age an affinity for nonfiction materials.

Kingore, B. (2004). *Differentiation: Simplified, Realistic, and Effective.* Austin: Professional Associates Publishing.

Figure 7.5:

PERFORMANCE ASSESSMENT

STUDENT _____

DATE _____

PRODUCT _____

TEACHER _____

SCHOOL _____

Abstract Thinking, Complexity, and Depth (ACD)

(Demonstrated beyond grade-level expectations)

- ABSTRACTIONS - symbols and metaphors
- CHANGE OVER TIME - Past, present, future trends
- ESSENTIAL QUESTIONS
- ETHICS
- GENERALIZATIONS - Interpret; extend; create
- INTERDISCIPLINARY CONTENT
- ISSUES
- LANGUAGE AND TERMINOLOGY
- METHODOLOGY
- PATTERNS
- PERSPECTIVES - Multiple viewpoints
- RESOURCES AND TECHNOLOGY
- _____
- _____
- _____

Summary

	Not Applicable	Below Expectations	Grade-level Expectations	Advanced Response	Exceeds Expectations	Innovative
Learning Standards						
Abstract thinking						
Complexity						
Depth of content						
Problem solving; procedural knowledge						
Communication						
Extension						
Autonomy						

Kingore, B. (2004). *Differentiation: Simplified, Realistic, and Effective.* Austin: Professional Associates Publishing.

Below Expectations	The student is not performing within grade-level expectations. Identified gifted students should not perform at this level. If this level is indicated by a student's work, analyze and explain which of the following factors may be contributing or related to the problem. ▢ Instructional issue ▢ Student issue ▢ Background issue
Grade-level Expectations	Most general-education students can and should achieve this level of competency. Product does not exceed grade-level expectations. Responses are appropriate to the core curriculum standards. Performance is typical of general-education students.
Advanced Response	Some students achieve this level of competency. Product demonstrates a strong, above-average response. Occasional sparks of advanced potential are evident. Performance is typical of high-achieving students.
Exceeds Expectations	Few students achieve this level of competency. Product exceeds the standards and expectations of the grade level. The student exhibits consistent excellence; heightened abilities and insights; greater depth, complexity, and scope. Responds positively to task complexity and challenge. Performance is typical of gifted students.
Innovative	This level of competency is rare. Responses are remarkable and substantially exceed expectations. Strengths are clearly outstanding. Product is an original contribution to the discipline for a student of this age. Performance is typical of highly-gifted students.

Kingore, B. (2004). *Differentiation: Simplified, Realistic, and Effective.* Austin: Professional Associates Publishing.

	Not Applicable	Below Expectations	Grade-level Expectations	Advanced Response	Exceeds Expectations	Innovative
Abstract thinking			Concrete ideas; appropriate but literal; event based	Concludes appropriate relationships; uses some metaphors to develop relationships; discusses concepts and principles based upon events	Symbolic or metaphorical; abstract thinking is evident; concludes beyond concrete realities or specific objects; idea based	Creates complex symbolic or metaphorical relationships; uses idea-based thinking to pose principles or generalizations; makes connections between abstract ideas and intangibles
Learning standards			Valid content; accurate facts and details but little depth or elaboration; conveys a general idea or understanding.	Covers topic effectively; well developed; explores the topic beyond basic facts and details.	Precise data; in-depth; well supported; develops more advanced concepts and relationships; insightful; evaluates the issues of the topic.	Forms original generalizations using complex concepts and relationships; hypothesizes and infers beyond the data; unique ideas or responses; evaluates issues across disciplines and topics.
Complexity			Simple and basic information; limited critical thinking.	Critical thinking is evident; compares and contrasts; integrates topics, time, or disciplines.	Analyzes, synthesizes, and evaluates across time and disciplines; interprets and creatively integrates multiple perspectives and issues; uses beyond grade-level resources.	Internalizes complex information and relationships; expands concepts beyond age-expectations; works with multiple abstractions; sophisticated use of resources.
Content depth			Valid content; accurate facts and details but little depth or elaboration; conveys a general idea or understanding.	Covers topic effectively; well developed; explores the topic beyond basic facts and details.	Precise data; in-depth; well supported; develops more advanced concepts and relationships; insightful; evaluates the issues of the topic.	Forms original generalizations using complex concepts and relationships; hypothesizes and infers beyond the data; unique ideas or responses; evaluates issues across disciplines and topics.

Kingore, B. (2004). *Differentiation: Simplified, Realistic, and Effective.* Austin: Professional Associates Publishing.

Eliciting Advanced Achievement

	Not Applicable	Below Expectations	Grade-level Expectations	Advanced Response	Exceeds Expectations	Innovative
Communication: Written, oral, and/or graphic			Explains or discusses in response to questions or probes; uses some appropriate terminology, graphics, and/or notation; shows some consideration of audience	Elaborates in response to questions or probes; incorporates appropriate terminology, graphics, and/or notation; communication is clear and interesting; shows awareness of the audience	Explains independently, clearly, and confidently; precise vocabulary, graphics, and/or notation; develops product or performance with nuances for a specific audience	Outstanding; communicates a level of insight that enhances the understanding of others; sophisticated and professional level of vocabulary, graphics, and/or notation; engages others in reflection
Extension			Completed as assigned	Response is embellished; ideas or concepts are elaborated and developed to enhance assignment	Response is developed beyond the assignment; poses unanswered questions; extends through personal insight, examples, graphics, performance, or an atypical application	Response demonstrates intense involvement in the topic or data; pursues a self-selected problem beyond the assignment; response is multiple-faceted and developed over time
Autonomy			Simple and basic information; limited critical thinking.	Critical thinking is evident; compares and contrasts; integrates topics, time, or disciplines.	Analyzes, synthesizes, and evaluates across time and disciplines; interprets and creatively integrates multiple perspectives and issues; uses beyond grade-level resources.	Internalizes complex information and relationships; expands concepts beyond age-expectations; works with multiple abstractions; sophisticated use of resources.
Problem solving; Procedural knowledge			Follows directions; completes the assignment on time	Anticipates directions and time lines; applies the skills of independence	Self-directed; self-governing; functions independently; frequently initiates own learning; exceeds the parameters of assignments	Self-motivating; self-selects problems and procedures; efforts and products exceed the parameters of the assignment; develops systems and habits for effective, efficient learning

Kingore, B. (2004). *Differentiation: Simplified, Realistic, and Effective.* Austin: Professional Associates Publishing.

TIERED INSTRUCTION

Tiered instruction provides different levels of learning tasks within the same unit or topic in order to align the curriculum to the different readiness levels of students and to respond to learner differences. It allows students to focus on essential skills yet still be challenged at the different levels on which they are individually capable of working.

The teacher varies the complexities of activities to ensure that all students explore ideas at a level that builds upon what they already know and facilitates their continued learning. In mixed-ability classrooms, tiered assignments maintain the essential understandings and skills required by the curriculum and district or state standards for all learners. Simultaneously, tiered instruction provides pathways at appropriate challenge levels for students to access learning at increased degrees of abstract thinking, complexity, and depth.

Tiered instruction blends assessment and instruction. The teacher completes a pre-instruction assessment to determine what students know and then prescribes content materials and learning experiences at students' different readiness levels. The teacher

Kingore, B. (2004). *Differentiation: Simplified, Realistic, and Effective.* Austin: Professional Associates Publishing.

also plans different kinds and degrees of instructional support and structure, depending upon each student's level.

Instruction can be tiered by content (the complexity of what they learn), process (how students learn), and products (how they present their learning). When differentiating through tiered instruction, tier appropriately challenging tasks to require different levels of complexity and abstraction in the content level of information; the products assigned; and the thinking-, communication-, and research-processes required. Ideally, tiered learning tasks engage students slightly beyond what they find easy or comfortable in order to provide genuine challenge and to promote their continued learning (Jensen, 2000; Csikszentmihalyi, 1997). Optimally, a task level is neither too simple so that it leads to boredom nor too difficult so that it results in frustration.

Consider tiered instruction to be like a stairwell. The top story represents learning tasks for advanced readiness students with very high skills and complex understanding, and the bottom story represents learning tasks for students with less readiness and fewer skills. Note that there isn't always a student working on every tier level as students progress through tiers of learning at different paces. Also, within each tier, there simultaneously can be multiple small-group activities presenting different ways to learn. Some floors in the stairwell even have multiple stairways as students access higher learning levels differently. As teachers consider students' readiness levels, it becomes obvious that everyone is not at the same place in their learning and that different tiered tasks are needed to optimize every student's classroom experience.

Research results clearly substantiate that tiered instruction is needed in mixed-ability classrooms to differentiate instruction. Students are more successful in school and find it more satisfying if they are taught in ways that are responsive to their readiness levels (Vygotsky, 1986), interests (Csikszentmihalyi, 1997), and learning profiles (Sternberg et al., 1998). Yet, most teachers incorporate almost no variations in their learning experiences despite the fact that their students exhibit very different readiness levels (Ross, 1993). Content, processes, and products geared to the entire class seldom help struggling learners or challenge advanced students to increase their thinking and expand their knowledge (Westberg et al, 1993). Obviously, instruction must be varied in response to learner differences.

> TEACHER: *I can't use tiered instruction. My students don't think it's fair unless everyone does the same thing!*

What's fair? Is it fair that everyone does the same work regardless of their needs? Assigning the same work to all students increases the likelihood that some students will be overwhelmed while others have to expend so little effort to achieve that they infer school is easy! Redirect students' thinking by stating a position, such as the following.

> *We are different. We look different from one another; we like different things; we learn different ways. One size does not really fit everyone. Until everyone looks the same and wears exactly the same style and size of clothing, I will believe that you have different needs. Together, we will continue to determine different learning tasks that specifically match you and your best ways to learn.*

An analogy such as this can serve to explain why learning tasks differ for students. It is a compliment to students that you respect them and their needs so much that you plan instruction with specific awareness of each individual in the class.

Resentment from students is likely if some assignments are perceived as more fun or disproportionately difficult. Therefore, avoid the ineffective practice of assigning paper-and-pencil tasks to students with less skills as other students work on interesting, hands-on projects. Indeed, there may be instances in which skill sheets are needed by all students. However, it is also true that all students benefit from a variety of processes and products that integrate multiple ways to learn.

Rather than react defensively when students question differences in learning tasks, challenge students to analyze themselves and explain why a particular approach or task is better for them.

> STUDENT: *Why can't I do what Patrick is doing?*
> TEACHER: *Document to me how that is your best way to learn, and I will reconsider.*

Teacher tip...

"Fair" does not mean doing everything alike with all students. It means respecting each person and endeavoring to help each learn at her or his highest level. To do less is to be less of a teacher.

GUIDELINES FOR TIERED INSTRUCTION

1. **Differentiate by content, process, and/or product.**
   Content is the complexity of *what* students are to know; it is directly influenced by the level of materials they access to learn. Process is *how* students use key skills and relate ideas as they make sense of the content; it includes thinking skills, communication skills, research skills, and the ways students process information. Product is the *result* of content and process; it is what students create to demonstrate and extend what they learned. (A product may be a concrete thing, an action, or a verbal conclusion or summary of understanding.)

   Gifted students require differentiation by content and process to escalate learning in response to their readiness. Solely differentiating by product is less likely to result in their continued learning.

2. **Plan the number of levels most appropriate for instruction.**
   There is not an absolute number of levels required for an appropriate application of tiered instruction.
   - Different quantities of tiers are needed for different concepts and skills in relation to different learners' needs. Sometimes, two tiers are sufficient; at other times, three to five or more work better to match the wide range of learners.
   - The quantity of needed tiers varies in different curricula areas.
   - To adjust the working environment, teachers vary the number of tiers in response to their preferred number of students working on one learning task. Changing the number of tiers is one way to vitalize flexible groupings and ensure that students are not always in the same group.

Kingore, B. (2004). *Differentiation: Simplified, Realistic, and Effective.* Austin: Professional Associates Publishing.

3. **Begin tiered instruction at the readiness level of the students.**

   The complexity of a tiered assignment is relative because it is determined by the specific needs of the learners in a class, and because a learners' readiness levels vary in different curricula areas. In classes with below grade-level learners, the lowest tier would respond to those students. In classes in which all students are at or above grade level, the lowest tier would respond to grade-level or even above grade-level readiness (Kingore, 2002).

4. **Ensure that the tiers and the groups working within each tier are flexible.**

   The word *tiered* is not a euphemism for low-middle-high groups. The low-middle-high groups of the past were stagnant groups that labeled who could learn and who was not learning. Tiered assignments, however, denote all children as able to learn the same essential skills in different ways. The tiers and the groups working within the tier are flexible. The make-up of students working at each tier varies with the content, assignment, and quantity of tiers.

5. **Vary the time required to complete tiered assignments.**

   Some tiers incorporate short-term tasks completed in less than a single setting. Other tiered tasks many involve several class sessions or evolve over more than a week.

6. **Promote high-level thinking in each tier.**

   The background and readiness levels of students should not limit the range of thinking opportunities provided through tiered assignments. Avoid always allocating simple thinking tasks for students with the fewest skills, mid-level thinking tasks for students in the middle range of readiness, and high-level challenges for learners at advanced readiness levels. There are occasions when knowledge, comprehension, and application level tasks (at students' readiness level) are needed by all students. Conversely, all students need opportunities to analyze, synthesize, and evaluate information.

7. **Promote continual development.**

   Plan instruction that stretches students slightly beyond their comfort zones. As Tomlinson cautions, "Only when students work at appropriate challenge levels do they develop the essential habits of persistence, curiosity, and willingness to take intellectual risks" (2001, 5).

8. **Provide teacher support at every tier.**

   Every tier requires teacher modeling and support for the students working at that tier. All learners benefit from a teacher's instruction, interaction, guidance, and feedback-- even gifted children whom some educators perceive as always *making it on their own.*

   Figure 8.1 delineates a sequence for developing tiered tasks. Consider these steps in the process.

Think about it...

Reflect upon the level of thinking you expect from your students. All students can and should engage in high-level thinking processes as often as possible. One difference is that gifted students engage in high-level thinking most of the time while other students analyze and synthesize only as often as their background information enables them to do so. Furthermore, the analysis by gifted students may be more abstract and complex.

Kingore, B. (2004). *Differentiation: Simplified, Realistic, and Effective.* Austin: Professional Associates Publishing.

Figure 8.1
STEPS IN DEVELOPING TIERED ASSIGNMENTS

1. Identify what all students must learn. Select the essential concepts, skills, or generalizations to address. Determine which learning standards to integrate.

2. Reflect upon the assessments of students' readiness levels, learning profiles, and interests.

3. Determine the priorities of the lesson-- the ways students will interact and the selected products of learning.

4. Begin by creating an activity that challenges most students, is interesting, and promotes understanding of key concepts or skills.

5. Vary that activity appropriately for students with fewer skills.

6. Create additional activities that are more complex, require more abstract thinking, are interesting, and use advanced resources and technology. Determine the complexity of each activity to ensure tasks that will challenge above-grade-level students and gifted learners.

7. Ensure that each student participates in a variation of the activity that corresponds to that student's needs and readiness.

APPLICATIONS OF TIERED INSTRUCTION

In this section, examples of learning experiences are provided that are tiered in content, process, and/or product according to students' readiness. The following three classroom examples and the tiering applications that incorporate graphics require different kinds and degrees of instructional support and structure. While some students need direct teacher modeling and support during instruction, others are ready for teacher facilitation and more open-ended instruction that encourages greater student independence.

Not all levels of these tiered assignments would be used in every class. When implementing a tiered lesson, for example, some classes might have students working only on the first three tiers of the lesson while other classes might have students working on only the last two tiers of that same lesson. The intent is not to divide students into leveled groups but to accommodate the unique diversity of learners.

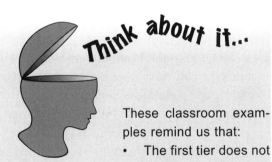

Think about it...

These classroom examples remind us that:
- The first tier does not represent the same skill or concept level in every lesson.
- The tiers begin at varying levels to denote that students' readiness is not static.
- Each student's readiness level varies with different content and in response to different classroom opportunities.
- Tiering can provide different learning experiences at varied levels of complexity or similar experiences that vary in the degree of complexity within each application of a task.

Kingore, B. (2004). *Differentiation: Simplified, Realistic, and Effective.* Austin: Professional Associates Publishing.

Tiered Instruction

TIERING A TOPIC: SCIENCE OR SOCIAL STUDIES

After assessing the wide-range of readiness levels among her middle school science and social studies students, Ms. Manning knew she needed to tier instruction to provide an appropriate level of challenge for each student. She strongly felt that some learning experiences should be shared by the whole class and that all of her students benefitted from an audience for their work. Hence, she incorporated some whole class experiences throughout the study and provided ongoing opportunities for students to interact and share their ideas and products. She selected open-ended activities for most whole class experiences so students could approach the tasks in various ways with differing levels of complexity.

All of her students work with her in direct-teaching lessons that develop background information and skills as they investigate a topic. At times, this direct instruction involves the whole class and, at other times, flexible small groups that change depending upon the objective. As she teaches small groups, she varies the materials by using the class text and grade-level materials as well as technology and additional print materials that expand grade-level skills and information while providing the appropriate levels of challenge.

When Ms. Manning is engaged in direct instruction with one group, other students are involved in their reading and product development. Sometimes she simultaneously has all students working in small groups, reading, discussing, processing, and producing so she can rotate among the students and facilitate their progress. She notes that this is an important assessment time for her as she acquires immediate feedback on successes and needs. Many of her reteaching decisions are made based upon this assessment.

Ongoing Whole Class Activities

♦ Using the class online message board, students periodically post observations, reactions, and questions about their reading. Students are also encouraged to post responses to others' messages. (If an online forum is not available, use a cork board or bulletin board in the classroom.)

♦ Questions that require high-level thinking are used to prompt students' awareness of key ideas and the vocabulary specific to the topic. Other analytical prompts encourage students' constructions of relationships among this topic and other topics of study. The students' responses are shared in oral discussions and posted for others' reactions.

• *Which phrases or sentences within the text are particularly interesting and significant to this topic?*

• *Which words do you believe to be most significant to this topic? Explain your thinking so others can understand.*

• *What direct and personal analogies can you create that respond to the topic?*
   a. *   (Item or person from the topic)   is like   (item or person from another topic)   because   .*
   b. *I am like   (item/event/person related to the topic)   because _____.*
   c. *   (Item or person from the topic)   relates to our theme of change when_____.*

Tiered Activities in Small Groups-- Simple to More Complex

♦ After Ms. Manning models and provides parameters for the task, some students work in pairs or trios to revisit the class text and other grade-level materials. They complete alphabetical sets of compound and complex sentences that specify significant information related to the topic for each letter of the alphabet. Later, their results are combined and organized into a poster or chart to share with the rest of the class and display outside the classroom.

Alphabetability

TOPIC: _____

A
B
C
D
E
F
G
H
I
J
K
L
M
N
O
P
Q
R
S
T
U
V
W
X
Y
Z

◆ With teacher direction and facilitation, some students review multiple resources that expand grade-level information. They then organize the topic into subtopics.

◆ Some of those students then work in different pairs or trios exploring their selected subtopic to prepare one part of a cooperative power point™ presentation about the topic to share with the class.

◆ Other students form a small group to organize their information into a test over the topic that incorporates the key concepts of each subtopic.

◆ With the teacher facilitating, some students identify essential questions and issues that the students are interested in

exploring. Students then conduct research independently or in small interest groups, using multiple grade-level and above grade-level materials (both print and technology), to investigate their chosen question or issue. Each student or group plans a method for sharing that information and determines the most appropriate audience for their presentation.

Culminating Whole Class Activities

◆ Products from the small groups' or individual's investigations are shared with the class.

◆ One group of students presents the test they prepared. The rest of the class participates in a discussion rating the complexity of each test item and reaching consensus regarding the best possible answers.

TIERING A CENTER: A WATER LIFE, SCIENCE DISCOVERY CENTER

Mr. Vidal teaches primary students and prefers to use centers to challenge his students to apply science concepts and scientific behaviors. He creates tiered tasks in centers to accommodate each learner's readiness level. The hands-on, visual nature of his choices matches his younger students' learning needs.

This primary center contains an aquarium, tiered learning tasks, and several books with information and illustrations about aquarium life; magnifying glasses are available nearby. The learning tasks are planned to use skills of observation, compare and contrast, inference, and writing words and sentences. Every child has opportunities over time to participate in the center one or more times. Mr. Vidal sometimes encourages children to choose which task to do. At other

Kingore, B. (2004). *Differentiation: Simplified, Realistic, and Effective.* Austin: Professional Associates Publishing.

times, he assigns children to complete a certain task based upon his assessment of their readiness. There is a cork board beside the aquarium where students post their completed work for others to read. One chart on the board is a list of attributes of the aquarium life that children collaboratively add to as they observe and read about additional attributes.

As children complete a task, they write a response in their centers log book.

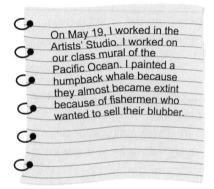

On May 19, I worked in the Artists' Studio. I worked on our class mural of the Pacific Ocean. I painted a humpback whale because they almost became extint because of fishermen who wanted to sell their blubber.

Tiered Activities in Small Groups-- Simple to More Complex

♦ Children use Figure 8.2 to record their observations. Children draw and are encouraged to write some words or sentences about what they hear, see, smell, and touch as they observe the aquarium.

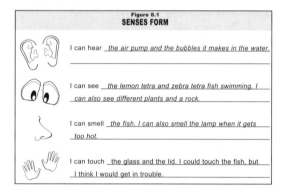

Figure 8.1
SENSES FORM

I can hear _the air pump and the bubbles it makes in the water._

I can see _the lemon tetra and zebra tetra fish swimming. I can also see different plants and a rock._

I can smell _the fish. I can also smell the lamp when it gets too hot._

I can touch _the glass and the lid. I could touch the fish, but I think I would get in trouble._

♦ Students use Figure 8.3 to write descriptive, contrasting sentences about their

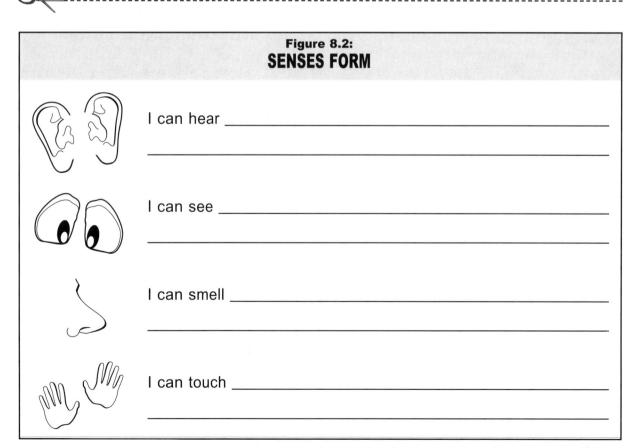

Figure 8.2:
SENSES FORM

I can hear _____

_____

I can see _____

_____

I can smell _____

_____

I can touch _____

_____

Kingore, B. (2004). *Differentiation: Simplified, Realistic, and Effective.* Austin: Professional Associates Publishing.

observations as they examine the environment of the aquarium.

♦ Children use Figure 8.3 to record their observations. However, children write their observations from the perspective of the fish: *What might the fish be seeing? Tasting? Hearing? Touching?* Children are also challenged to research if fish have the same senses as people.

♦ Children use the resource books provided to research, write, and illustrate one or more sentences comparing what they read about one of the living forms in the aquarium with what they observed.

♦ Children fold a large paper in half and label the top of one side *Observations* and the other side *Inferences.* Under the appropriate category, they then write sentences explaining their observations and

sentences about their inferences of life in the aquarium.

TIERING MATHEMATICS INSTRUCTION 3

Mrs. Bryant assessed a wide readiness span in her upper-elementary math class with learners representing more than a year below grade level to almost two years above grade expectations. Her district requires her to document that grade-level state standards are incorporated into her curriculum. So, she worked to tier her math instruction and involve students in skills and concepts at appropriate levels of challenge.

All of the students work with math reasoning, computation, application, and practice but at varying degrees of difficulty. Mrs. Bryant

Figure 8.3: SENSES FORM

I can hear _____
_____
But I can't hear _____

I can see _____
_____
But I can't see _____

I can smell _____
_____
But I can't smell _____

I can touch _____
_____
But I can't touch _____

Kingore, B. (2004). *Differentiation: Simplified, Realistic, and Effective.* Austin: Professional Associates Publishing.

initially introduces concepts, skills, and materials by teaching lessons to the whole class. To develop students' understanding, her direct instruction then focuses on flexible small groups that pursue skills and concepts at different paces and levels in response to their assessed readiness levels. She provides multiple applications of guided practice for some students to ensure success and reach mastery. With other students, a smaller quantity of guided practice applications are provided as understanding is accomplished with fewer examples

All students work with her in small groups sometimes, but the duration of each lesson varies with students' needs. At times students are in similar-readiness groups and at other times they work in mixed-readiness groups or interest groups. When she is directing a small-group lesson, the other students complete independent practice and the tiered activities provided in her classroom.

Mrs. Bryant uses whole class instruction for a review. She does not, however, use whole class math contests or competitions because the range in her class is so varied that the same students usually won and the same students usually lost. She found it more effective to use games and competitions that students self-select to do in pairs or small groups, such as those in the projects area.

Earlier in the year, when students' assessments documented that some students had mastered grade-level and above grade-level skills and concepts in the math area being studied, she used some math enrichment activities in her textbook. She observed, however, that if the enrichment tasks were predominately variations of the same skills and concepts, those experiences may not command students' interests nor increase students' achievements or level of mathematical understanding. More frequently now, she groups advanced students for direct math

instruction at their appropriate challenge level and engages them in tiered activities when working with the whole class.

In addition to her curriculum skill sheets for computation, she also incorporates open-ended activities for many applications and practice experiences to encourage students to learn how to organize data as well as compute a solution. She encourages students to approach the tasks in various ways with differing levels of complexity.

Tiered Activities--
Simple to More Complex Tasks Within Each Activity

◆ Demonstrations

Individually or in pairs, students select math problems in the text to prepare demonstrations that explain the problem to others.

◆ Four Ways

Individually or in pairs, students select a math problem in the text and then write and/or illustrate four ways to solve the problem.

◆ Creating Math Story Problems

Individually or in pairs, students write, illustrate, and complete their own examples of math story problems using the skills and concepts currently being studied.

◆ Math Process Letters

Students write a letter to a real or fictitious person of their choice to explain how to work a math problem that represents the skills and concepts currently being studied. Writing a clear and effective process explanation challenges students to demonstrate their mastery of a process without additional problems to compute.

Kingore, B. (2004). *Differentiation: Simplified, Realistic, and Effective.* Austin: Professional Associates Publishing.

♦ Computer Applications

According to assessed needs, students use computer programs for grade-level math applications or to develop advanced math skills and concepts.

♦ Error Analysis Cards

All students complete error analysis cards one or more times a week. Each card that Ms. Bryant prepares has a math problem containing errors which correspond to one or more students' practice needs. The cards can be used multiple times by different students assessed with that specific need.

The cards vary in complexity, up through prealgebra. Ms. Bryant assigns students' which cards to complete. Students respond to their assigned cards by using Figure 8.4 on which they write their name, the number

of the card they review, the problem, and a few descriptive sentences that answer the following questions: *What is incorrect in this problem?* and *How can the error be corrected?*

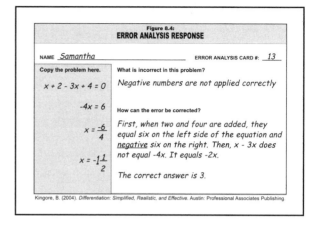

♦ Projects Area

All students participate in work at the projects area at least once a week. (This area is actually a small table with shelves of materi-

---

Figure 8.4: **ERROR ANALYSIS RESPONSE**		
NAME _____	**ERROR ANALYSIS CARD #:** _____	
Copy the problem here.	**What is incorrect in this problem?**	
	How can the error be corrected?	

Kingore, B. (2004). *Differentiation: Simplified, Realistic, and Effective.* Austin: Professional Associates Publishing.

als, supplies, and manipulatives nearby. Many stacks on the shelves have sticky notes with students' names on them to specify work in progress.) These activities are long-term, interest-based projects worked on by individuals, pairs, or trios of students. All of the projects evolve from students' interests and involve applications of math in the real world. In the current projects, students are:

*   Developing a collage-illustrated math glossary using examples of math terminology and concepts cut out from newspapers, magazines, and copies of sheet music.

*   Using large department store catalogs to document their calculations of how they might spend a $1,000 shopping spree in that store. Tax must also be calculated and figured within the total amount.

*   Taking digital camera photographs, collecting copies of published photographs, and organizing examples of architectural elements in those photographs to explain math applications in architecture.

*   Creating a *Sports Illustrated Book of Math* in which students explore and explain how math is used in different sports.

*   Playing board games that are based upon math concepts.

*   Using blank game boards and index cards to create new games that use math in a variety of applications.

TIERING APPLICATIONS THAT INCORPORATE GRAPHICS

Since many students are visual learners, graphics provide another avenue to use when tiering instruction. The difficulty of these activities that incorporate graphics varies with the complexity of the graphic and the requirements of the task as some tasks

using graphics may require higher-levels of skills and materials. Graphic organizers also have the advantage of requiring students to determine relationships instead of simply acquiring knowledge.

Graphic organizers are favored by many teachers and students. Popular graphics such as concept maps, charts, time lines, graphs, and Venn diagrams can be used to tier the complexity of students' responses.* The following tiered tasks use a Thinking Triangle graphic as one example of tiering activities with graphic organizers.

Thinking Triangle

The Thinking Triangle is a graphic technique for succinctly relating and organizing information. The first line has one word, the second line has two, the third line three, and so on to create a triangle shape. It invites more thinking and vocabulary explorations as students consider ways to express their ideas in the appropriate number of words.

Each tiered task using Thinking Triangles is preceded by direct-instruction with the teacher developing students' content-related concepts and skills as the process of using the graphic is modeled. When based upon materials at different reading and concept levels, these examples involve students in applications of reading skills, research skills, and thinking skills on multiple levels. The examples also vary in complexity by progressing from simple to more complex forms of the graphic and then building upon those experiences to challenge students' development of their own graphic forms to synthesize their learning.

Figure 8.5 Illustrates three variations of a Thinking Triangle. The variations progress from simple to more complex in structure and content.

---

*Additional graphic organizers are found in Chapter 7: Eliciting Advanced Achievement

Kingore, B. (2004). *Differentiation: Simplified, Realistic, and Effective*. Austin: Professional Associates Publishing.

Figure 8.5*

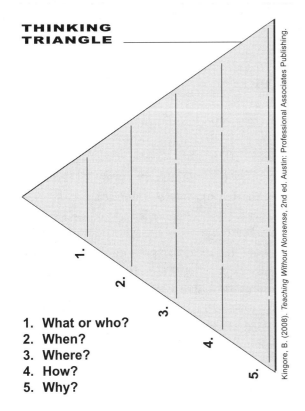

THINKING TRIANGLE

1. What or who?
2. When?
3. Where?
4. How?
5. Why?

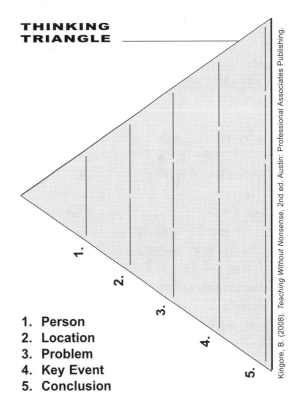

THINKING TRIANGLE

1. Person
2. Location
3. Problem
4. Key Event
5. Conclusion

Kingore, B. (2008). *Teaching Without Nonsense*, 2nd ed. Austin: Professional Associates Publishing.

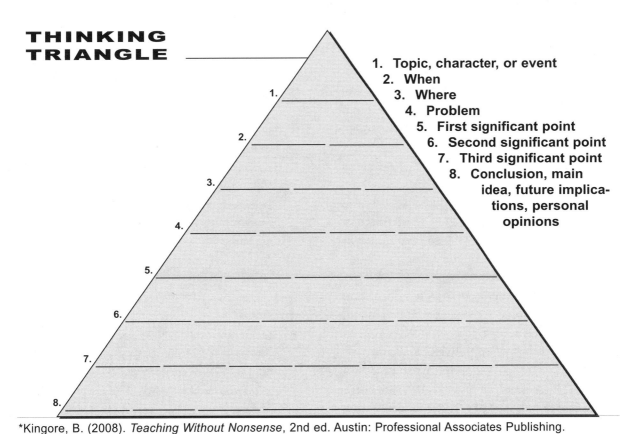

THINKING TRIANGLE

1. Topic, character, or event
2. When
3. Where
4. Problem
5. First significant point
6. Second significant point
7. Third significant point
8. Conclusion, main idea, future implications, personal opinions

*Kingore, B. (2008). *Teaching Without Nonsense*, 2nd ed. Austin: Professional Associates Publishing.

Kingore, B. (2004). *Differentiation: Simplified, Realistic, and Effective*. Austin: Professional Associates Publishing.

Tiered Activities in Small Groups--
Simple to More Complex

Tier I

- **Reading.** After completing a story in guided reading, children work in pairs or trios to retell the story by completing a Thinking Triangle form with investigative words: *what or who, when, where, how,* and *why.* Later, they come together as a class to share and compare their ideas.
- **Topic.** Students work in small groups to complete a Thinking Triangle form as they read about a social studies event or historical figure in their class text. Later, the different groups come together to share and compare responses.
- **Research.** Students research a topic and use the Thinking Triangle to organize their information before orally sharing what they learned.

Tier II

- **Reading.** Children vary the form to use *character, setting, problem, key event,* and *main idea* as the line descriptors. They individually use that form to retell a second story they read independently that develops the theme of conflict. Later, students share their retellings with other students and identify common elements of conflict across the stories.
- **Topic.** Working in small groups, students vary the form to use *person, location, problem, key event,* and *conclusion* as the line descriptors when they read about a social studies event or historical figure in their class text. Later, the different groups discuss and compare responses.
- **Research.** Students research a topic and use the five-line or more complex Thinking Triangle form as a pre-generator to organize the information they learn. Then, they write a simple research report to share with the class and post in the class research center. Their completed Thinking Triangle is used as the cover for their

report. Encourage depth and substantiation of information by ensuring that students list the resources they use in their study.

Tier III

- **Reading.** Individually, students use the more complex variation of a Thinking Triangle form that requires an eight-line response to analyze a novel or poem they read independently. Students are encouraged to integrate their complex and abstract thinking by creating an icon or symbol for each row of the triangle. Later, students share, compare/contrast, and discuss as a class the varied interpretations in their products.
- **Topic.** Using resources other than their social studies text, students work in pairs using the eight-line version of the Thinking Triangle to organize information about a president or other historical figure. Encourage students to integrate complex thinking by creating an icon or symbol for each row of the triangle. Later, students come together as a group to share, compare, and discuss their information.
- **Research.** Individually or in pairs, students use the eight-line version of the Thinking Triangle to synthesize and organize information relating to a current area of study. Encourage students to use multiple, above grade-level sources as they research a topic that is assigned or self-selected. Encourage complex thinking by challenging students to create an icon or symbol for each row of the triangle. Conduct a research forum so students can share their results.

Tier IV

- Students create their own version of a Thinking Triangle to use with their class content. They analyze the content to determine the most significant descriptors to use and also vary the number of lines needed to best convey in-depth information.

Kingore, B. (2004). *Differentiation: Simplified, Realistic, and Effective.* Austin: Professional Associates Publishing.

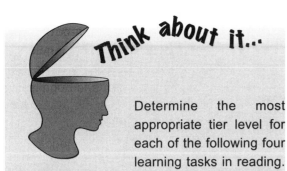

Think about it...

Determine the most appropriate tier level for each of the following four learning tasks in reading. Label each task tier one through four as you determine the continuum from simplest to most complex. Notice that all the tiers invite high-level thinking with tasks that address character analysis and cause-and-effect relationships.

____ A. Students work in trios to create a character map for the main character in each of the two novels they read. With the teacher, the groups then combine the information on their maps to compare the two characters on a Venn diagram. Finally, they identify similar causes in both stories that influenced each character's actions.

____ B. The teacher presents a list of five causes in the book that affected the main character. Working with the teacher, students determine and record the effect of each.

	Cause: Why?	Effect: What happened?
1.		
2.		

____ C. Working with the teacher, students forecast a list of events that might occur if the main characters from two different novels appeared in a sequel together. Students must continually review the stories to find specific information regarding character traits and events to substantiate their forecasts.

____ D. Students work with the teacher and use a Venn diagram to compare the main character at the beginning and end of the book. Then, they brainstorm, list together, and sequence the events that caused the character to change.

Reflect upon your problem-solving process as you determined the levels on the *Think about it* task. What are some of the differences among the levels? For example, which aspects of tier one made it more simple than tier three? Differences, such as the ones your identify, are the factors that influence the difficulty of tiered tasks and affect the development of tier levels. Compare your analysis with the factors which influence complexity in Figure 8.6 produced by other teachers.

Tiered instruction evolves from teachers' decisions regarding how to modulate tasks around the combinations of factors they select that influence complexity. All of the factors relate to the readiness of the learner. Some of the factors are instructional options that are more easily modified by the teacher, such as the degree of assistance a teacher provides, the complexity of the resources used, and the concrete or abstract nature of the process and product. Some factors are non-negotiable and require teachers to understand and accommodate within every tier, such as the background knowledge and skills the student brings to the task.

Identifying complexity factors helps teachers to efficiently proceed with the development of tiered activities. When you assess that students require variation of the concepts and skills designated in a lesson, reflect upon these factors to determine which to employ in that lesson.

Tier 1: B   Tier 2: D   Tier 3: A   Tier 4: C

Kingore, B. (2004). *Differentiation: Simplified, Realistic, and Effective.* Austin: Professional Associates Publishing.

Figure 8.6:

FACTORS THAT INFLUENCE THE COMPLEXITY OF TIERED ACTIVITIES

Degree of assistance and support
➡ The teacher directs the learning experience.
➡ The teacher facilitates the students' process in the learning experience.
➡ Students' are autonomous in their inquiry.

Degree of structure
➡ Clearly defined parameters for the task are prescribed.
➡ Open-ended criteria and parameters are posed for the task.

Required background knowledge and skills
➡ Minimal, basic information and understanding is required.
➡ Grade-level information and understanding is required.
➡ More extensive information and understanding is required, including research skills and skills of independent inquiry.

Concrete or more abstract
➡ The process and product are concrete.
➡ The process and product involve abstract thinking.

Quantity of resources
➡ A single resource is used.
➡ Multiple resources are employed.

Complexity of resources
➡ Grade-level resources are provided.
➡ Resources require above grade-level reading ability.
➡ The resources are concept dense.

➡ Sophisticated technology applications are required.

Complexity of process
➡ The required degree of thinking varies.
  • Simpler thinking processes are required.
  • Complex thinking processes are required.
➡ The time required to complete the task varies.
  • The task is short-term and often completed in one setting or one day.
  • The task is long-term, involving multiple steps and an extended period of time to complete.
➡ The research skills required to complete the task vary.
  • Simple research skills and beginning-level independent work skills are required.
  • More sophisticated research skills and independent work behaviors are required.

Complexity of product
➡ The parameters of the product vary.
  • The product parameters are structured and clearly defined.
  • The product parameters are more open-ended and unspecified.
➡ The integration of skills and concepts varies in sophistication.
  • The product integrates simple skills and concepts.
  • The product integrates more advanced skills and concepts.

Kingore, B. (2004). *Differentiation: Simplified, Realistic, and Effective.* Austin: Professional Associates Publishing.

PRODUCT OPTIONS AND TIERING

Providing product options facilitates tiering as teachers can more readily match products to students' learning strengths and needs. Figures 8.8 and 8.9 at the end of this chapter illustrate two formats for organizing product options--the Science Task Board presenting nine product options or a Math Task Board using twenty-five options. The objective should be to focus on a variety of product options rather than to suggest that students have to select the products in order or complete multiple tasks. Requiring students to complete more products does not necessarily result in higher or more effective responses. Rather, use the two formats to promote options for students that best match their learning profiles and interests as they demonstrate the depth of their learning.

To facilitate tiering, the teacher numbers the product options on a task board and analyzes the complexity of each task.
* Write a list of the more complex tasks to refer to, suggest, or assign when a student needs that level of challenge.
* Numbering the tasks also enables the teacher to focus on the product options that complement the task. *Students, you may elect to complete tasks 1, 4, or 14 on the Math Task Board to demonstrate your level of understanding of this process.*

When preparing nine or twenty-five product options seems overwhelming, simplify the process. Providing as few as two to four product options still begins to honor learners' profiles and readiness levels. Post product options on a grid or pocket chart with two to four responses. Product options allow students to choose the products they complete to document their learning. When the products options are weighted for depth and complexity, the assignments align with tiering objectives.

To allow diversity in product responses, prepare a list of products appropriate to the age, readiness levels, learning profiles, and strengths of the students. Review the curriculum and teaching objectives to determine products with potential for rich instructional applications. Focus on what students should learn and demonstrate as a result of this product experience. To avoid losing a good instructional possibility when brainstorming ideas alone or with others, write quick notes of any application ideas that emerge.

CREATING PRODUCT OPTION GRIDS OR POCKET CHARTS

1. Develop a list of products appropriate to your students, content, and instructional objectives.

2. Write quick notes of content application ideas.

3. Skim the list and select which options to develop and use.

4. Organize the options for depth and complexity.

When preparing a lesson, skim the list of products and determine the two to four options from which students may select. The arrangement of products on the grid tiers the products for depth and complexity. For example, one time the odd numbered products might be more simple than the even numbered choices. Another time, the odd numbered options or the left-to-right diagonal of products might be the more complex. This flexible arrangement makes the complexity levels of products more subtle and respects learner differences with less labeling. It also facilitates assigning a more challenging product to an underachieving student needing guidance. For example, when the odd numbers are the more complex, a teacher might

Kingore, B. (2004). *Differentiation: Simplified, Realistic, and Effective.* Austin: Professional Associates Publishing.

tell a less motivated student: *Today, I want you to select either product number 1 or 3.* In this way, the student still has some choice but the teacher increased the likelihood of a more complex student response.

A group of primary teachers modeled this process of creating product options as they used their interdisciplinary unit on space travel to integrate their objectives of vocabulary development; research skills; graphing skills; and written, oral, and graphic communication skills. They brainstormed the list of possible products included in Figure 8.7 and then discussed which products represented the best student outcomes for the objectives of the unit.

Deciding that all students will complete a graphing activity during this unit, the teachers analyze the graphing options for depth and complexity. They determine that graphing classmates' favorites is simplest because of the process and skills, graphing distances more complex because it involves more reading for information, and graphing the time of travel the most difficult as students have to gather data and then complete calculations because the information is not necessarily listed as time travel between locations. They then incorporate those three tasks as tiered learning experiences in their unit.

Figure 8.7:
PRODUCTS FOR A SPACE UNIT

- Alphabet chart of space words and items

- Picture dictionary

- Word web
  1. Used as a group preassessment of content background
  2. Used as an individual culminating task to evaluate vocabulary related to the topic

- Rebus story about traveling to specific planets using a page of space items or pictures to cut, paste, and incorporate into a story

- Non-fiction rebus story relating information from research about a space topic

- Pop-up book about one planet with an illustration and two or three facts

- Pop-up book relating information from research about a space topic

- Graph of the favorite planet of 10 classmates

- Graph of the time needed to travel to several locations in space from the earth

- Graph of the distances between the sun and other locations in space

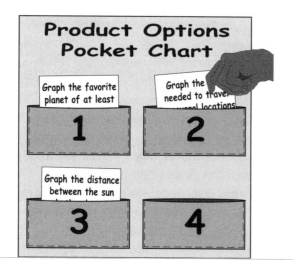

Kingore, B. (2004). *Differentiation: Simplified, Realistic, and Effective.* Austin: Professional Associates Publishing.

Figure 8.8:
SCIENCE TASK BOARD

1. CRITIQUE-- Critique how the scientific method was applied during a specific experiment conducted in class.	**2. ACROSTIC--** Using a key term from the topic of study, write sentences related to the topic that begins with each letter of the key term.	**3. FLOW CHART--** Use a flow chart to illustrate and explain a cyclical process in nature.
4. DEBATE-- Debate the issues of using animals for research studies.	**5. CHORAL READING/ READERS THEATER--** Use the format of <u>Joyful Noise: Poems for Two Voices</u>* to write, organize, and compare significant facts about specific animals, plants, or two biomes.	**6. COLLECTION COLLAGE--** Use a digital camera to complete a collage of photographs of scientific principles found at home.
7. VENN DIAGRAM-- Overlap three circles to create a three-way Venn that compares the similarities and differences of the forms of matter.	**8. GRAPH--** Graph the weather in your area for one month. Compare it to a Farmer's Almanac from 100 years earlier. Record three observations or conclusions.	**9. DEMONSTRATION--** Demonstrate how to use a piece of scientific equipment.

*Fleischman, P. (1988). <u>Joyful Noise: Poems for Two Voices</u>. New York: Harper & Row.

Kingore, B. (2004). *Differentiation: Simplified, Realistic, and Effective.* Austin: Professional Associates Publishing.

Figure 8.9:
MATH TASK BOARD

TEST (ORIGINAL)-- Instead of taking a test, write the test items for the math process or concept of study.	REVERSE CROSSWORD PUZZLE-- Provide the completed puzzle grid of numbers. Others write the formulas or math facts that resulted in those numbers.	COLLAGE--Organize a collage showing fractions in daily life.	ACROSTIC--Using a concept or topic word, such as *factorial*, write a sentence beginning with each letter that is significantly related to the topic.	TANGRAMS--Use tangrams to create the ten digits and all the letters of the alphabet.
VENN DIAGRAM-- Overlap four circles to create a four-way Venn that compares the similarities and differences of math operations.	BIO POEM--Create a bio poem for *integer* or another key math term.	FLOW CHART--Draw and label a flow chart that illustrates how to apply a specific math strategy or geometric proof.	DEMONSTRATION-- Use manipulatives to demonstrate division to a younger student.	CONTENT PUZZLES-- Write key math facts on a shape. Cut it into puzzle pieces for others to put back together by correctly matching the problem and the solution.
BULLETIN BOARD-- Complete a bulletin board to demonstrate mathematical applications, such as: *Ways to Make 78*.	CHILDREN'S STORY (ILLUSTRATED)-- Create a story to explain a math concept. As examples, read books by C. Neuschwander about Sir Cumference[1].	STUDENT'S CHOICE	LETTER (MATH PROCESS)-- Complete one math problem. Then, write a letter to someone explaining step-by-step how you completed that problem.	ERROR ANALYSIS-- Analyze a problem that is flawed. Write what is wrong and how to correct it.
RATIO RESEARCH-- Read *If You Hopped Like a Frog*[2]. Research other attributes of animals and humans and express your findings as intriguing ratios.	GAME--Create a stock market game or math fact rodeo.	METAPHOR/SIMILE-- Express a mathematical concept through a metaphor or simile, such as: *Addition is like compound words, and subtraction is like contractions.*	SCAVENGER HUNT-- Provide a list of math terms to find examples of in the real world.	RIDDLE--Develop simple or more complex riddles, such as: *I am a prime number larger than 13 and smaller than the square root of 324.*
QUESTIONNAIRE-- Conduct a questionnaire asking adults how math is needed in their jobs, and graph the results.	NEWSPAPER ADVERTISEMENTS--Use the ads to buy a balanced meal for four people that totals less that $20.00. List your items, quantity, and total, including tax.	COMPUTER GAME-- Create a computer game that uses algebra.	WRITTEN REPORT-- Write a report with diagrams illustrating how geometry applies to baseball or some other sport.	TEN WAYS-- Determine at least 10 different math applications required when designing or manufacturing a car.

[1]Neuschwander, Cindy. (2001). *Sir Cumference and the Great Knight of Angleland*. (1999). *Sir Cumference and the Dragon of Pi*. (1997). *Sir Cumference and the First Round Table*. Watertown, MA: Charlesbridge.
[2]Schwartz, D. (1999). *If You Hopped Like a Frog*. New York: Scholastic.

Kingore, B. (2004). *Differentiation: Simplified, Realistic, and Effective*. Austin: Professional Associates Publishing.

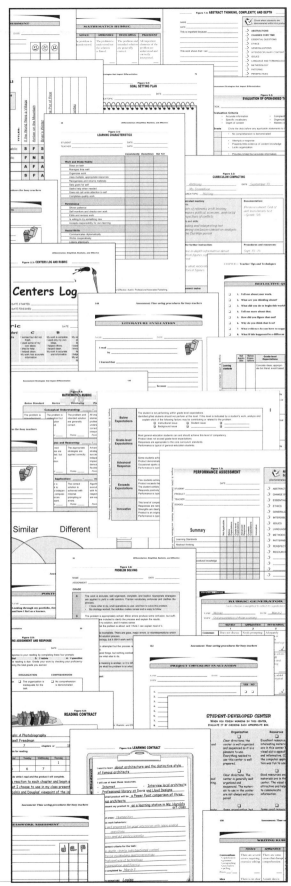

ASSESSMENT STRATEGIES THAT IMPACT DIFFERENTIATION

ASSESSMENT
is the continual analysis of information to determine students' learning needs and accomplishments.

EVALUATION
is the interpretation and judgment of students' learning to grade quality.

Assessment and evaluation differ in their intent and application. While both are necessary in education, assessment is the greater teaching priority as well as the more important influence on instruction. Assessment must work in tandem with an effective curriculum to help teachers and learners monitor students' work and gauge growth in learning.

Assessment is a key to differentiation. Assessment tasks provide tangible evidence of students' understanding and growth before instruction begins (preassessment), as instruction progresses (formative assessment), and at the end of a segment of instruction (summative

Assessment Strategies

Kingore, B. (2004). *Differentiation: Simplified, Realistic, and Effective.* Austin: Professional Associates Publishing.

assessment) (Stiggins, 2001; Tomlinson et al., 2002). Differentiation can not succeed without a strategically developed and implemented assessment system that includes preinstruction assessment, continuing assessment, and culminating evaluation that is frequently collaborative and incorporates students' self-assessments.

Preassessment clarifies students' interests and levels of readiness. Continuing assessment supports instruction by substantiating when to implement reteaching and pacing adjustments. Culminating evaluation incorporates and collaborates with students' self-assessments to document learning achievements and encourage student responsibility and ownership. Teachers' observations and analyses are constants that support this assessment system.

ASSESSMENT THROUGH ANALYTICAL OBSERVATION AND METACOGNITION

Ed Young ends his award-winning picture book *Seven Blind Mice** with this mouse moral:

> *Knowing in part may make a fine tale, but wisdom comes from seeing the whole.*

To better understand the multiple facets of individuals and their learning needs, teachers need to see the whole child. Dynamic teachers are analytical observers who frequently use informal conversations and formal conferences to talk with their students and elicit their perceptions. Students have significant information to share if we only know to ask. Talking with students about what they are doing or how they feel about their work often provides a

window to their thinking. This information is helpful when making instructional decisions.

VALUES OF ANALYTICAL OBSERVATION

- Analytical observation helps define and refine students' levels of development, acquired proficiencies, and learning needs.
- It enables teachers to assess the process of students' learning.
- It signals the students' integration and transfer of skills taught in previous classroom learning experiences.
- It increases awareness of special populations and needs that may be clouded by standardized tests.
- It supports and integrates with other assessments.
- It enhances teachers' interpretations and insights about their students.

METACOGNITIVE QUESTIONS

Teachers frequently interpret and respond to what students are trying to do when engaged in learning tasks by questioning and probing for clarity of their thinking. Students' responses to metacognitive questions provide a window that increases adults' understanding of students' behaviors as the probes invite students to bring their thinking to a conscious level. The objective is for metacognitive or self-monitoring strategies to become an internalized part of students' learning.

A parent reported that her second-grade daughter did not want to participate in a discussion about a book she had immensely enjoyed because: *I have already discussed it with myself.* Since gifted learners are so consciously involved in introspection, teachers should continually analyze students' behaviors and talk with them to make sense of what is

---

*Young, E. (1992). *Seven Blind Mice.* New York: Puffin Books.

Kingore, B. (2004). *Differentiation: Simplified, Realistic, and Effective.* Austin: Professional Associates Publishing.

occurring in different learning situations (Abilock, 1999).

- *Tell me about your work.*
- *What is your next step or idea?*
- *What about it did you think was easy to do, and what was difficult?*
- *How did you figure that out?*
- *Why do you think that is so?*
- *What in the text led you to infer or conclude that?*
- *What evidence can you use to support that?*
- *If this had not worked, what would you have done?*
- *What would you ask?*
- *How is this like   (previous content) ?*
- *What changes would you want to make?*
- *What is the most important thing you learned from this?*
- *How would you share this information with others?*
- *What is a question that is essential to this topic?*

Teacher tip...

Exciting moments happen in a lesson when I encourage students to produce their own questions. As producers, students are more motivated to offer ideas, suggest solutions, and reflect on what they have heard, seen, and done.

PREASSESSMENT

Preinstruction assessment is a precursor to appropriate instruction as it clarifies students' interests and levels of readiness. Many educators associate assessing with testing; however, students may not demonstrate the range of their talents on a test. Hence, *preassessment* instead of *pretesting* is used to accent the incorporation of multiple formats in addition to tests to gain information about students.

Preassessment enables teachers to match instruction to students' interests. Through interest inventories, interviews, activities, and informal conversations, teachers assess students' interests and learning profiles to match instructional tasks to students' needs. These assessments guide opportunities for teacher-suggested and students' self-selected learning experiences through the process outlined in Figure 9.1.

Preassessment is vital for matching instruction to the readiness level of students. Researchers document that gifted and talented elementary students have mastered from 35 to 50 percent of the curriculum to be offered in the five basic subject areas before they begin the school year (Ross, 1993). Hence, preassessing is necessary to clarify which skills are known or needed.

Some teachers never use preassessment because they believe they do not have time. *I can't do that,* one secondary teacher explained as we discussed types of preassessments, *I barely have time to teach as it is. I can't waste time before I begin a lesson.* His frustration is understandable! Yet, preassessment can be a tremendous asset instead of a liability. Foremost, you potentially save some students from frustration when the skills and concepts exceed their readiness; other students are saved from boredom and allowed the right to extend their learning.

Kingore, B. (2004). *Differentiation: Simplified, Realistic, and Effective.* Austin: Professional Associates Publishing.

Figure 9.1:
STEPS IN PREASSESSMENT

1. Each student completes a pre-instruction assessment .

2. Students document their work by writing on the assessment their name, date, and a score--the number of correct answers or the degree of mastery according to a rubric. One high school teacher began implementing more preassessments and observed that her students became more motivated to work because they then knew specifically what they needed to learn.

   For students who need to continue through the scheduled instruction, the preassessment score could be translated into a grade for the grade book. But it is better left as a holistic assessment and beginning benchmark by which to gauge future learning. The grade after instruction is the more appropriate score to record in the grade book.

3. When the score indicates that some students need to participate in only some or none of scheduled instruction, those students complete a compacting form or learning contract indicating instructional needs and replacement tasks. With the preassessment, the students store the compacting form or learning contract for continued reference. These students are then either exempt from or participate only in the scheduled instruction as contracted. They also complete appropriate replacement tasks as contracted and plan ways to share the information gained from their replacement tasks.

4. Students store the preassessment for comparison at a later date. The preassessment can be stored in the students' work folders or in a separate file.

5. At teacher-designated times during instruction and/or after instruction is completed, students retrieve their preassessments and use a different colored pen to embellish, delete, or correct items on them. The use of a different color helps students concretely validate their increased accuracy and quantity of information. Students add a legend to the top of the assessment with the beginning date written in the first color and the review dates written in the second and third colors to clarify changes in their knowledge and understanding over time. These assessments are useful as portfolio products that document growth and as discussion prompts between parents and children.

Preassessment is a precursor to appropriate instruction as it clarifies students' interests and levels of readiness.

Kingore, B. (2004). *Differentiation: Simplified, Realistic, and Effective.* Austin: Professional Associates Publishing.

Preassessment can benefit every student by providing a benchmark by which to measure their growth. *This is where you began. Let's see how far you can go.* Preassessment becomes a standard by which to compare future learning and concretely show students their achievements and successes.

Why do it?

* Preassessment enables teachers to instruct at the most appropriate readiness level of each student.
* It provides information for selecting and pacing appropriate instructional materials.
* It enables teachers to form appropriate flexible groups.
* It provides a comparative benchmark to enable each student to gauge future achievements.
* It supports the use of compacting and tiered instruction to match students' readiness.
* It allows students to demonstrate and get credit for the concepts and skills previously mastered.

What are the benefits?

* Preassessment can motivate students to be more involved in and attentive to instruction and learning experiences as they clearly identify what they know and what they need to know. It appropriately raises their level of concern by signaling what they need to learn.
* It helps avoid boredom; students are more mentally engaged when the learning is relevant to their needs and interesting to them.
* It saves instruction time when teachers do not reteach what students already know.
* It reduces the amount of grading, as students demonstrating mastery do not complete the tasks planned to help others learn.

DOCUMENTING PREASSESSMENT

While students occasionally demonstrate total mastery on a preassessment, the process more frequently serves to provide instructional information regarding students' readiness levels. To access this information, many teachers need a larger repertoire of preassessment procedures to implement. Teachers also want ways to use the preassessment to benefit all students. One process for increasing the instructional value of preassessment is discussed in this section, followed by a variety of preassessment techniques that either require a single-correct answer or are open-ended.

To maximize the instructional benefit of using preassessment techniques, implement the procedure illustrated by Figure 9.2: Flow Chart for Increasing the Instructional Value of Preassessment.

PREASSESSMENT TECHNIQUES

Single-Correct-Answer Techniques

End-of-Chapter or Unit Tests

Administer the test as a preassessment to eliminate areas already mastered by individuals or the whole group. This technique works best when you already have tests developed so you can easily use them pre- and post-instruction.

Skills Sheet

Provide a skills sheet intended to measure achievement at the level of mastery. Students complete the task to determine needs.

Most Difficult Problems

Select a small number of the most difficult problems from the next segment of instruction. Students have the option of trying those first to determine if subsequent instruction is appropriate. This technique was originally developed by Susan Winebrenner (2001) to allow students to quickly demonstrate skills and be excused from more lengthy practice tasks or homework. The weakness she found was that

Figure 9.2:
FLOW CHART FOR
INCREASING THE INSTRUCTIONAL VALUE
OF PREASSESSMENT

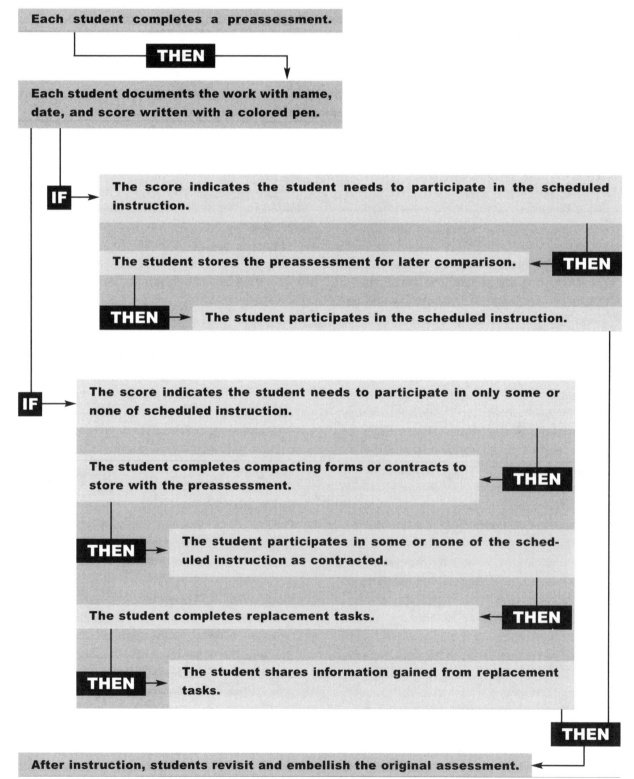

students still had to sit through the whole-class instruction of concepts. Therefore, when using this strategy, consider selecting difficult problems that allow students to demonstrate concept mastery and proceed to replacement tasks.

Grading Single-Correct-Answer Techniques

Provide an answer key that you or students use to grade, and then record their results. Invite students who have substantiated high scores to complete compacting forms or learning contracts in order to organize their replacement tasks and continued learning process. For students who score below mastery, help them set learning goals to revisit after instruction as celebrations of growth and learning successes.

Double-Duty Activities:
Open-Ended Techniques for Assessment and Instruction*

Preassessment techniques can be open-ended in structure. I call these double-duty activities because several activities used for instruction can also be used for assessment. A double-duty learning task saves instructional time--once students know how to do the activity, it can be used again for instruction, assessment, or reflection without lengthy explanation of the procedure. Open-ended techniques can preassess concepts and vocabulary, relationships, or summary and sequence.

Discussions are an important focus and an important reflection activity. However, they are less effective as an assessment tool, as documentation is less clear. Specifically, did a student not speak up because he was not familiar with the information or because he is introspective and prefers not to speak out in larger groups? Teachers who choose to use a group discussion as one of their assessment

tools subgroup the class into smaller groups and use a checklist to document students' responses.

Concept and Vocabulary Tasks

Responses to concept and vocabulary tasks indicate students' retrievable background knowledge in a topic of study. Vocabulary is an indicator of content depth because a person with extensive information about a topic uses more specific vocabulary and terminology when discussing that topic. Score these assessments based upon the accuracy, complexity, and depth of information rather than the number of responses. For example, one student might produce a lengthy list of responses but at a general level of content, while another student's list is shorter but with much more complex and specific data.

➡ **Most Significant Words/Concepts**

Allow selected students five or ten minutes to write the most significant words, ideas, or concepts they already know about the topic.

➡ **KWR***

This is a variation of KWL (Ogle, 1986). Before instruction, students complete the first two columns of a KWR which designates *What I Know* and *What I Want to Know.* They then list *What I Will Read or Research*

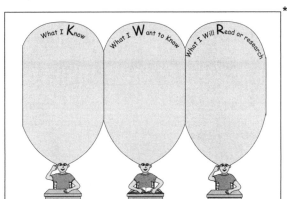

*Adapted from: Kingore, B. (2003). *Just What I Need!* Austin: Professional Associates Publishing.

Kingore, B. (2004). *Differentiation: Simplified, Realistic, and Effective.* Austin: Professional Associates Publishing.

to signal the teacher about that students' background, interests, and awareness of resources.

➡ Alphabetability

Students list the alphabet down the left side of a piece of paper and then organize the most significant ideas and concepts they know about a topic by filling in words, phrases, and sentences for as many letters of the alphabet as they can.

➡ Acrostic

Using a key term related to the topic, students organize the most significant ideas, vocabulary, and concepts to each letter of the acrostic.

➡ PMI

Using Edward De Bono's (1992) PMI technique, students organize the most significant concepts or information they know about a topic by listing in three rows on their paper the Pluses, Minuses, and Interesting ideas and concepts related to that subject.

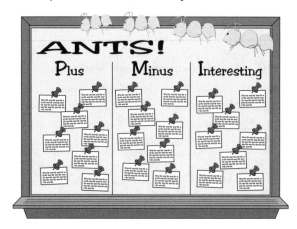

Relationships

These tasks assess the relationships among concepts and require students' to orga-

nize and relate their background knowledge. Scoring these assessments is based upon accuracy, complexity, organization, and depth of information rather than quantity.

➡ Analysis Grid

An analysis grid is a graphic organizer for analyzing the attributes or characteristics of a topic or subject. Present a grid with the topic, subtopics, and attributes listed. Students individually complete the grid using the coding system you indicate. Increase the complexity of the assessment by providing some attributes and requiring students to add and complete the analysis of additional attributes to reflect their depth of understanding.*

Analysis Grid —
TOPIC **Polygons**
CODE A=always   N=never   S=sometimes

	Straight sides	Closed figure	Four sides	Angles are equal	Sides are equal length	Parallel sides	Symmetrical	Sum of angles = 180°	Sum of angles = 360°	FORMULA: Area = base x height
triangle	A	A	N	S	S	N	S	A	N	N
square	A	A	A	A	A	A	A	N	A	A
rectangle	A	A	A	A	N	A	A	N	A	A
pentagon	A	A	N	S	S	S	S	N	N	N
hexagon	A	A	N	S	S	S	S	N	N	N
octagon	A	A	N	S	S	S	S	N	N	N
parallelogram	A	A	A	S	S	A	A	N	A	A
quadrilateral	A	A	A	S	S	S	S	N	A	S

Kingore, B. (2008). *Teaching Without Nonsense*, 2nd ed. Austin, TX: Professional Associates Publishing.

➡ Concept Map

Students complete a concept map before instruction. For a simpler version, students respond to the categories the teachers designates on the concept map. For greater

---

*Reprinted from: Kingore, B. (2008). *Teaching Without Nonsense,* 2nd ed. Austin: Professional Associates Publishing.

Kingore, B. (2004). *Differentiation: Simplified, Realistic, and Effective.* Austin: Professional Associates Publishing.

complexity, students use plain paper or a blank concept map graphic to generate their interpretation of the most relevant categories and then respond to those categories on the concept map (Kingore, 2002).

➡ Venn Diagram

Students use a Venn diagram to list facts and relationships comparing two key aspects of the topic. For a simpler version, students respond to the categories the teacher designates. For greater complexity, students use plain paper or a blank Venn graphic and generate the categories before responding to them.*

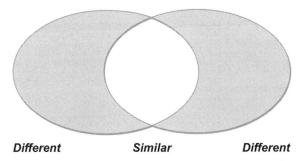

Different   **Similar**   **Different**

Summary and Sequence

These tasks assess students' overview, generalizations, and understanding of a process or topic. The responses indicate students' background knowledge, applications, and command of terminology. Scoring these assessments is based upon the accuracy, complexity, and depth of information rather than the length of their summary or the number of steps in their process analysis.

➡ Topic Frame

Students use a topic frame to supply information about a topic. A topic frame is a basic outline of a topic designed to help students organize what they know. It consists of a series of guide phrases that prompt the infor-

mation teachers want to assess, connected with transition words and blanks.

*

> **Topic Frame**
>
> TOPIC: _____
>
> A significant point about this topic is _____
> _____
> _____ .
>
> Another important idea is _____
> _____
> _____ .
>
> Something interesting is _____
> because _____
> _____
> _____ .
>
> Two key factors to remember are _____
> _____ and _____
> _____ .
>
> An important person or place related to this topic is _____
> _____ because _____
> _____ .
>
> Three words to remember about this topic are _____ ,
> _____ , and _____
> I relate this topic to _____
> because _____
> _____ .
>
> In my opinion, _____
> _____
> _____ .
>
> Kingore, B. (2003). Just What I Need! Austin: Professional Associates Publishing.

➡ Cloze

Students complete a cloze procedure as a summary of the most significant information about the topic. The cloze sample omits the key words of the topic and requires students to understand and fill in those terms.

➡ Process Letter

Students choose real or fictitious, well-known characters. They then write a letter to that character, explaining how to complete a strategy, experiment, or challenging problem. Clearly and effectively explaining a process challenges students to demonstrate their mastery of a particular process and provides data for educators, regarding which parts of the process, if any, need refining through additional instruction.

*Reprinted from: Kingore, B. (2003). *Just What I Need*! Austin: Professional Associates Publishing.

Kingore, B. (2004). *Differentiation: Simplified, Realistic, and Effective.* Austin: Professional Associates Publishing.

Assessment Strategies

➡ **Flow Chart**

Students develop a flow chart to graphically represent key concepts, significant terminology, relationships, and/or sequence. Flow charts are particularly applicable to historical topics and topics involving a sequenced process, such as a science experiment or problem solving in math.

Grading Open-Ended Assessments

Since more than one correct answer is possible, assessments using open-ended techniques must be scored with a rubric based upon clearly established criteria that are shared with students before they begin the task. The degree of success students demonstrate in relation to these criteria enables the teacher to determine where to initiate instruction.

Holistic rubrics, such as Figure 9.3, are an efficient scoring choice for preassessment. The criteria are listed at the top and incorporated into each level. In the grade column, a holistic score of 0 to 4 or letter grades can be used. The wording of each proficiency level is user-friendly so students can self-assess. Incorporate any of these criteria plus others of your choosing to develop rubrics to grade your students' completed preassessments.

Teachers do not have to grade all of the preassessments unless they prefer to do so. Instead, students have a copy of the rubric and self-assess their own work. Students who score their work as *4* or *A*, show their work to the teacher for collaboration and then begin to plan their replacement tasks. Students who score themselves below *4* or *A*, set learning goals to revisit after instruction to celebrate learning successes. Preassessment results should motivate future learning rather than label students.

Preassessments should motivate future learning rather than label students.

PROCEDURES FOR STUDENTS WHO DEMONSTRATE MASTERY ON PREASSESSMENT TASKS

In order to qualify to be exempt from scheduled instruction, students need to score a high level of accuracy on a preassessment that gauges their depth and complexity regarding the concepts and skills planned for the scheduled instruction. The single-answer responses and some of the double duty tasks discussed earlier can be used to assess an advanced level of mastery. While one-hundred percent accuracy is unnecessary, a criterion of eighty-five percent or higher is typically used.

The scored preassessment is stored as written documentation of mastery. The student can complete and attach to this product a list of strengths or proficiencies as demonstrated by the preassessment. The student then collaborates with the teacher or resource specialist to plan replacement activities for enrichment and acceleration. This process is facilitated by the curriculum compacting techniques discussed in Chapter 2.

When students score above seventy percent, they would not qualify to be totally exempt from the scheduled instruction, but teachers should consider reviewing the preassessment results with them to determine areas of mastery. They can then work on replacement tasks during instruction of the skills and concepts they have mastered.

A TEACHER QUESTIONS:
When students test out of this topic or concept, how will I get the grades in my grade book if they don't do this work?

Recommended Solution

Use the preassessment grade as the documented level of achievement for this material,

Kingore, B. (2004). *Differentiation: Simplified, Realistic, and Effective.* Austin: Professional Associates Publishing.

EVALUATION OF OPEN-ENDED TASKS

TASK: _____

Evaluation Criteria

- Accurate information
- Specific vocabulary
- Depth of content
- Complexity
- Organization
- Mastery of written mechanics

Grade   *Circle the dots before any applicable statements to indicate achievement.*

	• No comprehension is demonstrated
	• Attempts a response • Presents little evidence of content knowledge • Lacks organization
	• Provides limited but accurate information • Demonstrates a beginning-level vocabulary, information, and mechanics • Makes some effort to organize the information
	• Reflects understanding through accurate information • Uses specific vocabulary • Supports response with appropriate details • Analyzes • Organizes the information effectively • Applies basic writing mechanics accurately
	• Provides complex information • Uses advanced and precise vocabulary • Demonstrates a depth of content; is meaningful and well developed • Reflects a complex level of analysis and interpretation of information • Organizes effectively to add interest and clarity • Applies advanced levels of writing mechanics

My product shows_____

_____

_____.

I could improve _____

_____.

I earned this grade because _____

_____.

Assessment Strategies

Kingore, B. (2004). *Differentiation: Simplified, Realistic, and Effective.* Austin: Professional Associates Publishing.

and record that grade the number of times equal to the number of intended learning task grades for the class. For example, Adrian scores 93 on the preassessment. His teacher records 93 for each of the three grades she intends to take on this segment of instruction (thereby reducing the amount of grading for the teacher). However, Lila's preassessment grade is 87, and she (or her parent!) only wants 100s in the grade book. Lila's teacher allows her to choose to independently complete the scheduled work at her fastest pace, have the results from that work recorded, and then proceed with replacement tasks. The replacement tasks should evolve from student's interests and encourage the student to work to continue learning rather than produce to get a grade.

Not Recommended

Grade the same number of replacement tasks. For example, students complete other work, and the grades from that work are recorded. This solution seems viable because students are graded on different tasks and not required to repeat the work they have mastered. However, a serious limitation of this practice is that the other graded work more frequently stems from teachers' selections and enrichment tasks in the texts rather than students' interest. These tasks can be interpreted by students as busy work and punishment. Students perceive it as busy work when the tasks just treadmill what the students already know. They feel the work is punishment when they interpret the tasks as just more to do and they develop the attitude frequently expressed by gifted students: *My reward for being gifted is that I have to do more!*

> *Replacement tasks that follow preassessment need to be interesting, involve vibrant learning possibilities, and engage personal relevance. Student self-selection with teacher facilitation is recommended.*

DEVELOPING TOOLS FOR CONTINUING ASSESSMENT

Continuing assessment supports instruction by substantiating when to implement reteaching and pacing adjustments. These assessments occur throughout an instructional segment to guide a teacher's instructional decision-making. A wide variety of assessment tools are used to more effectively provide the feedback a teacher needs to determine the pacing of instruction, such as checklists, students' participation in flexible groups, observations, quick reviews of work in progress, learning logs, self-evaluations, and products that frequently require students to generate responses rather than only choose among descriptors or complete blanks.

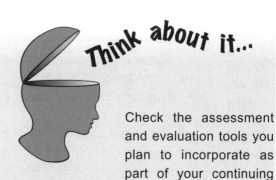

Check the assessment and evaluation tools you plan to incorporate as part of your continuing assessment. How does each guide your decisions regarding instruction?

- ✍ Analytical observation
- ✍ Assessment procedures accompanying published grade-level materials
- ✍ Checklists
- ✍ Discussions with students
- ✍ Interest inventories
- ✍ Peer collaboration
- ✍ Performance tasks
- ✍ Portfolios
- ✍ Products from learning experiences
- ✍ Quick Writes or Learning Logs
- ✍ Records of independent reading of fiction and nonfiction materials
- ✍ Rubrics
- ✍ Student self-evaluations
- ✍ Others

Kingore, B. (2004). *Differentiation: Simplified, Realistic, and Effective.* Austin: Professional Associates Publishing.

Pacing Adjustments

Continuing assessment reveals the numbers of students who would benefit from reteaching, additional practice, or acceleration of skill levels. The teacher then implements these pacing adjustments in skill groups that are short-term. Students are often aware of their skill needs and can benefit from being able to self-nominate their participation in specific skill groups.

Students' Self-assessment and Reflection

Continuing assessment is frequently collaborative and incorporates students' self-assessments. One focus of self-assessment is the use of metacognitive responses discussed earlier in this chapter. Other devices, such as the Status Notes in Chapter 6, guide students self-assessing and maintaining records of their own progress rather than only comparing their work with peers and lacking ownership of their assessment. Product descriptors and rubrics also increase students' responsibility for their own learning by requiring students to assess their own work before it is graded or shared with others. Consider implementing more rubrics for students' self-assessment and reflection.

Peer Collaboration

Peer interpretation and feedback can also be incorporated as continuing collaborative assessment. Students know that their teacher is there to help them, but they can also view their classmates as sources of help. Often both students benefit when one student helps another clarify an idea or process. Consider providing a small board where students post messages and collaboration requests. This procedure is particularly useful across multiple sections of classes that meet in the same room if students would otherwise have little opportunity to discuss class topics with one another.

Assessment Supported by Portfolios

In a differentiated classroom, a portfolio documents a learner's range of potential by the wide scope and complexity of products included. In this manner, the portfolio process honors the diversity of students and helps adults discover the strengths of each learner. As products document each student's growth in skills and concepts over time, portfolios provide important support for differentiating instruction. Portfolios become an integral part of learning processes and continually document learning assessments and evaluations. Over time, students can review their development as learners and come to understand that success is likely to follow hard work.

DEVELOPING TOOLS FOR CULMINATING EVALUATION

Culminating evaluation documents students' levels of achievement following instruction. This evaluation typically is a teacher's responsibility that occurs at the end of an instructional segment and results in grading students' work to record in the grade book. In a differentiated classroom, this evaluation, in addition to determining grades, guides the flexible regrouping of students for reteaching or advancing to the next instructional segment.

The tools of culminating evaluation must reflect the instructional focus of the classroom. Since differentiated instruction responds to the differences of the learners in the environment, the evaluations must honor those differences and elicit many different ways of knowing. Fill-in-the-blank and multiple-choice responses tap a narrow range of thinking. Using more open-ended evaluations requires a conversion from answer keys to rubrics that accent high-level thinking.

Culminating evaluation in a differentiated classroom often becomes a collaborative

Kingore, B. (2004). *Differentiation: Simplified, Realistic, and Effective.* Austin: Professional Associates Publishing.

task between teachers and students. When it is collaborative, students assess their work before it is graded or shared with others. Rubrics are required to guide students' self-assessment.

Several examples of culminating evaluation tools and procedures follow. The discussion begins with a focus on high-level thinking in testing. It then compares product descriptors with rubrics. Finally, the discussion explores rubrics customized for advanced and gifted students.

TESTING AT HIGH LEVELS OF THINKING

If assessment is to drive instruction, then the testing of classroom content must mirror an emphasis on high-level thinking. Classroom tests must avoid simple, single-answer responses and encourage higher thinking applications. For example, generate test questions that require high-level thinking and reasoning instead of memorization of facts. In Figure 9.4, several question triggers--organized around the thinking skills presented in Chapter 2--illustrate testing at high-levels of thinking. Grading students' responses requires a holistic rubric similar to Figure 9.3 or an analytical rubric similar to Figure 9.6.

Teacher tip...

Gifted students do not just want to answer questions; they want to pose new questions and make discoveries in their learning.

GRADING: PRODUCT DESCRIPTORS VERSUS RUBRICS

Product Descriptors

Some educators confuse product descriptors with rubrics. (Figure 9.5 compares these grading tools.) Product descriptors are a solid start toward communicating the requirements or attributes of a learning task. Descriptors are basically lists that clarify to students what to do or what to include in products. Product descriptors are important because students exhibit higher achievement when they understand what is expected by the task.

Problems

1. Many product descriptors fail to include content as a descriptor. The list then implies to students that good work can be devoid of important and relevant information.
2. A second problem is that a product descriptor lacks a communication of quality. If a student's product includes everything on the product descriptor, does that equal an A? How are differences in the quality of products indicated? Hence, grading is very subjective and quite difficult to explain to a student or parent. Students are likely to ask: *Why did you give me ___? Why did Alicia get ___?*

Product Descriptors with a Grade Scale

Some product descriptors include a scale to produce a grade. The scale is typically a 1 through 4 rating, a graduated number of points, or grades (such as A, B, C, D, or F) beside each descriptor.

Problems

1. What does a student do to improve her work and move from a 2 to a 3 or from 5 points to 10 points or from a C to a B? How do you explain to a student or parent what the student is to do to improve?

Kingore, B. (2004). *Differentiation: Simplified, Realistic, and Effective.* Austin: Professional Associates Publishing.

Figure 9.4:

TRIGGERS FOR TEST QUESTIONS

Inquiry
- Formulate questions
- Pose unknowns

Which three questions would you pose to this scientist about _____?
What is unknown about this process?

Inference
- Hypothesize
- Predict
- Assume

What inferences might be made about the results?
Predict future issues for _____.
What assumptions does the author make about the concept of _____?

Synthesis
- Conclude
- Generalize
- Think deductively
- Think inductively

What conclusions can be drawn from this event?
What is the central idea or theme of that historical period?
What is the potential consequence of _____?
Using what you know about _____, plan the next _____.

Comparative Reasoning
- Differentiate similarities and differences

Determine three similarities and differences between _____ and _____.

- Distinguish reality and fantasy or fact and fiction
- Determine sequence
- Determine the cause and effect

Which events in the report could not actually have happened?

Could the order of events be changed or any event left out?
Identify three causes leading to _____.

- Identify patterns
- Develop analogies
- Distinguish point of view

What can you identify in our history that will repeat?
The central character is like _____ when _____.
How would the event be different if told through another's viewpoint?

Classification
- Identify ambiguity

What aspects of the content led to the diverse interpretations of the three central figures?

- Categorize
- Analyze the attributes or characteristics

Organize this data, and label each category.
What are the components of _____?

Evaluative Reasoning
- Determine relevancy
- Substantiate
- Establish and apply judgmental criteria

What evidence is presented that _____ is motivated by _____?
Identify the government's position on this issue, and defend it.
Judge the arguments in favor of and against _____.

- Rank or prioritize
- Interpret

Rank the five greatest _____ and explain your ranking.
What do the artifacts of _____ infer about their civilization?

Assessment Strategies

Kingore, B. (2004). *Differentiation: Simplified, Realistic, and Effective.* Austin: Professional Associates Publishing.

2. Product descriptors and scales fail to clarify to students what skills or behaviors are required to reach higher levels of achievement. They do not communicate the differences in quality between the different grades. Students are still likely to ask: *Why did you give me ___? Why did Alicia get ___?*

Rubrics

A rubric is a description of the requirements for various levels of student proficiency. Rather than list descriptors (beginning, body, and summary) the criteria of a rubric focus on categories of skills and concepts (such as Figure 9.6). The purpose is to answer the question, *What are the conditions of success on this learning task and to what degree are those conditions met by this student's work?* Thus, a rubric enables teachers to clarify to students and parents which skills and behaviors are required in a learning experience and what to do to reach higher levels of achievement (Kingore, 1999). Rubrics provide a clearer standard to help teachers grade students' work more accurately and fairly.

Rubrics offer two very important advantages over product descriptors and product descriptors with a grade scale. First, rubrics are more effective in clarifying to both students and adults the standards for assessing or evaluating the outcome of their learning, ensuring that evaluation is accurate, efficient, and equitable. Second, rubrics communicate to students what they need to do to improve the quality of their work inasmuch as the next level of the rubric specifies which skills, concepts, or

---

Figure 9.5:

ORAL PRESENTATION PRODUCT DESCRIPTORS AND RUBRIC

			EXAMPLES
Good	**Product descriptor**	A product descriptor is a list of attributes or factors that tells students what to do, include, or attend to in their product.	• Introduction • Beginning • Body • Mannerisms • Summary
Better	**Product descriptor with a grade scale**	This product descriptor includes a score or grade beside each descriptor on the list to indicate the degree of quality of the response.	A B C D F • Introduction A B C D F • Beginning A B C D F • Body A B C D F • Mannerisms A B C D F • Summary
Best!	**Analytical rubric**	A rubric is a set of criteria and hierarchically-arranged statements to clearly describe the quality of each level of achievement. These statements communicate to students what to do to succeed and how to evaluate the quality of their work when they finish.	• Figure 9.6: Oral Presentation Rubric

Kingore, B. (2004). *Differentiation: Simplified, Realistic, and Effective.* Austin: Professional Associates Publishing.

Figure 9.6: ORAL PRESENTATION RUBRIC

TOPIC: _____

	Below Passing	C 70-79	B 80-89	A 90-100
Communi-cation Points /15	Not able to discuss; confused or disjointed; fails to address the topic **Below 11**	Needs prompting to explain or discuss; lacks a clear focus; over-uses notes **11**	Adequate explanation or discussion; appropriate vocabulary **12**	Explains independently, clearly, and confidently; precise vocabulary **13-15**
Complexity Points /25	Insufficient or irrelevant information **Below 17**	Simple and basic information; little critical thinking evident **17-19**	Critical thinking evident; compares and contrasts; integrates topics, time, or disciplines **20-22**	Beyond expected level; analyzes multiple perspec-tives and issues; abstract thinking **23-25**
Content depth Points /30	Needs more information or more accurate information; too general **Below 21**	Valid content but little depth or elaboration; sparse **21-23**	Covers topic effectively; well developed; explores the topic beyond facts and details **24-27**	Precise data; in-depth; well sup-ported; develops complex concepts and relationships **28-30**
Organization Points /15	Unclear; lacks organization **Below 11**	Attempts to organize and sequence but is hard to follow **11**	Organized effectively; a clear sequence; well structured **12**	Coherent; skill-fully planned; logically sequenced and organized to communicate well **13-15**
Presentation Points /15	Needs prompting and assistance; unprepared **Below 11**	Addresses topic; needs prompting; lacks fluency, eye contact, or visual aids **11**	Well prepared; clear; well paced; effective visual aids and speaking techniques **12**	Exceptional visual aids, speech, and mannerisms; dynamic; fluent **13-15**
Total Grade Points **/100**	**Comments**			

Generated using: Kingore, B. (2007). *Assessment*, 4th ed. Austin: Professional Associates Publishing.

Kingore, B. (2004). *Differentiation: Simplified, Realistic, and Effective.* Austin: Professional Associates Publishing.

behaviors to work on to raise their achievement level and their grade. Students are likely to understand: *If I earned a 'C' and I want to earn a 'B', I need to review the skills listed in the 'B' column and work to attain that level of concepts and skills.*

Problems

1. Rubrics must be on target and practical. Rubrics are on target when they are clear, complete, and describe tasks that are worth doing. Rubrics are practical when they are appropriate for the grade level, pose a realistic challenge for students, and are easily used by teachers and students (Stiggins, 2001). Poorly conceived rubrics do not clarify quality.

2. Rubrics with trivial criteria are trivial.

Combinations for Success

Teachers have found a place for both product descriptors and rubrics in their instruction. They use a product descriptor to introduce the learning experience and specifically outline the components of the task or product. Then, they present a rubric to clarify degrees of success and enable students to goal set their intended levels of achievement. The product descriptor often becomes a checklist for students to mark their progress and inclusion of the requirements as they work. The rubric is their assessment device.

Teacher tip...

Students are surprisingly accurate and honest on their self-assessments when rubrics are well constructed.

RUBRICS: DOCUMENTING EVALUATION*

Rubrics are guidelines to:
- **Quality.**
  They clarify to students how to succeed.
- **Evaluation.**
  They provide a clearer view of the merits and demerits of students' work than grades alone can communicate. Rubrics show students how they are responsible for the grades they earn rather than to continue to view grades as something someone gives them (Kingore, 2002).

A problem observed in numerous rubrics (or product descriptors referred to as rubrics) is the omission of an emphasis on the quality of the content. Teachers, eager to clarify the parameters of the learning task, only list evaluation criteria that focus on appearance and process when they specify *what to include, how much to do,* and *how the product should look.* Criteria related to content are nonexistent. The unintentional message communicated to students is that appearance is more important than depth and breadth.

If students are to demonstrate their understanding of the information they acquire, evaluation criteria must accent content rather than just focus on appearance and how to complete the product. All rubrics for students' work should include criteria focusing on the *accuracy and quality of information* that is presented. Additionally, with many students and decidedly with advanced and gifted learners, the rubric's emphasis should include abstract thinking, complexity, and depth of content, such as in Figure 9.7--the scoring level on the left represents the lowest proficiency; the scoring level on the right represents the highest proficiency. Elaborated examples of these

*Adapted from: Kingore, B. (2007). *Assessment*, 4th ed. Austin: Professional Associates Publishing.

Kingore, B. (2004). *Differentiation: Simplified, Realistic, and Effective.* Austin: Professional Associates Publishing.

criteria are included in a performance assessment rubric in Chapter 7.

RUBRICS ARE USEFUL

Rubrics are shared with students prior to beginning the task so students know the characteristics of quality work and how to succeed. Rubrics foster growth by focusing students' attention on the current skills they most need to develop. Later, revise the rubric to increase complexity as students' understanding and skill levels escalate.

♦ Rubrics can be used three ways: a student's goal setting, a student's self-assessment, and the teacher's evaluation.
  1. Before beginning the learning experience, each student uses a copy of the rubric to set a goal for their desired level of achievement on the task by marking the level they intend to work toward.
  2. After completion of the learning experience, students use a rubric to self-assess their achievement level on each criterion and then record their total earned proficiency level or grade at the top or bottom of the rubric.
  3. After the student has self-assessed the work, the teacher uses a different color to evaluate the student on the same rubric copy.

♦ A rubric is concrete. It clarifies to students what they are to do to demonstrate levels of quality and learning; it motivates them to try harder. Students want to aim for higher scores during self-assessment.

♦ A rubric can be shared with students, parents, and other adults to clarify learning tasks and expectations.
  1. Staple the rubric in the front of each journal or display it as a poster so students and visitors can refer to it.
  2. A copy of a rubric can be shared with parents to more clearly communicate the skills and growth their children accomplish.

♦ Standards are documented as the rubric is adjusted upward as appropriate over time to reflect the increased concept and skill complexity included in the next level of standards.

♦ A rubric increases student responsibility for learning as it increases teacher efficiency.

Figure 9.7:
RUBRIC CRITERIA

Abstract thinking	Inadequate	Concrete reporting of ideas and details	Abstracts and infers from the data	Concludes relationships; generalizes beyond the data
Complexity	Too simple or not appropriate	Simple information; limited critical thinking critical	Information shows critical thinking; compares and contrasts	Beyond expected level; analyzes multiple issues and points of view
Content depth	Too general or not accurate information	Valid but limited content; needs elaboration	Well developed information covers the topic; effective details	Precise; in-depth; details support the content and the conclusions

Kingore, B. (2004). *Differentiation: Simplified, Realistic, and Effective.* Austin: Professional Associates Publishing.

STUDENT-DEVELOPED RUBRICS

Teachers need concrete, well-developed examples of criteria and levels of proficiency to share with students to guide their growth. After students have participated in several successful experiences using rubrics, involve the class in rewriting a rubric with your guidance to make it more specific to students' understanding. This process helps students experience more ownership as they interpret the levels of proficiency on a rubric. Allow them to use simple phrases instead of more formal terminology. However, continue to accent that the descriptions must clearly designate what to do to reach higher levels of achievement for each level of proficiency.

Involve students in rewriting a state-standard rubric to guide their understanding of the elements of high achievement on those procedures. Expanding upon multiple successful experiences with rubrics, some advanced or gifted learners may be ready to independently develop rubrics and reflection

DIORAMA				
	F	**C**	**B**	**A**
Accuracy of information Points /20	No way; does not make sense Below 14	Most information is acurate 14-15	Accurate information; uses text to support some details 16-17	Very accurate; supports ideas with text and additional materials 18-20
Content depth Points /30	Little content Below 21	Needs to add more important information 21-23	Covers topic well; includes important information; clearly explained 24-26	Precise; in-depth; supports content; way to go! 27-30
Creativity Points /30	Used others ideas Below 21	Little creativity 21-23	Developed some original ideas 24-26	Unique ideas; clever; a stand-out 27-30
Effort/task commitment Points /10	Did not do work Below 7	Did not complete work on time 7	Appropriate effort; used time well 8	Big-time effort; self-motivated to do well 9-10
Appearance Points /10	Poorly done not neat Below 7	Needs to attend to details 7	Attractive; neat job 8	Eye catching; very appealing; Wait until you see this! 9-10
TOTAL GRADE: COMMENTS				

Adapted from: Kingore, B. (1999). Assessment. 2nd ed. Austin: Professional Associates Publishing.

Generated using: Kingore, B. (2002). Rubrics and More! Austin: Professional Associates Publishing.

devices to assess their replacement projects and independent study.

RUBRICS CUSTOMIZED FOR ADVANCED AND GIFTED STUDENTS

Customize rubrics for advanced and gifted students by clarifying higher, more complex levels of the concepts and skills. Implement rubrics with grade-level standards extended through higher proficiencies. The following three techniques can be employed to customize rubrics for advanced and gifted students and clarify higher levels of concepts and skills: grade-level standards combined with higher levels of proficiency, the use of a blank column extending a standards rubric, and student-developed rubrics that extend beyond a grade-level standards rubric. These techniques progress from teacher-constructed to student-developed rubrics.

Use these three techniques to convey the message that the ultimate learning target

STUDENT-DEVELOPED CENTER
WHEN YOU FINISH WORKING IN THIS CENTER, EVALUATE IT BY CHECKING EACH APPROPRIATE BOX.

Content	Organization	Resources
❑	❑	❑
Great question! The content is in-depth and very informative. I learned a lot.	Clear directions; the center is well organized and sequenced so it is a pleasure to use. Everything needed to use this center is well prepared.	Excellent resources and interesting materials. are in this center. The visual aid is appealing and informative. (Or, the computer application was fun to use.)
❑	❑	❑
Good question and content. The facts and concepts are interesting.	Clear directions. The center is generally well organized and sequenced. The materials to use in the center are not always well prepared.	Good resources and materials are in this center. The visual aid is attractive and helped to communicate information.
❑	❑	❑
The content is accurate but simple. I wanted to learn more.	Some organization, but the information and process is hard to follow at times. Clearer directions would be helpful.	Some good resources and materials are in this center. A visual aid would be a more attractive way to present some information.
❑	❑	❑
The content is not accurate.	The lack of directions makes this center hard to use.	The resources are not helpful.

My favorite thing about this center is _____

_____

Kingore, B. (2004). *Differentiation: Simplified, Realistic, and Effective.* Austin: Professional Associates Publishing.

of each advanced student begins with a foundation in state or district standards and then escalates as high as possible. These rubrics communicate that rather than just get an *A*, the objective is to extend your learning. These rubrics are best developed for multiple applications to maximize the return on teachers' preparation time.

Grade-Level-Standards-Plus Rubric*

Illustrated below is a Standards-Plus Rubric--a teacher-constructed, holistic rubric that including two additional levels of accomplishment for advanced and gifted students. In mixed-ability classrooms, begin by analyzing and paraphrasing the district or state grade-level learning standards. The fourth card lists those standards. The first, second, and third cards list ascending levels of skills that lead to the proficiencies on the fourth card. Then, extend the rubric by incorporating beyond grade-level standards to allow the acceleration of skills and concepts more appropriate for students who have already mastered the basic standards. Add two higher levels of proficiency to the standards rubric to create a rubric with six levels of proficiency instead of four. Levels five and six have the same grade and label as level four to signal that each of these is a desired learning outcome. The intent is to encourage students to focus on learning rather than just a grade and to challenge students to aim for higher-levels of achievement.

The Standards-Plus Rubric Poster also adjusts to students' growth and development. When most students are proficient at level four, reorder the cards--remove the second card, shift the third through fifth cards down, and add the new sixth card. Leave the first card to communicate that not trying is unacceptable and the main reason for not achieving.

Figure 9.8 illustrates proficiencies prepared for a standards-plus rubric. The first six cards are initially used on the rubric with the fourth card representing grade-level standards and the fifth and sixth cards exceeding the standards respectively. The seventh and eighth cards represent the continuing escalation of skills and concepts that can be incorporated over time.

These extended rubrics are available to all students in a mixed-ability classroom and allow anyone wanting to initiate a higher level of achievement to do so. Teachers either allow students to set their own level of challenge or require some students to aim for the more advanced levels of proficiencies. In a class where the range of readiness is extreme, one might provide more than two additional levels of proficiency. Adapt the technique to meet your students' learning readiness levels. Update the rubric frequently enough to reflect your students' pacing needs and readiness for advanced levels of challenge.

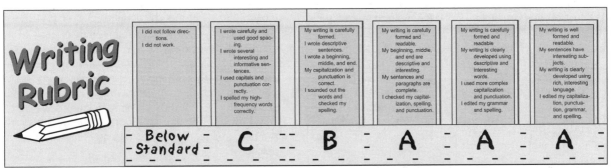

*Directions for constructing a Standards-Plus Rubric Poster are located in Appendix C.

Kingore, B. (2004). *Differentiation: Simplified, Realistic, and Effective.* Austin: Professional Associates Publishing.

Blank Column Rubric

Blank column rubrics, such as Figure 9.9, begin as a teacher-constructed rubric and then extend standards by inviting students' input for higher achievement goals. The rubric leaves the column at the highest end blank for advanced and gifted students to fill in to designate their interpretations of challenge and extended learning. A blank column rubric is a collaborative device as students determine criteria and then elicit input from teachers to negotiate their higher level of challenge. This technique is applicable in classrooms in which students are sophisticated in the development and use of rubrics. It prompts students to respond to the questions: *What would you* *need to do to exceed this level? How can you demonstrate that?*

Student-Developed Rubrics Beyond Grade-Level Standards

This rubric is constructed by students with teacher facilitation. The teacher guides the process and prompts students' analysis of learning tasks as the students develop the rubric. This technique is only applicable in classrooms in which students have gained a sophisticated understanding of rubric assessment through extensive experiences over time using rubrics for teacher-student collaborative assessments and evaluations.

Figure 9.8:

STANDARDS-PLUS RUBRIC CARDS:
THIRD GRADE BEGINNING WRITING SKILLS

Card 1	Card 2	Card 3	Card 4
I did not follow directions. I did not work.	I wrote carefully and used good spacing. I wrote several interesting and informative sentences. I used capitals and punctuation correctly. I spelled my high-frequency words correctly.	My writing is carefully formed. I wrote descriptive sentences. I wrote a beginning, middle, and end. My capitalization and punctuation is correct. I sounded out the words and checked my spelling.	My writing is carefully formed and readable. My beginning, middle, and end are descriptive and interesting. My sentences and paragraphs are complete and well developed. I checked my capitalization, spelling, and punctuation.

Card 5	Card 6	Card 7	Card 8
My writing is carefully formed and readable My writing is clearly developed using descriptive and interesting words. I used more complex capitalization and punctuation. I edited my grammar and spelling.	My writing is well formed and readable. My sentences have interesting subjects. My writing is clearly developed using rich, interesting language. I edited my capitalization, punctuation, grammar, and spelling.	My writing is neat and legible. My sentences have interesting, well developed subjects. My writing is clearly developed using precise words. I have no major errors in grammar, usage, or spelling.	My writing is neat and legible. I wrote complete sentences and paragraphs that vary to match meaning and purpose. My writing is clearly developed using precise words and vivid images with no major errors.

Kingore, B. (2004). *Differentiation: Simplified, Realistic, and Effective.* Austin: Professional Associates Publishing.

Figure 9.9:
MATHEMATICS RUBRIC

Below Standard	*Novice*	*Developing*	*Proficient*	*Extended*
Conceptual Understanding: _____ / _____ POINTS				
The problem is misunderstood.	The problem is understood but the solution is flawed.	The problem and intended solution are generally correct.	All important elements of the problem are understood and correctly interpreted.	
Points: _____	Points: _____	Points: _____	Points: _____	Points: _____
Strategies and Reasoning: _____ / _____ POINTS				
Inappropriate strategies are attempted.	The correct strategies are attempted, but flawed in application.	The appropriate strategies are applied correctly.	Advanced strategies are successfully and independently implemented, demonstrating flexible thinking.	
Points: _____	Points: _____	Points: _____	Points: _____	Points: _____
Application: _____ / _____ POINTS				
Student attempts a solution with limited mathematical applications.	Student is hesitant to proceed independently; computational errors are present.	The correct solution is achieved with minimal prompting or errors.	Algorithms are executed correctly with higher-level responses than are expected.	
Points: _____	Points: _____	Points: _____	Points: _____	Points: _____
Communication: _____ / _____ POINTS				
Incorrect or no explanation is provided.	The explanation is minimal with basic terminology and/or no graphic support.	The appropriate terminology and graphics are used in a clear explanation.	An exceptional explanation is given using advanced terminology and graphics.	
Points: _____	Points: _____	Points: _____	Points: _____	Points: _____

Total points earned: _____ / _____ POINTS

Kingore, B. (2004). *Differentiation: Simplified, Realistic, and Effective.* Austin: Professional Associates Publishing.

Assessment Strategies

Allow significant time for students to create these rubrics. The process requires extensive student-to-student and teacher-to-students conversations about learning objectives. The outcomes of this process, however, are a clarity of objectives and increased student ownership and motivation toward escalating learning.

analysis, beauty contests, state and national level tests, and many professional competitions. Now, most educators are increasingly using rubrics, realizing that well-developed rubrics clarify instruction as well as assessment. We are learning to value classroom rubrics as standards of excellence.

IMPLICATIONS OF RUBRIC ASSESSMENT

The instructional target of rubric assessment and evaluation is to challenge all students to escalate their learning as high as possible. The three rubric techniques customized for advanced and gifted students (grade-level standards plus, blank column rubric, and student-developed rubrics beyond grade-level standards) demonstrate that target to students and adults. Each technique is an effective device to use when conferencing with the parents of advanced or gifted children as it concretely communicates your plan for extending their child's learning.

The subjective nature of evaluations is a reoccurring issue in teaching. The obvious problem is when teachers are unclear about a level of quality or less specific about what they want in a product, students are likely to also be confused and unsuccessful. This dilemma decreases when rubrics are used to provide a shared standard of quality and communicate to students how to succeed in a specific learning experience.

Rubrics can change the evaluation verb that students use. Students typically say *gave*, as in: *The teacher gave me an 87.* As students use rubrics for goal setting, self assessment, and evaluation, they realize the verb is actually *earn* and begin to assume more responsibility for their own learning.

Rubrics have been successfully used for years in the Olympics, Wall Street stock

Think about it...

Analyze the accomplishments you have made in assessment and your objectives for continued growth in assessment and evaluation.

- Challenge yourself to progressively implement rubrics.
- Consider using rubrics for students' goal-setting and self-assessments.
- Interact with other teachers to collaboratively develop additional examples of effective rubrics that are on target and practical for your curriculum.
- Set a goal to progress toward student-developed rubrics.

Kingore, B. (2004). *Differentiation: Simplified, Realistic, and Effective.* Austin: Professional Associates Publishing.

INTEGRATING LEARNING STANDARDS

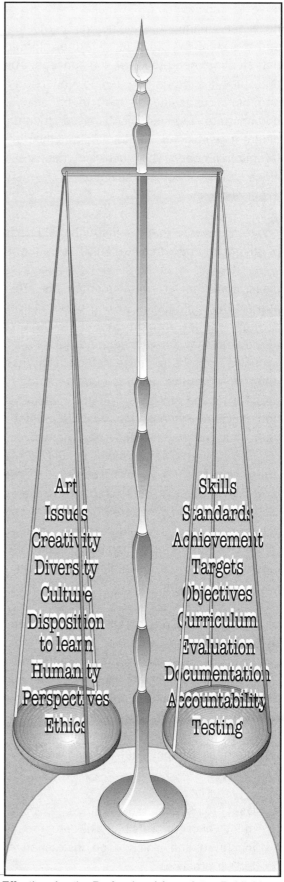

Virtually every state education department and national professional group has developed academic standards. These standards result from a reexamination of important achievement expectations in content areas. The standards are articulated in the form of objectives prescribed in terms of concepts, skills, or attitudes to promote student excellence. Teachers are then responsible for interpreting these standards into achievement targets that fit students' pathways to proficiency.

DIFFERENTIATING DISTRICT AND STATE STANDARDS

At times, state or district standards seems at odds with differentiation. A frustrated administrator announced: *We don't have time to differentiate; all students have to learn these benchmarks!* It follows, however, that all students do not master skills in the same way or at the same time. Any teacher in a mixed-ability classroom can testify that students differ in their backgrounds, readiness, needs, learning profiles, and dispositions toward learning.

The established curriculum, the content area standards, and students' needs

Kingore, B. (2004). *Differentiation: Simplified, Realistic, and Effective.* Austin: Professional Associates Publishing.

drive lesson planning. To make instructional decisions, teachers examine the curriculum and the standards to determine the information students need to know, the concepts and principles the students need to understand, and the skills students need to be able to demonstrate. Teachers also analyze students' different dispositions for learning and their differentiation needs. The juncture of these decisions guides teachers' selection of learning experiences.

Be aware that the instructional needs of advanced and gifted students are frequently overlooked or ignored in heterogeneous classrooms that are dominated by the pressure of the high-stakes testing of standards. A high school foreign language teacher requested that his accelerated juniors be excused from the exercises all classes used during the first five minutes of each period to prepare for the state test. All of his students had successfully passed the test the previous year, but his department chair denied his request saying: *That wouldn't be fair to the other teachers. Everyone is required to do the exercises.* Clearly, their objective became distorted with the pressures of the test. The preparation exercises had become ingrained in the curriculum rather than being one tool in a repertoire used to escalate students' skills and concept mastery.

Advanced and gifted students do need to master state and district standards. However, as these standards represent minimum grade-level competencies, advanced and gifted students may be able to demonstrate mastery with little or no additional instruction. Consider the following recommendations for using preassessment when working with these students.

1. Use preinstruction assessment to document which concepts and skills are already mastered and which need instruction or further practice.

2. Provide instruction at an accelerated pace to match advanced and gifted students' need for minimum repetition.

3. Provide replacement tasks at students' appropriate level of challenge rather than additional experiences with mastered skills.

Teacher tip...

Less is often more with advanced students. They need fewer examples and less guided practice to *get it.*

WHY INTEGRATE STANDARDS?

In areas with high-stakes testing, teachers at times feel overwhelmed with what seems to be an immense number of skills to teach. One middle school teacher's response is a typical reaction to this perceived pressure: *I don't have time for the fun stuff any more. We'll do some of that after the test.* Another teacher told her stressed class: *I promise you after this test we won't have to write for the rest of the year.* Consider the nonverbal messages these statements deliver to students:

*   *Learning is not interesting.*
*   *Writing is something to avoid whenever you can.*

These teachers exemplify the reaction of many school personnel to the government-dictated standards--*Suspend everything else, and just teach those skills!* Teaching learning

Kingore, B. (2004). *Differentiation: Simplified, Realistic, and Effective.* Austin: Professional Associates Publishing.

standards one at a time is such a lengthy, daunting task that teachers resort to drill and repetitions that are more isolating than ever intended. To avoid that stressful and ineffective response, work to continually integrate into your teaching the learning standards for which you are responsible.

In a differentiated classroom, teachers skillfully integrate clusters of learning standards in engaging performance tasks which enable students to demonstrate understanding. The standards are viewed as springboards for discussions and learning experiences instead of ends in themselves. The standards are not the curriculum; they are the objectives that focus the curriculum. Teachers interpret those objectives to align them to the curriculum; they then develop learning experiences that teach the curriculum and enable students to achieve or exceed the standards.

Integrating clusters of standards enable teachers:

- To replace the skill and drill activities that require little thinking with different active participation tasks that challenge students to generate responses.

- To relate learning standards to students' experiences and interests.

- To celebrate diversity in thinking by encouraging different students to respond with multiple correct responses at different levels of complexity and depth.

- To assess the depth and complexity of students' understanding and application of the objectives.

Specific learning tasks illustrate how teachers weave clusters of standards into the curriculum. For example, some upper elementary and middle school teachers require students to use the computer to develop, illus-

trate, and complete a complex math story problem that applies the concepts and skills of current study. The task integrates many mathematical standards including number concepts, number problems, and computation. Technology skills of graphic design and word processing are integrated with English language skills as students write for a specific audience and use correct writing conventions. Oral communication and teamwork skills are also applied if the task is completed by pairs of students instead of individuals.

Similarly, in one primary class, the teacher integrates economic concepts with graphing skills and language skills--following written directions, interviewing, and using correct writing conventions. The lesson requires children to make peanut butter, conduct a taste comparison using a commercial brand of peanut butter, graph the results, and then write and illustrate advertisements for their product based upon their survey results.

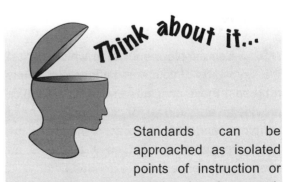

Think about it...

Standards can be approached as isolated points of instruction or integrated clusters woven into learning experiences. Reflect upon the issues that involve which approach you observe most frequently, which approach students deserve, and which approach teachers prefer.

Kingore, B. (2004). *Differentiation: Simplified, Realistic, and Effective.* Austin: Professional Associates Publishing.

TECHNIQUES TO INTEGRATE STANDARDS

Teachers incorporate several different techniques in their teaching that effectively integrate clusters of learning standards with less intensive preparation time. The following techniques are successful examples of ways to approach this integration.

1 • **Post the key words of the standards.**
2 • **Prompt students' responses with key word cubes of the standards.**
3 • **Use key words on product captions that students complete to document their learning.**
4 • **Analyze content-related literature for skill connections.**
5 • **Correlate standards to your most effective learning experiences.**
6 • **Correlate reading and writing standards to your favorite literature selections.**

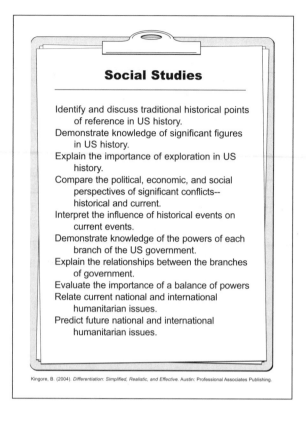

Social Studies

Identify and discuss traditional historical points of reference in US history.
Demonstrate knowledge of significant figures in US history.
Explain the importance of exploration in US history.
Compare the political, economic, and social perspectives of significant conflicts-- historical and current.
Interpret the influence of historical events on current events.
Demonstrate knowledge of the powers of each branch of the US government.
Explain the relationships between the branches of government.
Evaluate the importance of a balance of powers
Relate current national and international humanitarian issues.
Predict future national and international humanitarian issues.

Kingore, B. (2004). *Differentiation: Simplified, Realistic, and Effective.* Austin: Professional Associates Publishing.

POST KEY WORDS

Purposes

• To integrate learning standards into any class discussion
• To increase students' active involvement
• To accommodate verbal and visual learners

Procedure

Use simple graphics on which to post the key words of your standards to concretely represent those concepts and skills. Graphics provide an easy format for daily applications of learning standards. The graphic increases the visual appeal of the list so it becomes an effective reference for an extended time.

The clip board graphic, Figure 10.1, is one example of a visual prompt that works well. List on the clip board key words for each expectation within each objective.

If you prefer, enlarge the graphics with a poster maker. Then, laminate and post the clip board of standards in a highly visible site. Consider making more than one copy so you can post one copy of the graphic in the area of the classroom where you do most of your direct teaching and another copy in an area of the room where students work independently or engage in peer conferences.

• For visual emphasis during instruction, use a non-permanent marker to check the objectives that you focus on as you teach a specific lesson.

• Place the clip board in an independent work area or center, and check the objectives for students' focus as they work.

• For increased student responsibility and transfer of the objectives, have students check the appropriate objectives on the graphic as they identify and explain which are embedded in the instruction or a specific learning task.

Kingore, B. (2004). *Differentiation: Simplified, Realistic, and Effective.* Austin: Professional Associates Publishing.

Figure 10.1:
STANDARDS CLIPBOARD

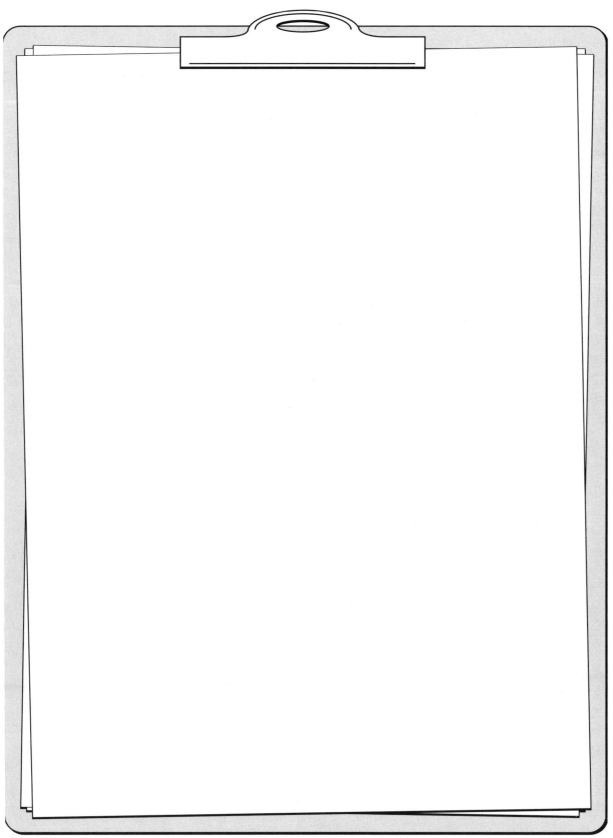

Kingore, B. (2004). *Differentiation: Simplified, Realistic, and Effective.* Austin: Professional Associates Publishing.

Maintain interest in the learning standards graphic by frequent use and by setting class expectations for responding. For example, as students begin independent work, announce your learning focus.

- *When I talk with you about your work today, be prepared to show me examples of _____.*
- *Be ready to explain to me how you _____.*

Bulletin board application

If you have available bulletin board space, use large letters to post the key words for your content area standards on that board. Prepare three or more brightly colored, laminated arrows to use to target skills featured in your current instruction. As you teach, move the arrows to indicate your skills focus to the students. The bulletin board application also documents to other adults your continual emphasis on the learning objectives. Anyone

who visits the room can immediately identify the standards integrated into the learning priorities of the class.

PROMPT STUDENTS' RESPONSES WITH KEY WORD CUBES

Purposes

- To integrate learning standards into any class discussion
- To increase students' active involvement
- To accommodate kinesthetic learners

Procedure

Prepare several cubes labeled with learning standards. Provide a cube for each small group when discussing a topic or skill application in class. The group members gently toss the cube, and the objective in view on

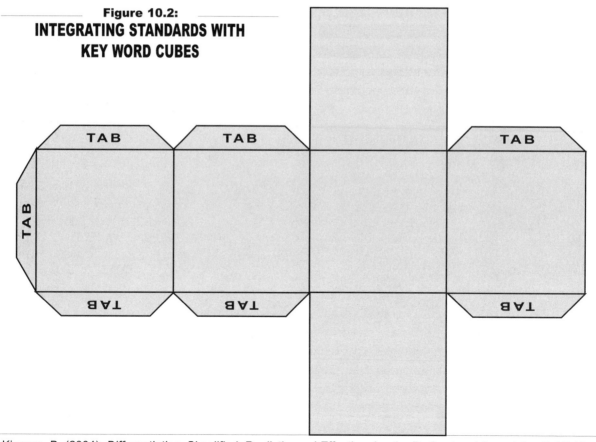

Figure 10.2:
INTEGRATING STANDARDS WITH KEY WORD CUBES

the top of the cube determines that group's response. The random nature of the procedure can increase students' interest in the objectives and accent that content area standards are woven throughout the curriculum.

1. For increased student choice, consider allowing groups to toss two cubes and then decide between the two options.

2. Use the blank cube pattern (Figure 10.2) to create prompts that relate to students' instructional needs. For example, write question prompts on each cube surface to activate students' questioning. There is merit in students posing questions for others to answer rather than only answering a teacher's questions. It usually requires more understanding to pose an insightful question than to simply answer one. Primary classes can use who, why, where, when, how, and what as cube prompts. Older students can use question prompts based upon Bloom's taxonomy to develop questions requiring high-level thinking.

Teacher tip...

Captions with standards encourage students to think about what they are learning and consider what they still want to learn.

USE PRODUCT CAPTIONS THAT DOCUMENT LEARNING

Purposes

*   To integrate learning standards into any student product
*   To document standards
*   To increase students' active involvement in assessing their learning

Procedure

Teachers strive to increase students' responsibility for their learning and to document their achievement of learning standards. One simple documentation technique is to incorporate key words for standards or skills on the caption strips that students use to organize a product for their portfolio, such as Figures 10.3 through 10.4. Advanced and gifted students can independently complete these captions to substantiate the learning objectives by checking the skills or standards applied in their replacement tasks and independent studies.

Incorporating learning standards on the caption strips increases students' active involvement in assessing learning. When selecting a product for a portfolio, each student is responsible for analyzing and then checking the skills or objectives applied in that work. Captions with standards encourage students to think about what they are learning and consider what they still want to learn. The captions crystallize the harmony of the concrete product and the product's abstract quality of more enduring learning, such as frameworks of knowledge, strategies, attitudes, and self-efficacy (Tomlinson et al, 2002). As adults review products, these captions document a student's learning so redundant activities can be avoided. The following two examples of portfolio captions strips can be used to document standards.

Kingore, B. (2004). *Differentiation: Simplified, Realistic, and Effective.* Austin: Professional Associates Publishing.

Figure 10.3: PRODUCT CAPTION

NAME _____   DATE _____

This work shows that I can _____

_____

_____

_____

I feel _____

_____

Standards:

□ _____   □ _____

□ _____   □ _____

□ _____   □ _____

Kingore, B. (2004). *Differentiation: Simplified, Realistic, and Effective.* Austin: Professional Associates Publishing.

Figure 10.4: PRODUCT CAPTION

NAME _____   DATE _____

This assignment was:

hard because _____

_____

interesting because _____

_____

OBJECTIVES: □ **Writes to inform an audience, express thoughts, influence or entertain**

□ **Adds, deletes, combines, elaborates and rearranges to revise drafts**

□ **Complete compound and complex sentences**   □ **Prepositional phrases**

□ **Appropriate spelling, capitalization, and punctuation**   □ **Legible handwriting**

□ **Appropriate voice and style**   □ **Literary devices**   □ **Transitions; conjunctions**

□ **Cohesive organization**   □ **Logical support of ideas**   □ **Vivid, precise wording**

□ **Subject-verb agreement**

Kingore, B. (2004). *Differentiation: Simplified, Realistic, and Effective.* Austin: Professional Associates Publishing.

ANALYZE CONTENT-RELATED LITERATURE FOR SKILLS CONNECTIONS

Purposes

- To guide a teacher's analysis of the application of skills within printed resources
- To enable teachers to use quality literature to model and apply skills across the curriculum during instruction

Procedure

An Analysis Grid is an effective graphic organizer for analyzing the attributes of a topic (Kingore, 1999b). Using an Analysis Grid similar to Figure 10.5, a successful sixth-grade social studies teacher listed the reading skills she needed to integrate into her teaching and some of the books she most wanted to share with her students. The selected books included picture books and novels to fit her overarching concepts of change across time as well as comparison and contrast across cultures. The books were chosen to integrate with the content she was teaching and to motivate students to want to read more about the topic. Then, she completed an Analysis Grid to interpret the quantity of skill examples she found in each book. By indicating whether examples of each skill were abundant, some, seldom, or none she developed a quick reference tool to help effectively integrate her district standards.

Consider incorporating Analysis Grids. Model a skill in context by incorporating a content-related resource that contains a rich quantity of examples. Use the blank grid to organize your applications of reading skills to the content materials in your class library. Across the top of a grid, list the resources you most want to share with your classes. List down the left side several skills that are a significant focus in your instruction. Then, use the initials listed to the right to rate how many examples of each skill occur in each resource.

Figure 10.5: CONTENT AREA SKILLS ANALYSIS GRID

A = Abundant
S = Some
F = Few
N = None

SKILLS:	If the World Were a Village	Amber on the Mountain	Brian's Winter	Mama Provi and the Pot of Rice	The Giver	Pink and Say	The View from Saturday	The Yellow Star
Adjectives--multisyllablic	S	F	S	S	A	S	A	A
Adverbs--multisyllablic	F	N	S	F	A	F	S	S
Complex sentences	A	F	A	A	A	F	A	A
Conjunctions	S	F	A	S	S	S	A	A
Dialogue	N	S	F	S	S	A	A	S
Prepositions	A	S	S	A	A	A	S	A
Puns	N	N	N	S	N	N	F	F
Similes and metaphors	S	A	F	S	S	F	F	N

CORRELATE STANDARDS TO LEARNING EXPERIENCES

Purposes

- To guide a teacher's analysis of the application of learning standards within a variety of learning experiences
- To enable teachers to use quality activities to model and apply learning standards

Procedure

An Analysis Grid can also be used to align standards to the most effective learning experiences and products. This correlation enables teachers to continue to use the best teaching practices, select the most appropriate activities, and integrate standards rather than isolate skills. A form for aligning standards to learning experiences is provided in Figure 10.5. A completed example of this form correlating math standards to specific learning experiences follows.

Kingore, B. (2004). *Differentiation: Simplified, Realistic, and Effective.* Austin: Professional Associates Publishing.

Figure 10.5:
CONTENT AREA SKILLS ANALYSIS GRID

A	=	*Abundant*
S	=	*Some*
F	=	*Few*
N	=	*None*

SKILLS:

Kingore, B. (2004). *Differentiation: Simplified, Realistic, and Effective.* Austin: Professional Associates Publishing.

Figure 10.5: CONTENT AREA SKILLS ANALYSIS GRID MATHEMATICS ACTIVITIES: SKILLS:	Acrostic	Content puzzle	Error analysis	Letter (math process)	Number challenge game	Test (student generated)	Venn diagram
Compute and estimate	✔	✔	✔	✔	✔	✔	✔
Solve problems using comparisons	✔	✔	✔	✔		✔	✔
Measure and compare quantities	✔	✔	✔	✔		✔	✔
Estimate measurements	✔		✔	✔		✔	
Use technology, instruments, and formulas	✔	✔	✔	✔		✔	
Use variables and patterns	✔		✔	✔		✔	✔
Use tables, graphs, and symbols	✔					✔	✔
Use systems of number properties	✔	✔	✔	✔	✔	✔	
Use algebra	✔	✔	✔	✔	✔	✔	✔
Use geometric concepts	✔	✔	✔	✔		✔	✔

Figure 10.6:
STEPS IN CORRELATING STANDARDS TO LEARNING EXPERIENCES

Consider the following steps when aligning learning experiences and products to standards.

1. Review and analyze the objectives to incorporate.

2. Focus on a list of key words to represent each objective.

3. List the selected learning experiences.

4. Mark all of the standards that can be incorporated into each activity. Do not necessarily incorporate all of these standards when students complete a specific activity; the analysis just identifies the possibilities from which to choose.

5. When planning a specific activity, look over the Content Area Skills Analysis Grid, and build into the lesson plan the skills and learning objectives to incorporate and focus on in that lesson.

Imagine the following scenario. The teacher in the room across the hall notices the engaging, interactive learning experiences that you completed with your students and comments to you after school: *I wish I had time for fun activities, but I was busy teaching our learning standards.* Comfortably respond: *That's great. I was teaching those standards, too. Here is the list of the objectives we incorporated today. It was so engaging. The students had a good time and were much more involved in learning. They tend to retain more when they are interested and actively involved.*

Figure 10.6 delineates the process of how teachers correlate standards to their learning experiences. Teachers determine their preferred activities and then analyze which clusters of standards can be woven into each learning task.

Kingore, B. (2004). *Differentiation: Simplified, Realistic, and Effective.* Austin: Professional Associates Publishing.

CORRELATE STANDARDS TO LITERATURE

Purposes

- To provide concrete examples of learning standards' skills and objectives in context
- To integrate learning standards into any class discussion
- To accommodate auditory learners during read-aloud sessions

Procedure

Correlate standards to the wonderful literature that you will share with your students. Categorize concepts or skills that are integrated into each great novel, poem, story, transcript of a famous speech, or essay that will be a part of instruction. Share your analysis with your instructional team and principal so they understand how you consistently weave standards into authentic instructional experiences.

When reading a literary work aloud to students, first read the selection uninterrupted so the quality of the literature can be enjoyed in its entirety. Following the read aloud, state the concept or skills to accent and then, when appropriate, reread a section as students analyze it. At other times, state the concept or skill and ask students to recall and discuss examples they remember from the story.

One first grade teacher developed action responses for several favorite books to help her students focus on specific skills in each story. For example, she read to her class *Why Mosquitoes Buzz in People's Ears**. The class discussed cause and effect, and then the teacher reread a page of the picture book, asking the students to raise their arms over their head each time they heard an effect.

When students are reading a selection as a part of instruction, it is most effective for them to read the entire section before analyzing or practicing skills. This approach assists comprehension as the flow of the content is less interrupted.

There are two ways to organize this correlation of standards to literature.

1. Teachers list their content area standards and then write titles of applicable books under each standard, as in the following example.
2. Teachers use an analysis grid, listing standards down the left margin and book titles across the top. They then mark each objective application of each book.

The student is expected to interpret literary devices such as flashback, foreshadowing, and symbolism.

Brumbeau, Jeff. (2000). <u>The Quiltmaker's Gift</u>. Duluth, MN: Pfeifer-Hamilton.
Dahl, Roald. (1964). <u>Charlie and the Chocolate Factory</u>. New York: Knopf.
Deedy, Carmen. (2000). <u>The Yellow Star</u>. Atlanta: Peachtree.
George, Jean Craighead. (1972). <u>Julie of the Wolves</u>. New York: Harper & Row.
Levine, Gail Carson. (1997). <u>Ella Enchanted</u>. New York: Harper Collins.
Lewis, C.S. (1950). <u>The Lion, the Witch, and the Wardrobe</u>. New York: HarperCollins.
Lowry, Lois. (1993). <u>The Giver</u>. New York: Bantam Doubleday Dell Books.
Peck, Robert. (1998). <u>A Long Way from Chicago</u>. New York: Puffin.
Sachar, Louis. (1998). <u>Holes</u>. New York: Farrar, Straus, & Giroux.
Tolkien, J. R. R. (1999). <u>The Hobbit</u>. (1998). <u>The Lord of the Rings</u>. Boston: Houghton Mifflin.

Think about it...

In addition to your ideas for literature applications to standards, involve colleagues and students in analyzing several additional entries for each objective until you have a substantial list from which to choose.

**Aardema, V. (1975). *Why Mosquitoes Buzz in People's Ears.* New York: Dial Books.

Kingore, B. (2004). *Differentiation: Simplified, Realistic, and Effective.* Austin: Professional Associates Publishing.

APPENDICES AND REFERENCES

BUDDIES: OLDER STUDENTS AS MENTORS AND COLLABORATIVE LEARNERS

Teachers of young children wonder how they will ever have enough time to accomplish all they want to do with their children. Buddies is one helpful solution. Buddies is the name for a project involving older students interacting in learning situations with younger children to provide the individual attention teachers so desire for their students (Kingore, 1995). This is a valid way to differentiate learning experiences for both advanced and special need learners because the one-on-one interaction allows young children to proceed and achieve at their individual level of readiness. The Buddies help young children complete learning experiences they would otherwise lack the skills to accomplish. For example, young gifted children often demonstrate advanced thinking ability, but their writing abilities are more typical of their age. When Buddies write the young children's dictation, the younger children can engage in more complex, in-depth explanations and see those ideas expressed in print.

Buddies can involve a whole classroom of older students or only a few students at a time. When an entire class is involved, the older class typically goes to the classroom of the younger students and works with the children. Another version of Buddies, however, involves only a few older students who have completed work in their class and then go to the classroom of the younger children to assist.

Consider arranging with another teacher for your classes to participate in a Buddies project. There is excellent educational value for both older and younger children.

POTENTIAL LEARNING EXPERIENCES

The following learning experiences are particularly effective projects for Buddies and younger students.
- Interviewing
- Reading books together
- Taking dictation

EDUCATIONAL VALUE

OLDER STUDENTS	YOUNGER STUDENTS
Communication skills	Communication skills
Social skills	Social skills
Self-esteem: *Someone needs my help.*	Self-esteem: *Someone likes to work with me.*
Critical thinking	Critical thinking
Creative and productive thinking	Creative and productive thinking
Flexibility in thought and process	Reading/writing models
Time management	Individual attention
Planning	
Organizational skills	
Responsibility	

Kingore, B. (2004). *Differentiation: Simplified, Realistic, and Effective.* Austin: Professional Associates Publishing.

- Completing math surveys or story problems
- Assisting in individual study, computer searches, or research
- Completing more complex math applications
- Conducting science experiments
- Graphing individually collected data
- Making books of original stories, family stories, or topic information
- Completing captions for portfolio products

One principal commented that the Buddies project in her school helped bring out the best in students. In one instance, for example, the principal saw a tough fifth grader holding his buddy's hand as they walked together to the library to help the younger child check out a book. The principal was very surprised by the fifth grader's thoughtful behavior as he was often in her office because of disruptive behavior. She commented, "I was so excited about seeing such a positive behavior from him. Now I have something positive to talk about with him instead of just discipline problems."

BUDDIES WORKSHOP FOR STUDENTS

Conducting a brief workshop to prepare the older students increases the success of a Buddies project. Designate a fifteen minute period for the workshop and schedule it a day or so before the first time the Buddies work together. Consider serving a drink or cookies during this meeting. Refreshments add to the fun and camaraderie of the workshop.

The younger children typically go to the older students' room to get acquainted with that teacher. The young children enjoy sitting in the bigger desks and seeing what *big* classrooms are like. The teacher of the older students usually reads a book to the young children while they are visiting.

The older students go to the younger children's classroom for the workshop. The teacher shares the following information:
- Where needed materials are located.

- Which materials and equipment may be used without asking.
- Where Buddies work with younger children. Spreading out around the room on the floor is usually more productive than crowding together at the children's' tables or desks.
- How to prompt children's thinking. Students need help knowing what to say to younger students. Discuss prompts, such as:
  Tell me about your picture.
  Tell me another idea.
  Explain what you mean.
  Because...
  Then...next...so...

Discuss what the first project will be. Excellent beginning projects accent learning about each other, such as completing stories and pictures about their families or investigating each other's favorite things.

The teacher then answers any questions the students may have about the process and accents the factors which both teachers consider most important.
- Since many older students worry that they will make a mistake in front of the younger student, the teacher might emphasize that the most important thing is to record the ideas of the younger child; the older students can recopy the writing later to correct spelling and handwriting as needed.
- Let the older students know how important each of them really is in this project by telling them, *You will have many chances to help a child experience success. When you do that, you have accomplished a most important thing.*
- Emphasize to the students that their attitude is vital. Tell them, *Be enthusiastic and enjoy your time together.*

Schedule a follow-up workshop after the Buddies have worked together two or three times. Typically the students have more questions by then and also benefit from a time to share strategies among themselves.

Kingore, B. (2004). *Differentiation: Simplified, Realistic, and Effective.* Austin: Professional Associates Publishing.

PRODUCT OPTIONS FOR DIFFERENTIATED INSTRUCTION

acronym

acrostic

advance organizer

advertisement

advice column

animation

analogy

anecdote

annotated bibliography

announcement

anthem

appendix

art gallery

audiotape

autobiography

award

background music

ballad

banner

billboard

bio

biography

block picture story

blueprint

board game

book

book jacket

booklet

bookmark

book review

bound book

brochure

bulletin board

bumper sticker

calendar

calendar quip

calorie chart

campaign speech

candidate platform

card game

caricature

cartoon

caption

census

ceramics

cereal box

certificate

chamber music

character sketch

charade

charcoal sketch

chart

children's story

choral reading

cinquain

cloze paragraph

coat of arms

collage

collection

column analysis--

  folding paper into

  columns to organize

  data

comic strip

commentary

communication code

comparison

complaint

compliment tree

Computer animation

computer game

computer program

concept map (web)

conference presentation

constitution

contract

conundrum

cooked concoction

costume

couplet

critique

cross section

crossword

  puzzle/reverse

  crossword puzzle

cryptogram

cumulative story

dance

data sheet

debate

definition

demonstration

description

detailed illustration

diagram

dialogue

diamante

diary

dictionary

diorama

directions

director

display

document

documentary

dough art

dramatization

dramatic monologue

drawing

economic forecast

editorial

encyclopedia entry

epilogue

epitaph

essay

etching

evaluation

experiment

expository

fable

fact file

fairy tale

fantasy

family tree

fashion article

fashion show script

festival

fictionary

Kingore, B. (2004). *Differentiation: Simplified, Realistic, and Effective.* Austin: Professional Associates Publishing.

field trip
filmstrip
flannel board
   presentation
flip book or chart
flow chart

folder game
folklore
game
game rules
game show
geometric shapes
glossary
good news-bad news
graffiti
graph
graphic organizer
greeting card
Haiku
headlines
hidden picture
HyperCard™ stack
hypothesis
informative speech
infomercial
illustrations
indexes
interview
introduction (to people,
   places, books)
invention
investment portfolio
invitation
jewelry
jigsaw puzzle
jingles

job application
joke book
journal
jump rope rhyme
lab report
labels
labeled diagram
landscape design
large scale drawing
learning center
learning profile
lecture
legend
lesson
letter
letter to the editor
limerick
line drawing
list
lyrics
mad lib
magazine
magazine article
magic trick
manual
map w/legend

marquee notice
maze
memorial
memoir
metaphor
menus
mobile
model
monologue
montage
mosaic
movie
movie review
movie script

mural
museum exhibit
musical composition
mystery
myth
needlework
news analysis
newscast
news report
newspaper
newspaper article
nursery rhyme
obituary
observation log

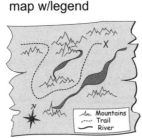

ode
oil painting
opinion
oral history
oral report
outline
overhead transparency
painting
palindrome
pamphlet
pantomime
paper chain story
paragraph
parody
pattern
persuasive speech
photo essay
photo journal
picture
picture book
picture dictionary
picture file
play or skit
playdough charac-
   ters/scene

poem
political cartoon
pop-up book
portfolio
post card
poster
pottery
Power Point™
   presentation
prediction
press conference
problem solution
product description
profile
propaganda sheet
protest sign
protocol
proposal
proverb
public announcement
pun
puppet
puppet show

puzzle
quip
quiz show
quiz
questionnaire
questions
quotation

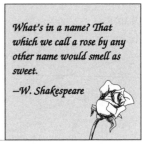

What's in a name? That which we call a rose by any other name would smell as sweet.

—W. Shakespeare

Kingore, B. (2004). *Differentiation: Simplified, Realistic, and Effective.* Austin: Professional Associates Publishing.

radio commentary

radio commercial

radio show

rap

reaction

readers theater

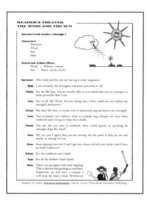

real estate notice

rebus story

rebuttal

recipe

recital

reflective essay

relief map

remedy

research report

response

request

requiem

requisition

resume

reverse crossword
   puzzle

review

revision

rhyme

rhythmic pattern

riddles

role play

rubric

rule

sale notice

salt map

satire

satirical play

scale drawing

scavenger hunt

schedule

science fiction story

scrapbook

sculpture

secret

self-portrait

self description

sequels

serialized story

set design

short story

sign

silly saying

simulation

skit

slide presentation

slogan

small scale drawing or
   model

sniglet

soap opera

social action plan

society news

soliloquy

song (original)

songs (collection)

sonnet

speech

spoof

spoonerism

sports account

sports analysis

stencil

story

summary

superstition

survey

symbol

table

tall tale

talent show

tape

task card

telegram

telephone directory

telestitch

terrarium

test

textbook

thank you note

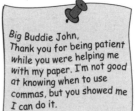

theatre program

three-dimensional
   scale

time line

titles

theory

tongue twister

topographical map

traffic rule

transcript

travelogue

travel folder

travel poster

trial

tribute

trifold

trivia game

TV commercial

TV guide

TV program

upside-down book

Venn diagram

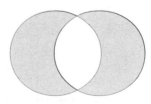

video documentary

video game

videotape

vignette

vocabulary list

want ad

wanted poster

warning

weather forecast

weather instrument

weather report or log

web--concept mapping

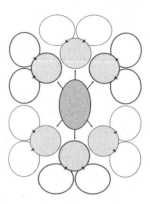

website

will--legal document

wish

wordle (word puns)

wordless books

wordplay

worksheet

written report

yellow pages

Kingore, B. (2004). *Differentiation: Simplified, Realistic, and Effective.* Austin: Professional Associates Publishing.

PRODUCTS GRID

	MODALITIES				MULTIPLE INTELLIGENCES							
	V	O/A	W	K	L	L-M	N	S	M	B-K	Inter	Intra
analogy		•	•		•	•	•				•	•
bio poem			•		•	•	•				•	•
book or booklet	•		•		•	•	•	•			•	•
brochure	•		•		•	•	•	•			•	•
bulletin board	•		•	•	•	•	•	•		•	•	•
center (student made)	•	•	•	•	•	•	•	•	•	•	•	•
chart	•				•	•	•	•			•	•
children's story (illustrated)	•		•		•	•	•	•			•	•
computer animation	•	•		•	•	•	•	•	•	•	•	•
concept map (web)	•				•	•	•				•	•
debate		•	•		•	•	•				•	•
demonstration	•	•	•	•	•	•	•	•	•	•	•	•
diagram (labeled)	•		•		•	•	•				•	•
diorama	•			•	•	•	•	•				•
documentary film	•	•	•	•	•	•	•				•	•
editorial		•	•		•	•	•				•	•
experiment	•		•	•	•	•	•				•	•
family tree	•		•		•							
flow chart	•		•		•	•	•		•		•	•
graph	•		•		•	•	•		•			
interview		•	•		•	•	•				•	•
journal, diary, or learning log			•		•	•	•					•
letter to the editor	•		•		•	•	•				•	•
magazine article			•		•	•	•					
map (with legend)	•		•		•	•		•				
model	•			•	•	•	•	•	•			•
museum exhibit	•		•	•	•	•	•	•	•		•	•
newscast		•	•		•	•	•	•			•	•
newspaper	•		•		•	•	•	•			•	•
painting	•			•				•	•		•	•
photo essay	•			•		•	•	•			•	•
Power Point™	•	•	•		•	•	•	•	•	•	•	•
poster	•		•	•	•	•	•	•			•	•
questionnaire		•	•		•	•	•					•
rap		•	•		•				•	•	•	•
readers theater	•	•	•	•	•	•			•	•	•	•
satirical play	•	•	•	•	•	•	•	•			•	•
scavenger hunt	•		•	•	•	•	•				•	•
sculpture	•			•					•		•	•
simulation	•	•	•	•	•	•	•	•	•		•	•
song (original)		•	•		•	•	•		•	•	•	•
time line	•		•		•	•	•	•			•	•
trivia game		•	•		•	•	•				•	
Venn diagram	•		•		•	•	•	•			•	•
website	•		•		•	•	•	•			•	•

Adapted from: Kingore, B. (2007). *Assessment*, 4th ed. Austin: Professional Associates Publishing.

Materials

- Three sheets of colored poster board
- Eight pieces of white or colored typing paper
- Computer with a printer or a set of markers
- Cutting device, glue, stapler

CONSTRUCTING THE RUBRIC POSTER

As depicted by Figure C.1, cut two of the sheets of poster board like the top image; these pieces will comprise the body of the poster and four of the cards. Cut the third sheet of poster board to create the remaining four cards, the two pieces of the pocket, and a ten-inch scrap piece. (Using a straight edge--such as a metal yard stick--and an exacto knife makes it easier to make long, straight cuts through the poster board.)

Figure C.1

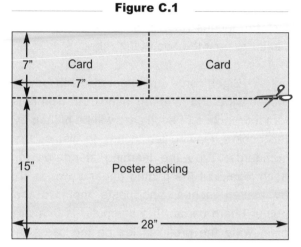

(Cut two pieces like the above pattern.)

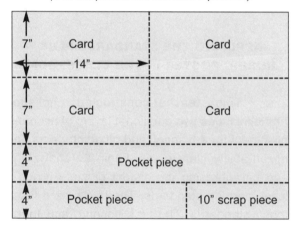

Attach the two pieces that measure fifteen by twenty-eight inches end to end and tape them together--this will become the back of the poster. Next, attach the two pocket pieces and staple them to the poster as illustrated in Figure C.2. (Space the staples about seven and a half inches apart to allow enough

Figure C.2

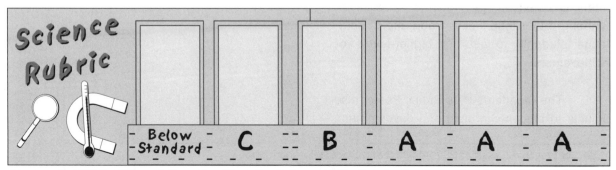

Kingore, B. (2004). *Differentiation: Simplified, Realistic, and Effective.* Austin: Professional Associates Publishing.

room for the cards to slide into the pocket easily.) Ten inches remain on the left end of the poster to post the title of the rubric.

Eight cards are created--each seven inches wide and fourteen inches tall. The bottom four inches of each card will be hidden by the pocket, leaving ten inches to display the standards. Type the learning standards for each level, cut the printed pages down to six by eleven inches, and paste them to the poster board cards. (If a computer is unavailable, write the proficiencies on the cards by hand.)

APPLYING THE STANDARDS-PLUS RUBRIC POSTER IN THE CLASSROOM

This teacher-constructed, holistic rubric includes two additional levels of accomplishment for advanced and gifted students. In mixed-ability classrooms, begin by analyzing and paraphrasing the district or state grade-level learning standards. The fourth card lists those standards. The first, second, and third cards list ascending levels of skills that lead to the proficiencies on the fourth card. Then, extend the rubric by incorporating beyond grade-level standards to allow the acceleration of skills and concepts more appropriate for students who have already mastered the basic standards. Add two higher levels of proficiency to the standards rubric to create a rubric with six levels of proficiency instead of four. Levels five and six have the same grade and label as level four to signal that each of these is a desired learning outcome. The intent is to encourage students to focus on learning rather than just a grade and to challenge students to aim for higher-levels of achievement.

The Standards-Plus Rubric Poster also adjusts to students' growth and development.

When most students are proficient at level four, reorder the cards--remove the second card, shift the third through fifth cards down, and add the new sixth card. Leave the first card to communicate that not trying is unacceptable and the main reason for not achieving.*

---

*See Chapter 9: Assessment Strategies that Impact Differentiation

THE GIFTED READERS' BILL OF RIGHTS

The right to read at a pace and level appropriate to readiness without regard to grade placement.

The right to discuss interpretations, issues, and insights with intellectual peers.

The right to reread many books and not finish every book.

The right to use reading to explore new and challenging information and grow intellectually.

The right for time to pursue a self-selected topic in depth through reading and writing.

The right to encounter and apply increasingly advanced vocabulary, word study, and concepts.

The right to guidance rather than dictation of what is good literature and how to find the best.

The right to read several books at the same time.

The right to discuss but not have to defend reading choice and taste.

The right to be excused from material already learned.

Kingore, B. (2004). *Differentiation: Simplified, Realistic, and Effective.* Austin: Professional Associates Publishing.

REFERENCES

Abilock, D. (1999). Librarians and gifted readers. *Knowledge Quest, 27,* 30-35.

Betts, G. & Kercher, J. (1999). *Autonomous Learner Model: Optimizing Ability.* Greeley, CO: ALPS Publishing.

Cecil, N. (1995). *The art of inquiry: Questioning strategies for K-6 classrooms.* Winnipeg, MB, Canada: Peguin Publishers.

Csikszentmihalyi, M. (1997). *Creative flow and the psychology of discovery and invention.* New York: Harper Collins.

DeBono, E. (1993). *Teach your child how to think.* New York: Penguin Books.

Erickson, H. (1998). *Concept-based curriculum and instruction: Teaching beyond the facts.* Thousand Oaks, CA: Corwin.

Gentry, M. (1999). *Promoting student achievement and exemplary classroom practices through cluster grouping: A research-based alternative to heterogeneous elementary classrooms.* Storrs, CT: The National Research Center on the Gifted and Talented.

Jensen, E. (2000). *Brain-based learning.* Del Mar, CA: Turning Point Publishing.

Kaplan, S. & Cannon, M. (2000). *Curriculum starter cards: Developing differentiated lessons for gifted students.* Austin: Texas Association for the Gifted and Talented.

Kingore, B. (2007). *Assessment: Timesaving procedures for busy teachers, 4th ed.* Austin: Professional Associates Publishing.

Kingore, B. Ed. (2002). *Reading Strategies for Advanced Primary Readers.* Austin: Texas Education Agency.

Kingore, B. (1995). *Reaching high potentials.* Worthington, Ohio: DLM division of Macmillan/McGraw-Hill.

Kulik, J. (1992). *Analysis of the research on ability grouping: Historical and contemporary perspectives.* Storrs, CT: The National Research Center on the Gifted and Talented.

Loveless, T. (1998). *Tracking and ability grouping debate.* Washington, D.C.: The Thomas B. Fordham Foundation.

Ogle, D. (1986)). KWL: A teaching model that develops active reading of expository text. *The Reading Teacher, 36,* 564-570.

Paul, R. (1995). *Critical thinking: How to prepare students for a rapidly changing world.* Santa Rosa, CA: Foundation for Critical Thinking.

Pettig, K. (2000). On the road to differentiated practice. *Educational Leadership, 58,* 1, 14-18.

Reis, S., Burns, D., & Renzulli, J. (1992). *Curriculum compacting: The complete guide to modifying the regular curriculum for high-ability students.* Mansfield Center, CT: Creative Learning Press.

Rogers, K. (1998). Using current research to make 'good' decisions about grouping. *NASSP Bulletin, 82,* 38-46.

Ross, P. (1993). *National excellence: A case for developing America's talent.* Washington, DC: US Department of Education.

Renzulli, J. (1977). *The enrichment triad model: A guide for developing defensible programs for the gifted and talented.* Mansfield Center, CT: Creative Learning Press.

Renzulli, J. & Smith, L. (1978). *The compactor.* Mansfield Center, CT: Creative Learning Press.

Schuler, P. (1997). *Cluster grouping coast to coast.* The National Research Center on the Gifted and Talented, Winter Newsletter.

Schunk, D. (1987). Peer models and children's behavioral change. *Review of Educational Research, 47,* 149-174.

Shepard, L. (1997). *Measuring achievement: What does it mean to test for robust understanding?* Princeton, NJ: Educational Testing Service.

Sizer, T. (1997). *Horace's school: Redesigning the American high school.* Boston: Houghton Mifflin.

Stiggins, R. (2001). *Student-involved classroom assessment,* 2nd ed. Upper Saddle River, NJ: Merrill Prentice Hall.

Sternberg, R., Torff, & Grigorenko. (1998). Teaching triarchically improves student achievement. *Journal of Educational Psychology, 90.* 374-384.

Szabos, J. (1989). Bright child, gifted learner. *Challenge, 34.*

Texas Education Agency. (2003). *Resource manual: Performance standards exit-level project.* Austin: TEA Publicatons.

Tomlinson, C. (2001). Differentiated instruction in the regular classroom: What does it mean? How does it look? *Understanding Our Gifted, 14,* 3-6.

Tomlinson, C. (1999). *The differentiated classroom: Responding to the needs of all learners.* Alexandria, VA: Association for Supervision and Curriculum Development.

Tomlinson, C., Kaplan, S., Renzulli, J., Purcell, J., Leppien J., & Burns, D. (2002). *The parallel curriculum: A design to develop high potential and challenge high-ability learners.* Thousand Oaks, CA: Corwin Press.

Torrance, E. & Meyers, R. (1970). *Creative learning and teaching.* New York: HarperCollins.

Vos Savant, M. (1997). Ask Marilyn. *Parade Magazine,* August 10, 5.

Vygotsky, L. (1986). *Thought and language.* Cambridge: MIT Press.

Westberg, K., Archambault, F., Dobyns, S., & Salvin, T. (1993). *The classroom practices study: Observational findings.* Storrs, CT: The National Research Center on the Gifted and Talented.

Wiggins, G. & McTighe, J. (1999). *Design for understanding.* Alexandria, VA: Association for Supervision, Curriculum and Development.

Winebrenner, S. & Brulles, D. (2008). *The cluster grouping handbook.* Minneapolis, MN: Free Spirit Publishing.

Winebrenner, S. (2001). *Teaching gifted kids in the regular classroom. 2nd ed.* Minneapolis, MN: Free Spirit Publishing.

Winebrenner, S. & Devlin, B. (2001). Cluster grouping of gifted students: How to provide full-time services on a part-time budget: update 2001. *ERIC Clearinghouse on Disabilities and Gifted Education.* ERIC EC Digest #E607.

INDEX

T

V

W

Differentiation Interactive CD-ROM

Dr. Bertie Kingore
ID CODE: BK-12

This interactive CD-ROM includes over 65 customizable forms, rubrics, task activity boards, and figures from this publication. Also included are bonus reprinted forms which were discussed as examples but not included in the book, such as the following.

- Venn variations
- Status notes
- Cube a Thought
- Read and Listen
- KWR variations
- Analysis Grid
- Concepts maps
- Topic Frame

Almost all of the forms are **completely customizable**.
- Customize them to suit your specific needs,
- Save* any changes you have made, and/or
- Have your students complete them on the computer!

PO Box 28056 • Austin, Texas 78755-8056

Toll free phone/fax: 866-335-1460

www.kingore.com